Du mot à la phrase

Collection dirigée par Jean-Pierre Demarche

Nouvelle édition

Du mot à la phrase

VOCABULAIRE ANGLAIS CONTEMPORAIN ET EXERCICES

Michel DUMONG

Jean POUVELLE

Christine KNOTT

ellipses

Des mêmes auteurs chez le même éditeur

Dumong Michel, *L'antifaute anglais*, 2002.

–, *Épreuves corrigées et commentées d'anglais aux concours d'entrée (1re et 2e années) des IEP de province (1996-1999)*, 2000.

–, *Le vocabulaire junior anglais - Vocabulaire thématique et exercices*, 1995.

Pouvelle Jean, *Guide de la littérature américaine des origines à nos jours*, 2008.

–, *Guide de la littérature britannique des origines à nos jours*, 2008.

–, *Guide des littératures d'Irlande et du Commonwealth. Des origines à nos jours*, 2008.

Knott Christine, Pouvelle Jean, *Au fil des mots – Lexique français-anglais des mots essentiels*, 2009.

–, *Vox Anglais - Le vocabulaire incontournable des examens et concours*, 2004.

Dumong Michel, Knott Christine, Pouvelle Jean, LOGOS – *L'essentiel du vocabulaire anglais*, 2001.

Dumong Michel, Huart Rose-Anne, Knott Christine, Pouvelle Jean, *Du mot au texte, Vocabulaire anglais thématique et exercices*, 2006.

–, *EXPRESS - Guide de l'expression anglaise*, 1997.

–, *Le vocabulaire anglais du supérieur*, 2001.

Casanave Daniel, Niemeyer Mark, Park Adrian, Pouvelle Jean, *Repères de civilisation Grande-Bretagne États-Unis*, 2003.

ISBN 978-2-7298-5489-8

32, rue Bargue 75740 Paris cedex 15

www.editions-ellipses.fr

PRÉFACE

Cet ouvrage s'adresse aux élèves du second cycle de l'enseignement secondaire, aux étudiants des classes préparatoires, ou aux grands débutants qui souhaitent améliorer rapidement leurs connaissances lexicales.

Le but visé est de faciliter la rédaction de textes ou de commentaires tout autant que d'enrichir l'expression orale : dans ce but, **cette édition réactualisée fournit, sous forme de symboles phonétiques courants, la prononciation des mots difficiles**.

Pour rendre la tâche plus aisée, chacun des trente-six chapitres thématiques est divisé selon les catégories auxquelles les éléments appartiennent : noms, adjectifs, adverbes, verbes, expressions, phrases.

Chaque chapitre est suivi d'une série d'exercices permettant de vérifier et de stimuler l'apprentissage. Les chapitres sont regroupés en neuf grandes parties. Cependant, autre nouveauté, **l'ultime chapitre échappe à cette classification et constitue un florilège des expressions imagées et dictons les plus populaires de la langue anglaise**.

Le choix des éléments n'a pas été limité à un registre particulier, de façon que chacun y trouve son compte dans des circonstances et domaines variés. Nous nous sommes efforcés de faire un tri, afin que ne figurent dans cet ouvrage que le vocabulaire essentiel – celui qui doit devenir actif – et les expressions qu'un bon élève de second cycle ou qu'un bon étudiant non spécialiste devrait à notre sens posséder. Ainsi avons-nous éliminé tous les mots qui nous semblaient susceptibles d'encombrer inutilement la mémoire.

Chaque chapitre vise à fournir non seulement le vocabulaire thématique propre, mais aussi les mots et les expressions qui permettent de traiter le sujet. Il concilie donc classement thématique et approche fonctionnelle.

Conçu pour être avant tout un outil d'apprentissage et de révision en vue de tests ou examens, cet ouvrage devrait aussi constituer une aide appréciable dans la rédaction d'essais ou de devoirs. Il peut enfin se révéler un vade-mecum utile lors d'un séjour en pays anglophone. N'oublions pas qu'**un élément lexical n'est vraiment acquis que lorsqu'il trouve sa place dans un énoncé suivi, écrit ou oral.**

Notre souhait le plus vif est que cet ouvrage soit pour vous un passeport en bonne et due forme pour une meilleure pratique de la langue anglaise.

Les auteurs

TABLE DES MATIÈRES

Préface.....3

I. THE HUMAN BEING — 7

1• The human body — *Le corps humain*.....7
2• Feelings — *Les sentiments*.....14
3• The mind — *L'esprit*.....23
4• Human life — *La vie humaine*.....30
5• Health and medicine — *La santé et la médecine*.....35

II. HUMAN ACTIVITIES — 41

6• Work — *Le travail*.....41
7• Leisure — *Les loisirs*.....47
8• Sport — *Le sport*.....53
9• Food and drink — *La nourriture et la boisson*.....61
10• The arts — *Les arts*.....66

III. IDEAS — 73

11• Commenting on a text — *Le commentaire de texte*.....73
12• Time — *Le temps*.....78
13• Religion and ethics — *La religion et la morale*.....85

IV. SCIENCE AND TECHNOLOGY — 91

14• Science and research — *La science et la recherche*.....91
15• Electronics and computer science — *L'électronique et l'informatique*.....96
16• Industry and industrial relations — *L'industrie et les relations industrielles*.....101
17• Energy and natural resources — *L'énergie et les ressources naturelles*.....107

V. MAN'S ENVIRONMENT — 115

18• Housing — *Le logement*.....115
19• City life — *La vie urbaine*.....120
20• Nature — *La nature*.....125
21• Farming — *L'agriculture*.....132
22• The environment and pollution — *L'environnement et la pollution*.....138

VI. LIVING IN SOCIETY — 145

23• Social life — *La vie sociale*.....145
24• The media — *Les médias*.....150
25• Transport — *Le transport*.....154

VII. SOCIAL INSTITUTIONS **161**

26• Education — *L'éducation* 161
27• Law — *La loi* 167
28• Government and politics — *Le gouvernement et la politique* 173

VIII. THE WORLD **183**

29• Nations and countries — *Nations et pays* 183
30• Travel — *Les voyages* 189
31• Haves and have-nots — *Les nantis et les démunis* 194
32• Meteorology and space — *La météorologie et l'espace* 199

IX. TRADE **205**

33• Economic issues — *Les questions économiques* 205
34• Shopping — *Les achats* 210
35• Advertising — *La publicité* 215
36. Popular phrases and sayings — *Expressions populaires et dictons* 219

Verbes irréguliers figurant dans les listes 227

I. THE HUMAN BEING

1• The human body
Le corps humain

Vocabulaire général

the body	*le corps*
the heart [ha:t]	*le cœur*
blood [blʌd]	*le sang*
the stomach ['stʌmək]	*l'estomac*
the skeleton	*le squelette*
the build [bild]	*la carrure*
a bone	*un os*
the frame	*l'ossature*
the flesh	*la chair*
the skin	*la peau*
the neck	*le cou*
the throat [θrəut]	*la gorge*
a lung	*un poumon*
the breath [breθ]	*l'haleine, le souffle*
sweat [swet]	*la sueur*
the head	*la tête*
the brain	*le cerveau*
the hair (sing.)	*les cheveux*
a hair	*un cheveu, un poil*
the nose	*le nez*
the mouth	*la bouche*
the voice	*la voix*
a moustache [məs'ta:ʃ]	*une moustache*
a beard [biəd]	*une barbe*
a tooth (pl. teeth)	*une dent*
the tongue [tʌŋ]	*la langue*
an eye	*un œil*
a tear [tiə]	*une larme*
an ear	*une oreille*
an arm	*un bras*
a hand	*une main*
a fist	*un poing*
a finger	*un doigt*
a leg	*une jambe*
a knee [ni:]	*un genou*
a foot (pl. feet)	*un pied*

health	*la santé*
strength	*la force*
weakness	*la faiblesse*
balance	*l'équilibre*
the weight	*le poids*
tiredness	*la fatigue*
exhaustion [igz'ɔ:stʃən]	*l'épuisement*
digestion	*la digestion*
a giant	*un géant*
a dwarf [dwɔ:f]	*un nain*
a cripple	*un handicapé*
a blind person	*un aveugle*
the blind [blaind]	*les aveugles*
a step	*un pas*
a stride	*une enjambée*
a leap, a jump	*un bond, un saut*
a movement	*un mouvement*
motion	*le mouvement*
an attempt [ə'tempt]	*une tentative*
a try	*un essai*
rest	*le repos*
sleep	*le sommeil*
perception	*la perception*
the senses	*les sens*
sight	*la vue*
hearing	*l'ouïe*
touch [tʌtʃ]	*le toucher*
smell	*l'odorat*
taste	*le goût*
beauty	*la beauté*
healthy	*bien portant*
unhealthy	*maladif*
lively	*vif*
sound [saund]	*sain*
tired	*fatigué*
exhausted	*épuisé*

smart	*chic, élégant*
lovely	*ravissant*
graceful	*gracieux (gracieuse)*
good-looking	*beau, belle*
handsome	*beau*
attractive	*séduisant(e)*
well-built	*bien bâti*
slim	*mince*
pretty	*joli*
ugly [ʻʌgli]	*laid*
visible	*visible*
invisible	*invisible*
clever	*adroit, intelligent*
awkward	*maladroit*
stiff	*raide*
small	*petit*
short	*petit (stature), court*
little	*petit (mignon)*
light	*léger*
heavy	*lourd*
thin, lean	*maigre*
fat	*gros*
overweight, obese [əu'bi:s]	*obèse*
large	*grand, gros*
enormous, huge [hju:dʒ]	*énorme*
gigantic	*gigantesque*
tiny	*tout petit*
well-fed	*bien nourri*
tall	*grand*
quick, fast	*rapide*
brisk	*animé, vif*
clean	*propre*
dirty [ʻdə:ti]	*sale*
(un)tidy	*(dés)ordonné*
naked [ʻneikid]	*nu*
rough [rʌf]	*rude, grossier*
tough [tʌf]	*dur, robuste*
soft	*doux*
smooth [smu:ð]	*lisse*
sun-tanned	*bronzé*
muscular	*musclé*
powerful	*puissant*
fit	*en forme*
fair-haired	*blond*
broad-shouldered	*large d'épaules*
pale	*pâle*
blue-eyed	*aux yeux bleus*
bald (-headed)	*chauve*
wrinkled	*ridé*
blind [blaind]	*aveugle*
deaf [def]	*sourd*

dumb [dʌm]	*muet*
deaf and dumb	*sourd-muet*
quite	*assez*
still	*encore, toujours*
extremely, exceedingly	*excessivement*
strikingly	*remarquablement*
carefully	*prudemment*
delicately	*délicatement*
gracefully	*avec grâce*
gently, softly	*doucement*
lightly	*légèrement*
roughly [ʻrʌfli]	*brutalement*
painfully	*péniblement*
quickly, swiftly	*rapidement*
fast	*vite*
energetically	*énergiquement*
steadily	*régulièrement*
slightly	*légèrement, un peu*
approximately	*environ*
prettily	*joliment*
sexually	*sexuellement*
backward(s)	*en arrière*
forward(s)	*en avant*
sideways	*de côté*
to and fro [frəu]	*de long en large*
to leave*	*quitter, partir*
to go*	*aller*
to go* on	*continuer*
to go* away	*s'en aller*
to quit*	*quitter, cesser*
to come*	*venir, jouir*
to come* upon	*tomber sur*
to meet*	*rencontrer*
to push	*pousser*
to pull	*tirer*
to move	*bouger*
to move on	*avancer*
to hold*	*tenir*
to seize [si:z]	*saisir*
to stand*	*être debout*
to stand* up	*se lever*
to lie* [lai]	*s'étendre, être allongé*
to lie* down	*s'allonger*
to lay* [lei]	*poser, mettre*
to lay* out	*disposer*
to bring*	*apporter*
to bring* up	*élever (enfant)*
to carry	*porter*
to carry on	*continuer*
to carry out	*effectuer*
to bear* [bɛə]	*porter, supporter*
to drag	*traîner*
to fetch	*aller chercher*

to weigh [wei]	*peser*
to hit*	*frapper*
to beat* [bi:t]	*battre*
to punch	*donner un coup de poing à*
to strike*, to knock	*frapper*
to kick	*donner un coup de pied à / dans*
to break*	*casser*
to bite* [bait]	*mordre*
to sting*	*piquer*
to throw*, to cast*	*jeter, lancer*
to put*	*mettre*
to try	*essayer*
to sit*	*s'asseoir, être assis*
to sit* down	*s'asseoir*
to dance [da:ns]	*danser*
to kneel* [ni:l]	*s'agenouiller*
to run*	*courir*
to run* away	*se sauver*
to rush	*se précipiter*
to swim*	*nager*
to climb [klaim]	*grimper*
to jump	*sauter*
to leap*	*bondir*
to start	*commencer, partir, sursauter*
to startle	*faire sursauter*
to flee*	*fuir, s'enfuir*
to hide*	*(se) cacher*
to make* up	*se maquiller*
to cut*	*couper*
to cut* off	*couper, amputer*
to turn	*(se) tourner*
to turn up	*arriver, venir*
to turn over	*(se) retourner (horizontal)*
to turn round	*se retourner (vertical)*
to give*	*donner*
to give* up	*abandonner*
to look	*paraître*
to look for	*chercher*
to search [sə:tʃ]	*fouiller*
to sleep*	*dormir*
to rest	*se reposer*
to become*	*devenir*
to remain	*demeurer, rester*
to stay	*rester*
to breed*	*engendrer*
to survive	*survivre*
to blow* [bləu]	*souffler*
to breathe [bri:ð]	*respirer*
to cough [kɔf]	*tousser*
to smoke	*fumer*
to sneeze	*éternuer*
to sniff	*renifler*
to spit*	*cracher*
to digest [daidʒest]	*digérer*
to fart	*péter*
to shit*	*chier*
to vomit	*vomir*
to be sick	*vomir, être malade*
to starve	*être affamé*
to sweat [swet]	*suer, exploiter*
to get*	*obtenir*
to get* up	*se lever*
to get* out	*sortir*
to feel*	*sentir*
to smell*	*sentir (odeur)*
to stink*	*puer*
to fight*	*se battre*
to struggle	*lutter*
to work	*travailler*
to toil, to labour ['leibə]	*peiner*
to practise	*pratiquer, s'exercer*

Vocabulaire spécialisé

the skull	*le crâne*
the forehead	*le front*
a wrinkle [rinkl]	*une ride*
an eyebrow	*un sourcil*
an eyelid	*une paupière*
an eyelash	*un cil*
a nostril	*une narine*
a cheek [tʃi:k]	*une joue*
a jaw [dʒɔ:]	*une mâchoire*
the lips	*les lèvres*
the limbs	*les membres*
a shoulder ['ʃɔ:ldə]	*une épaule*
an elbow	*un coude*
a wrist [rist]	*un poignet*
a rib	*une côte*
an ankle	*une cheville*
a heel	*un talon*
a toe [təu]	*un orteil*
a nail	*un ongle*
the trunk	*le tronc*

the nape of the neck	*la nuque*
the spine	*l'épine dorsale*
a vertebra (vertebrae)	*une vertèbre*
the backbone	*la colonne vertéb.*
the chest	*la poitrine (homme ou femme)*
the bust [bʌst]	*la poitrine (femme)*
the breasts [brests]	*les seins*
the womb [wu:m]	*l'utérus*
the hips	*les hanches*
the navel ['neivəl]	*le nombril*
the liver ['livə]	*le foie*
the intestines	*l'intestin*
the kidneys	*les reins*
fat	*la graisse*
saliva [sə'laivə]	*la salive*
semen ['si:men]	*le sperme*
urine ['juərin]	*l'urine*
shit	*la merde*

Clothing — *L'habillement*

clothes [kləuðz]	*les vêtements*
a garment	*un vêtement*
a hat	*un chapeau*
a cap	*une casquette*
a scarf (pl.: scarves)	*une écharpe*
gloves [glʌvz]	*des gants*
a sleeve	*une manche*
a coat	*un manteau*
a raincoat, a mac	*un imperméable*
a jacket	*une veste*
a fleece	*un polaire*
a shirt [ʃə:t]	*une chemise*
a tie, a neck-tie (US)	*une cravate*
a belt	*une ceinture*
a suit [sju:t]	*un costume*
a vest	*un maillot*
a jumper, a sweater	*un pull*
a T-shirt	*un tee shirt*
a tank top	*un débardeur*
a track suit	*un survêtement*
a hoodie	*un sweat à capuche*
a dress	*une robe*
a skirt [skə:t]	*une jupe*
(a pair of) trousers	*un pantalon*
(a pair of) jeans	*un jean*
(a pair of) shorts	*un short*
(a pair of) briefs	*un slip*
a thong [θɔŋ]	*un string*
(a pair of) knickers	*une culotte*
(a pair of) tights	*un collant*
a sock	*une chaussette*
slippers	*des chaussons*
trainers	*des chaussures de sport*
tennis shoes	*des chaussures de tennis*
boots [bu:ts]	*des bottes, des souliers montants*
to wear* [wɛə]	*porter*
to dress, to get* dressed	*s'habiller*
to undress, to get* undressed, to strip	*se déshabiller*
to put* on	*mettre*
to try on	*essayer*
to get* changed	*se changer*
to pull up	*remonter, tirer*
to roll up	*retrousser*
to fold	*plier*
to unfold	*déplier*

Motion — *Le mouvement*

to walk	*marcher*
to wander	*errer, flâner*
to stroll [strəul]	*flâner*
to head for	*se diriger vers*
to bump into	*rencontrer par hasard*
to tread* [tred] on	*marcher sur*
to trip, to stumble	*trébucher*
to stagger	*tituber*
to step	*faire un / des pas*
to crawl [krɔ:l]	*ramper, se traîner*
to creep*	*ramper*
to drag	*traîner, tirer*
to collapse	*s'effondrer*
to faint	*s'évanouir*
to bend*	*se courber*
to bow [bau]	*saluer, s'incliner*
to spring*	*bondir*
to cross	*traverser*
to hurl [hə:l]	*jeter (avec violence)*
to handle	*manipuler, manier*
to manipulate	*manœuvrer*
to twist	*tordre*
to grasp [gra:sp]	*saisir*
to grip	*serrer, agripper*
to cling* (to)	*s'accrocher (à)*

The senses — *Les sens*

to make* out	*discerner*
to watch	*regarder, observer*
to stare (at)	*dévisager, fixer*
to gaze (at)	*contempler*
to glance (at)	*jeter un coup d'œil*
to glare (at) [glɛə]	*lancer un regard furieux*
to peep (at)	*regarder furtivement*

to have a glance (at)	*jeter un coup d'œil*	to listen (to)	*écouter*
to catch a glimpse of	*entrevoir*	to shiver	*frissonner*
to taste	*goûter*	to blush [blʌʃ]	*rougir*
to hear* [hiə]	*entendre*	to tremble	*trembler*

Expressions

to do one's best	*faire de son mieux*
to do an exercise	*faire un exercice*
to do a favour	*rendre un service*
to do a job	*faire un travail*
to do some work	*faire du travail*
to do the cooking	*faire la cuisine*
Can you do something for me?	*Pouvez-vous faire quelque chose pour moi ?*
What is to be done?	*Que faut-il faire ?*
How do you do!	*Enchanté !*
to make a cake	*faire un gâteau*
to make an attempt	*faire une tentative*
to make an effort	*faire un effort*
to make a mistake	*faire une erreur*
to make a noise	*faire du bruit*
to make love	*faire l'amour*
to make someone do something	*forcer quelqu'un à faire quelque chose*
to make a good job of it	*faire du bon travail*
to make do with	*faire avec, se contenter de*
to have a cold	*être enrhumé*
to have a suntan	*être bronzé*
to have a walk	*faire une promenade*
to have a look	*jeter un coup d'œil*
to have a try / a go	*essayer, tenter le coup*
to have a rest	*se reposer*
to have a nap / a siesta	*faire un somme / une sieste*
to have a good time	*bien s'amuser*
to have someone do something	*faire faire quelque chose par quelqu'un*
to have something done	*faire faire quelque chose*
to have a bite to eat	*manger un morceau*
to have a breath of fresh air	*prendre l'air*
to have one's hair cut	*se faire couper les cheveux*
to get drowned	*se noyer*
to get something done	*faire faire quelque chose*
to get someone to do something	*faire faire quelque chose à quelqu'un*
to get killed	*se faire tuer*
to go cycling	*faire du vélo*
to go swimming	*faire de la natation*
to give someone a hand	*donner un coup de main à quelqu'un*
to be cold / hot	*avoir froid / chaud*
to be thirsty / hungry	*avoir soif / faim*
to be parched	*mourir de soif*
to be starving	*mourir de faim*

to be (blind) drunk	*être ivre (mort)*
to be safe and sound	*être sain et sauf*
to be in the nude / stark naked	*être nu / nu comme un ver*
to be five feet tall	*mesurer 1m50*
to be five months pregnant	*être enceinte de cinq mois*
a broken leg	*une fracture de la jambe*
a sprained knee	*une entorse du genou*
to be as fit as a fiddle	*être en pleine peau*
to weigh ten stone	*peser 63 kg*
to feel well / fine	*se sentir bien*
to feel unwell	*ne pas se sentir bien*
to feel seasick	*avoir le mal de mer*
to feel carsick / homesick	*avoir le mal de voiture / du pays*
to look fit / well	*avoir l'air bien / en forme*
to look in good shape / form	*avoir l'air en bonne forme*
to look like one's parents	*ressembler à ses parents*
to sound like one's parents	*parler comme ses parents*
to keep an eye on	*avoir l'œil à / sur, surveiller*
to keep on doing something	*continuer à faire quelque chose*
I can't swim	*Je ne sais pas nager*
He *can* drive	*Il sait bien conduire*
She *can't* dress	*Elle s'habille mal*
I could not help him	*Je ne pouvais (pourrais) pas l'aider*
I was not able to help him	*Je n'ai pas pu l'aider*
I can smell her perfume	*Je sens son parfum*
I can see him coming	*Je le vois venir*
I can't hear what you are saying	*Je n'entends pas ce que vous dites*
to smell of perfume	*sentir le parfum*
to blow one's nose	*se moucher*
to turn / go red	*rougir*
to turn / go pale	*blêmir*
to lose weight	*perdre du poids*
to put on weight	*prendre du poids*
to be on a slimming diet	*être au régime*
to sleep rough	*coucher dehors / à la dure*
to rough it	*vivre à la dure*
to roll up one's sleeves	*retrousser les manches*
to cut one's finger	*se couper le doigt*
to have one's finger cut off	*se faire sectionner le doigt*
to shout at someone	*crier après quelqu'un*
to let someone in	*faire entrer quelqu'un*
to see someone out	*raccompagner quelqu'un*
to kick a door open	*ouvrir une porte à coups de pied*
to knock someone unconscious	*assommer quelqu'un*
to kick / throw someone out	*mettre quelqu'un à la porte / vider quelqu'un*
to stop / to quit / to give up smoking	*arrêter de fumer*
to stop to light a cigarette	*s'arrêter pour allumer une cigarette*
to drag one's feet	*traîner les pieds*

Phrases

Give me a hand, will you?
Donne-moi un coup de main, veux-tu ?

Could you help me carry this luggage?
Pourrais-tu m'aider à porter ces bagages ?

She has always done her best to make their life easier.
Elle a toujours fait de son mieux pour leur rendre la vie plus facile.

I must get some work done before I go out.
Il faut que je m'avance dans mon travail avant de sortir.

Every five steps she would stop to glance at herself in a shop-window.
Tous les cinq pas elle s'arrêtait devant une vitrine pour s'y regarder un bref instant.

"I have nothing to offer but blood, toil, tears and sweat." (Winston Churchill, 13 May, 1940)
Je n'ai rien à vous proposer que sang, peine, larmes et sueur.

—What is the new headmaster like? —He is short, thickset and slightly overweight.
— Comment est le nouveau proviseur ? — Il est petit, trapu, légèrement corpulent.

It was so hot, I felt like having a nice cold beer.
Il faisait si chaud (que) j'avais envie d'une bonne bière glacée.

I could smell her heady perfume even before I saw her.
Je sentis son parfum entêtant avant même de la voir.

Amelia may look like her father, but on the phone she sounds like her mother.
Il est possible qu'Amélie ressemble à son père, mais au téléphone on dirait sa mère.

Exercices

I. Apparier chaque mot de la colonne de gauche avec un mot de la colonne de droite. Rétablir l'article indéfini devant les groupes nominaux.

sprained	body
healthy	handsome
sexually	forehead
smart	loud
blue-eyed	step
strikingly	dress
painfully	attractive
broken	ankle
brisk	blonde
wrinkled	arm

II. Compléter en utilisant les verbes do / make / get / have / can à la bonne forme :

1. Nowadays some young husbands ... the cooking and cleaning while their wives go out to work.
2. The refugees had to ... do with little food.
3. Nigel certainly proved that he ... drive : he won 13 Grand Prix that year!
4. I wonder how Henry always manages to ... a suntan right in the middle of winter.
5. He ... killed in a car crash last year.
6. On a Sunday he always ... a light meal and then a short rest.
7. I wish you would ... an effort to look more tidy.
8. The journalist ... mistakenly beaten up by the police last week.
9. He stepped off the jetty into the sea and as he ... swim, he ... drowned.
10. Watching greedy people eat and drink often ... me feel sick.

III. Compléter en employant les formes verbales appropriées :

He (1)... smoking when he read that it could induce cancer.

Joe has certainly put on weight in the past few years : he now (2)... over 18 stone.

He (3)... so much like his father that I can't tell the difference when he answers the phone.

It always takes Mary ages to (4)... ... as she can't choose between all her clothes.

Please give me something to eat, I'm (5)... .

I saw the two brutes (6)... the unfortunate passer-by within an inch of his life.

Yesterday Jack (7)... the whole house without being able to find his glasses.

George W. must have been blind (8) ..., for he (9) ... out of the bar, (10) ... the street in the middle of heavy traffic and nearly got run over by a bus.

2• Feelings
Les sentiments

a feeling	*un sentiment*	self-satisfaction	*l'autosatisfaction*
a mood [mu:d]	*une humeur*	sadness	*la tristesse*
temper	*le caractère*	displeasure	*le mécontentement*
happiness	*le bonheur*	dissatisfaction	*l'insatisfaction*
delight, joy, mirth	*la joie*[mə:θ]	sorrow [ˈsɔrəu]	*la peine, le chagrin*
pleasure [ˈpleʒə]	*le plaisir*	grief [gri:f]	*la douleur, la peine*
fun	*l'amusement*	mourning [ˈmɔ:niŋ]	*le deuil*
satisfaction	*la satisfaction*	worry [ˈwʌri]	*le souci*

anxiety [æŋ'zaiəti]	*l'inquiétude*	carelessness	*la négligence*
hope	*l'espoir*	calm [ka:m]	*le calme*
optimism	*l'optimisme*	quiet ['kwaiət]	*le calme, la paix*
enthusiasm [in'θju:ziæm]	*l'enthousiasme*	patience ['peiʃəns]	*la patience*
		self-control	*la maîtrise de soi*
determination	*la détermination*	a nuisance ['nju:sns]	*un désagrément*
eagerness ['i:gənis]	*l'empressement*	stress	*le stress*
goodwill	*la bienveillance*	strain	*la tension*
reluctance	*la réticence*	agitation	*l'agitation*
apathy ['æpəθi]	*l'apathie*	anger	*la colère*
pessimism	*le pessimisme*	impatience	*l'impatience*
hopelessness, despair	*le désespoir*	frustration	*la frustration*
resignation	*la résignation*	exasperation	*l'exaspération*
indifference	*l'indifférence*	shock	*le choc*
selfishness	*l'égoïsme*	frenzy	*la frénésie*
self-indulgence	*la complaisance, le laisser-aller*	approval [ə'pru:vəl]	*l'approbation*
		congratulations	*des félicitations*
care	*l'attention, le soin*	a reward [ri'wɔ:d]	*une récompense*
prudence ['pru:dəns]	*la prudence*	disapproval	*la désapprobation*
sensitivity	*la sensibilité*	a difference	*un différend*
intuition	*l'intuition*	a reproach [ri'prəutʃ]	*un reproche*
love	*l'amour*	a row [rau], an argument	*une dispute*
seduction	*la séduction*		
appeal [ə'pi:l]	*le charme, l'attrait*	a quarrel	*une querelle*
charisma [kæ'rizmə]	*le charisme*	recklessness	*la témérité*
warmth	*la cordialité*	fear [fiə]	*la peur*
friendship	*l'amitié*	fright	*l'effroi*
harmony	*l'harmonie*	dread, terror	*la terreur*
tolerance	*la tolérance*	panic	*la panique*
sympathy ['simpəθi]	*la compassion*	dismay	*le désarroi*
pity, mercy ['mə:si]	*la pitié*	a coward ['kauəd]	*un lâche*
indulgence	*l'indulgence*	cowardice	*la lâcheté*
benevolence	*la bienveillance*	courage ['kʌridʒ]	*le courage*
kindness	*la gentillesse*	a hero ['hiərəu]	*un héros*
hate, hatred ['heitrid]	*la haine*	surprise	*la surprise*
bitterness	*l'amertume*	astonishment	*l'étonnement*
resentment	*le ressentiment*	amazement	*la stupéfaction*
spite	*la malveillance*	wonder	*l'émerveillement*
deception	*la tromperie*	admiration	*l'admiration*
envy	*l'envie*	gullibility	*la crédulité*
jealousy ['dʒeləsi]	*la jalousie*	a sign [sain]	*un signe*
intolerance	*l'intolérance*	a hint	*une allusion*
severity, sternness	*la sévérité*	a smile	*un sourire*
cruelty ['kru:əlti]	*la cruauté*	laughter ['la:ftə]	*le rire*
scorn, contempt	*le mépris, le dédain*	a tear [tiə]	*une larme*
pride	*la fierté*	a breakdown	*une dépression*
confidence, trust	*la confiance*	a fit	*une crise, un accès*
self-confidence	*la confiance en soi*	a blunder	*une gaffe*
self-esteem	*l'amour-propre*	a bond	*un attachement*
vanity	*la vanité, l'orgueil*	a tie [tai]	*un lien*
shame	*la honte*	moody ['mu:di]	*lunatique*
guilt	*la culpabilité*	(un)happy	*(mal)heureux*
self-consciousness	*la gêne*	delighted	*ravi*
shyness	*la timidité*	merry	*gai*
imprudence	*l'imprudence*	cheerful	*enjoué, gai*

(dis)pleased	*(mé)content*
(dis)satisfied	*(in)satisfait*
self-satisfied	*suffisant*
sad	*triste*
sorry	*désolé*
worried [‘wʌrid]	*soucieux*
depressed	*déprimé*
pleasant [‘pleznt]	*agréable*
welcome	*bienvenu*
delightful	*charmant*
amusing [ə’mju:ziŋ]	*amusant*
funny	*drôle*
hilarious [hi’lɛərĭəs]	*hilarant*
hopeful	*plein d’espoir*
hopeless	*sans espoir*
optimistic	*optimiste*
pessimistic	*pessimiste*
enthusiastic	*enthousiaste*
determined	*décidé* [di’tə:mind]
eager [‘i:gə]	*avide, désireux*
anxious	*inquiet, impatient*
reluctant [ri’lʌktənt]	*réticent*
resigned [ri’zaind]	*résigné*
indifferent	*indifférent*
melancholy	*mélancolique*
downhearted [‘daun’ha:tid]	*découragé*
desperate [‘despərit]	*désespéré*
proud	*fier*
self-confident	*sûr de soi*
vain	*vaniteux*
boastful [‘bəustful]	*vantard*
ashamed [ə’ʃeimd]	*honteux*
unashamed	*éhonté*
shameless	*effronté*
guilty	*coupable*
self-conscious	*gêné*
loving, affectionate	*affectueux*
close [kləus]	*intime, proche*
lovely	*ravissant*
attractive	*séduisant*
fascinating	*fascinant*
charming	*charmant*
keen	*enthousiaste, ardent*
fond [fɔnd]	*affectueux, tendre*
friendly	*amitieux*
genial [‘dʒi:njəl]	*aimable*
even-tempered	*d’humeur égale*
sincere	*sincère*
earnest [‘ə:nest]	*sérieux, sincère*
kind, kindly	*bon, gentil, brave*
gentle	*doux*
nice	*gentil, sympathique*
sympathetic	*compréhensif*
(in)sensitive	*(in)sensible*

intuitive	*intuitif*
(in)tolerant	*(in)tolérant*
merciful	*clément*
benevolent [bi’nevələnt]	*bienveillant*
severe [si’viə], stern	*sévère*
merciless, pitiless	*sans pitié*
ruthless [‘ru:θlis]	*impitoyable*
pitiful	*pitoyable*
pathetic	*navrant*
cruel	*cruel*
bitter	*amer*
resentful [ri’zentful]	*rancunier*
jealous [‘dʒeləs]	*jaloux*
deceptive [di’septiv]	*trompeur*
hateful	*haïssable*
scornful	*méprisant*
contemptible	*méprisable*
selfish	*égoïste*
self-centered	*égocentrique*
careful, prudent	*prudent*
careless	*insouciant*
imprudent	*imprudent*
reckless	*téméraire*
shy	*timide*
timid	*timoré, craintif*
reserved	*réservé*
confident	*confiant*
trustworthy [‘trʌst’wə:ði]	*digne de confiance*
suspicious	*méfiant*
frightened	*effrayé*
scared [skɛəd]	*affolé, effrayé*
panic-stricken	*paniqué*
fearless	*intrépide*
dreadful [‘dredful]	*affreux, atroce*
awful [‘ɔ:ful]	*terrible, affreux*
terrible	*effroyable*
terrifying	*terrifiant*
appalling [ə’pɔ:liŋ]	*épouvantable*
terrific	*fantastique, super*
formidable	*redoutable*
horrible	*horrible*
awesome [‘ɔ:səm]	*impressionnant, terrifiant*
angry	*en colère*
annoyed	*agacé, contrarié*
furious	*furieux*
bad-tempered	*grincheux*
grumpy	*grincheux*
mad	*furieux*
upset	*contrarié, vexé*
offended [ɔ’fendid]	*offensé*
shocked	*choqué*
frantic	*hors de soi*

shocking	*choquant*
(dis)approving	*(dés)approbateur*
rewarding	*gratifiant*
reproachful	*réprobateur*
quarrelsome	*querelleur*
challenging	*provocateur*
calm, quiet [kwaiət]	*calme*
(im)patient	*(im)patient*
cool	*calme, décontracté*
casual ['kæʒjuəl]	*désinvolte*
nervous	*nerveux, tendu*
stressed	*stressé*
rash	*impétueux*
courageous [kə'reidʒəs]	*courageux*
heroic	*héroïque*
daring	*audacieux*
dedicated	*dévoué*
painstaking	*assidu, appliqué*
surprised	*surpris*
astonished	*étonné*
amazed [ə'meizd]	*stupéfait*
admirative	*admiratif*
gullible ['gʌlibl]	*crédule*
wonderful	*merveilleux*
amazing	*stupéfiant*
smiling	*souriant*
laughing	*riant, rieur*
tearful	*larmoyant*
exuberant	*exubérant*
bold [bəuld]	*hardi*
hard	*dur, durement*
hardly	*à peine*
(un)fortunately	*(mal)heureusement*
happily	*joyeusement*
pleasantly	*agréablement*
cheerfully	*gaiement*
delightfully	*délicieusement*
tremendously	*terriblement*
sincerely	*sincèrement*
intimately	*intimement*
faithfully	*fidèlement*
sadly	*tristement*
anxiously	*anxieusement ; avec impatience*
hopefully	*avec (bon) espoir*
optimistically	*avec optimisme*
enthusiastically	*avec enthousiasme*
hopelessly, desperately	*désespérément*
willingly	*volontiers*
eagerly	*avec impatience ardemment*
reluctantly	*à regret*
indifferently	*médiocrement*

lovingly	*tendrement*
attractively	*d'une manière attrayante*
charmingly	*d'une façon charmante*
intuitively	*intuitivement*
calmly	*calmement*
quietly	*tranquillement*
(im)patiently	*(im)patiemment*
coolly	*calmement*
casually	*avec désinvolture*
nervously	*nerveusement*
anxiously	*avec inquiétude*
awfully, terribly	*terriblement*
fearfully, horribly	*horriblement*
boldly	*audacieusement*
kindly	*avec gentillesse*
gently	*doucement*
nicely	*gentiment*
sympathetically	*avec compassion*
tolerantly	*avec indulgence*
intolerantly	*avec intolérance*
mercifully	*avec clémence*
severely, sternly	*sévèrement*
ruthlessly	*impitoyablement*
pathetically	*pitoyablement*
deeply	*profondément*
cruelly	*cruellement*
bitterly	*amèrement*
jealously	*jalousement ; avec vigilance*
deceptively	*faussement*
scornfully	*avec mépris*
proudly	*fièrement*
confidently	*avec confiance*
vainly	*vaniteusement ; vainement*
boastfully	*en se vantant*
self-consciously	*d'une manière gênée*
shamelessly	*sans vergogne*
shyly	*avec réserve*
timidly	*timidement*
selfishly	*égoïstement*
carefully	*soigneusement*
carelessly	*négligemment*
prudently	*prudemment*
recklessly	*imprudemment*
courageously	*courageusement*
heroically	*héroïquement*
angrily	*avec emportement*
madly	*follement, éperdument*
wonderfully	*merveilleusement*
amazingly	*étonnamment*

reproachfully	*d'un air de reproche*
to feel*	*(res)sentir*
to sense	*(pres)sentir*
to (dis)please	*(dé)plaire*
to satisfy	*satisfaire*
to cheer up	*égayer*
to mourn [mɔ:n]	*pleurer, se lamenter*
to sulk [sʌlk]	*bouder*
to worry	*s'inquiéter*
to hope	*espérer*
to despair [dis'pɛə]	*désespérer*
to love	*aimer*
to lure [luə]	*attirer (par la ruse)*
to fascinate	*fasciner*
to attract	*attirer, séduire*
to appeal to	*plaire à*
to approve (of)	*approuver*
to charm	*charmer*
to like	*aimer (bien)*
to dislike	*ne pas aimer*
to detest, to loathe [ləuð]	*détester*
to sympathize	*compatir*
to welcome	*accueillir*
to tolerate, to put up with	*tolérer, supporter*
to bear*[bɛə], to stand*	*supporter*
to pity	*plaindre*
to indulge in	*s'adonner à, s'octroyer*
to hate	*haïr*
to resent [ri'zent]	*s'offusquer de*
to deceive [di'si:v]	*tromper*
to hurt* [hə:t]	*blesser*
to envy	*envier*
to reproach (with)	*reprocher*
to quarrel, to argue	*se disputer*

to betray [bi'trei]	*trahir, tromper*
to challenge	*défier ; contester*
to disapprove (of), to frown on	*désapprouver*
to calm (down)	*(se) calmer*
to stress	*stresser*
to strain	*fatiguer, éprouver*
to frighten	*faire peur à*
to dread [dred]	*redouter*
to panic	*paniquer*
to dare [dɛə]	*oser ; défier*
to boast [bəust]	*se vanter*
to show* off	*crâner*
to anger	*mettre en colère*
to frustrate	*frustrer*
to shock	*choquer*
to offend [ɔ'fend]	*offenser*
to upset*	*bouleverser*
to surprise	*surprendre*
to astonish	*étonner*
to wonder at	*s'émerveiller de*
to admire [əd'maiə]	*admirer*
to look up to	*respecter*
to smile	*sourire*
to laugh [la:f]	*rire*
to giggle	*glousser*
to sneer at [sniə]	*se moquer de (méprisant)*
to mock, to jeer at	*se moquer de*
to cry, to weep*	*pleurer*
to sigh [sai]	*soupirer*
to sob	*sangloter*
to break* down	*s'effondrer, craquer*
to congratulate	*féliciter*
to reward [ri'wɔ:d]	*récompenser*
to blunder	*faire une bévue*
to promise, to pledge	*promettre*

Phrases et expressions

pleasure	***le plaisir***
to be pleased /satisfied / delighted with something	*être content / satisfait / ravi de quelque chose*
He is pleased with his new job.	*Il est content de son nouvel emploi.*
to be pleased / delighted to do something	*être content / ravi de faire quelque chose*
We'd be delighted to help you.	*Nous serions ravis de vous aider.*
It was a real pleasure seeing you again.	*Cela a été un réel plaisir de vous revoir.*
to enjoy oneself	*(bien) s'amuser*

We enjoyed ourselves at the party.	*Nous nous sommes bien amusés à la soirée.*
We had a whale of a time!	*On s'est vraiment éclatés*
to burst out laughing	*éclater de rire*
to have (a fit of) the giggles	*avoir le fou rire*
sadness	***la tristesse***
to mourn someone's death	*pleurer la mort de quelqu'un*
She will be sadly missed.	*Son absence sera très regrettée.*
What a shame (a pity)!	*Quel dommage !*
to feel sorry for someone	*plaindre quelqu'un*
to have a long face	*faire triste mine*
hope	***l'espoir***
Let's hope for the best!	*Espérons que les choses iront pour le mieux !*
I hope to be able to find him.	*J'espère pouvoir le trouver.*
I hope (that) you have a nice journey.	*J'espère que vous ferez bon voyage.*
Hopefully, we shall manage...	*Avec un peu de chance, on y arrivera...*
liking, disliking	***les penchants***
He likes a joke.	*Il aime la plaisanterie.*
He likes playing tricks.	*Il aime jouer des tours.*
I would like to visit India.	*J'aimerais visiter l'Inde.*
John is keen on good food.	*John aime beaucoup la bonne chère.*
They are keen to meet you.	*Ils tiennent à vous rencontrer.*
Emily was very fond of her native countryside.	*Emily était très attachée à sa campagne natale.*
I do not care much for serial music.	*Je ne suis pas trop porté sur la musique sérielle.*
It isn't my cup of tea.	*Ce n'est pas mon truc.*
I feel like (having) a nice cup of tea.	*J'ai envie d'une bonne tasse de thé.*
Do you fancy going for a walk?	*Ça te dit de faire une promenade ?*
enthusiasm	***l'enthousiasme***
She is eager to please.	*Elle est désireuse de plaire.*
He tries hard.	*Il fait son possible.*
He does his best.	*Il fait de son mieux.*
We are looking forward to meeting you.	*Nous attendons avec impatience de vous voir.*
Our proposal got an enthusiastic welcome.	*Notre proposition reçut un accueil enthousiaste.*
They were ecstatic about their trip.	*Ils étaient enchantés de leur voyage.*
wishes	***les souhaits***
I wish to leave as soon as possible.	*Je souhaite partir le plus tôt possible.*
I wish you would come with me.	*Je voudrais que vous veniez avec moi.*
I wish I were on holiday...	*Si seulement j'étais en vacances...*
I wish you had been with us last night.	*Je regrette que vous n'ayez pas été avec nous hier soir.*
to yearn for / to long for	*aspirer à / languir après*
to be willing to + inf	*être prêt à / disposé à + inf*
to be reluctant to + inf	*rechigner à + inf*
fear	***la crainte, la peur***
to be afraid of something	*avoir peur de quelque chose*
I'm afraid we shall be late.	*J'ai bien peur que nous soyons en retard.*

She's frightened of spiders.	*Elle a très peur des araignées.*
She was frightened by a huge spider.	*Elle a été effrayée par une énorme araignée.*
to be scared of something	*avoir une peur terrible de quelque chose*
I was scared stiff.	*J'avais une peur bleue.*
He fears the consequences of his acts.	*Il redoute les conséquences de ses actes.*
He fears having to face the consequences.	*Il redoute de devoir faire face aux conséquences.*
pride	***la fierté***
to be proud of one's success	*être fier de sa réussite*
to be pleased with oneself	*être content de soi*
to take pride in (doing) something	*tirer fierté de faire quelque chose*
to boast of being the best	*se vanter d'être le meilleur*
to show off one's accomplishments	*étaler ses talents*
Stop showing off, will you!	*Arrête de crâner, veux-tu !*
preference	***la préférence***
I'd rather have this one.	*J'aimerais mieux prendre celui-ci.*
I'd rather you did not insist.	*Je préférerais que vous n'insistiez pas.*
I think I'd prefer to go there in February.	*Je pense que je préférerais y aller en février.*
Generally speaking, I prefer working at home.	*De manière générale, je préfère travailler à la maison.*
I prefer fruit juice to Coca Cola.	*Je préfère le jus de fruits au Coca Cola.*
love	***l'amour***
to fall in love with somebody	*tomber amoureux de quelqu'un*
to feel attracted to someone	*être attiré par quelqu'un*
love at first sight	*le coup de foudre*
to be fond of + nom ou gérondif	*aimer, avoir de l'affection pour*
hate	***la haine***
I can't bear (stand) him.	*Je ne peux pas le supporter.*
I can't stand the sight of him.	*Je ne peux pas le voir en peinture.*
I hate his guts! (fam.)	*Je ne peux pas le sentir !*
There's no love lost between them.	*Ce n'est pas le grand amour entre eux.*
to hurt someone's feelings	*froisser / blesser quelqu'un*
He did it out of spite.	*Il l'a fait par malveillance.*
indifference	***l'indifférence***
I don't care.	*Je m'en fiche.*
I couldn't care less.	*Je m'en fiche pas mal.*
I don't give a damn. (fam.)	*Je m'en fiche comme de l'an quarante.*
I don't mind.	*Ça m'est égal.*
Don't bother answering!	*Ne vous donnez pas la peine de répondre !*
approval, disapproval	***l'approbation, la désapprobation***
Do you mind if I use the car?	*Cela ne te gêne pas si j'utilise la voiture ?*
Do you mind my using the car?	*idem*
Would you mind opening the window?	*Cela vous ennuierait d'ouvrir la fenêtre ?*
I do mind!	*Il n'en est pas question !*
The mind boggles!	*On croit rêver !*
He must be out of his mind!	*Il a dû perdre la raison !*

anger	***la colère***
to be fed up with	*en avoir assez de*
to get on someone's nerves	*taper sur les nerfs de quelqu'un*
to lose one's temper	*se mettre en colère*
to fly into a temper	*exploser, éclater*
to be angry with someone	*être en colère contre quelqu'un*
to be angry at something	*être en colère à cause de quelque chose*
to be at odds with someone (over)	*être brouillé avec quelqu'un (à propos de)*
to have a row	*se disputer*
to be bad-tempered	*avoir mauvais caractère*
to make a fuss	*faire des histoires*

depression	***la dépression***
to have the blues; to feel down	*avoir le cafard*
to feel depressed	*se sentir déprimé*
to feel lonely	*se sentir seul*
to burst into tears	*éclater en sanglots*
to have a nervous breakdown	*faire une dépression nerveuse*
to be on the verge of a breakdown	*être au bord de la dépression nerveuse*

recovery	***le rétablissement***
to get over a catastrophe	*surmonter une catastrophe*
to pull through	*s'en tirer, s'en sortir*
to cheer up	*prendre espoir*
Pull yourself together!	*Ressaisis-toi !*
to take courage	*prendre courage*

necessity	***la nécessité***
He needs (to have) other people's help.	*Il a besoin de l'aide des autres.*
Need he come?	*Est-ce la peine qu'il vienne ?*
He need not come if he doesn't feel like it.	*Ce n'est pas la peine qu'il vienne s'il n'en a pas envie.*
You need not have come.	*Ce n'était pas la peine de venir.*
What's the use of worrying?	*À quoi cela sert-il de s'inquiéter ?*
It's no use worrying.	*Cela ne sert à rien de s'inquiéter.*
Is the place worth visiting / a visit?	*Est-ce que l'endroit vaut la peine d'être visité ?*

Proverbes

An eye for an eye, a tooth for a tooth.
Œil pour œil, dent pour dent.

Familiarity breeds contempt.
La familiarité engendre le mépris.

A friend in need is a friend indeed.
C'est dans le besoin que l'on connaît ses amis.

There's no use crying over spilt milk.
Ce qui est fait est fait.

Exercices

I. Compléter les phrases suivantes en utilisant les prépositions appropriés :

1. He is not keen ... parties : I think he only came ... ... politeness.
2. You need not attend the concert if you do not care ... modern music.
3. He seems to be delighted ... his new car.
4. I wish she would stop boasting ... her academic achievements.
5. Auntie Rose does not approve ... Louis' new haircut.
6. Soon after his divorce he started to indulge ... alcoholic drinks.
7. Whatever his mistakes, Tony always looked pleased ... himself.
8. Let's hope ... a quick improvement ... the economic situation.
9. Hyacinth takes great pride ... her artistic abilities.
10. After all that hard work we longed ... a couple of days' rest.

II. Reformuler les phrases suivantes en utilisant les éléments entre parenthèses :

1. They can't help sympathizing with poor Emma. (sorry)
2. They often quarrelled when they had to work together. (odds)
3. He said he would not tolerate all that noise every night. (put)
4. I'd like him to give up smoking. (wish)
5. If only I could have a cup of tea now. (feel)
6. Would you object to my taking a few days' holiday? (mind)
7. When he heard the news, he got very angry. (flew)
8. Nobody ever dared to blame her as she would immediately start crying. (burst)
9. For God's sake, man, take courage! (pull)
10. As she could not stand him, she carefully avoided him. (nerves)

III. Apparier un élément de la colonne de droite avec un élément de la colonne de gauche pour former des ensembles cohérents :

Frances lacks self-confidence;	in fact I am afraid he could not care less.
I feel sorry for Clara:	I can't stand their tasteless cooking.
No matter how hard he tries to please,	I'm afraid of hurting his feelings.
She need not come to the wedding	she's always the one who gets the blame.
John and his wife were constantly quarrelling:	people do not seem to like him.
I expected him to be more enthusiastic;	he keeps tolerably fit and cheerful.
You needn't have bothered sending them a present,	if she doesn't feel like it.
I hate those fast-food places;	she needs other people's approval.
In spite of his age,	they are not even grateful.
I daren't tell him:	their life was a never-ending row.

3• The mind
L'esprit

thinking	*la pensée*
a thought [θɔ:t]	*une pensée*
a thinker	*un penseur*
a think-tank	*un groupe de réflexion*
a philosopher	*un philosophe*
awareness, consciousness	*la conscience*
an idea [ai'diə]	*une idée*
an afterthought	*une pensée après coup*
relevance	*la pertinence, l'à-propos*
a point	*un argument*
an opinion	*un avis*
advice [əd'vais]	*des conseils*
a piece of advice	*un conseil*
a discovery	*une découverte*
curiosity [,kju:ri'ɔsiti]	*la curiosité*
intelligence	*l'intelligence*
understanding	*la compréhension*
the brain	*le cerveau*
a genius ['dʒi:niəs]	*un génie*
a gift	*un don*
accuracy ['ækjrəsi]	*l'exactitude*
meaning ['mi:niŋ]	*la signification*
a hint	*une allusion*
a misunderstanding	*un malentendu*
a mistake	*une erreur*
attention	*l'attention*
concentration	*la concentration*
care [kɛə]	*la sollicitude, la précaution*
boredom	*l'ennui*
an investigation	*une investigation*
an inquiry [in'kwaiəri]	*une enquête*
a study	*une étude*
an examination	*un examen*
a clue [klu:]	*un indice*
evidence	*preuves/témoignages*
wisdom	*la sagesse*
reason	*la raison*
prudence, caution	*la prudence*
sanity	*la raison, la santé mentale*
common sense	*le bon sens*
knowledge ['nɔlidʒ]	*le savoir*
know-how	*le savoir-faire*
information	*des renseignements*
a piece of information	*un renseignement*
education	*l'éducation*
training	*la formation*
a qualification	*une qualification*
a diploma [di'pləumə]	*un diplôme*
a degree [di'gri:]	*un diplôme universitaire*
certainty	*la certitude*
trust, confidence	*la confiance*
doubt [daut]	*le doute*
a puzzle	*un mystère, une énigme*
a quiz	*un jeu, une devinette*
an enigma	*une énigme*
a mystery	*un mystère*
a suspect	*un suspect*
suspicion	*la suspicion*
a suspicion	*un soupçon*
hesitation	*l'hésitation*
wit	*l'esprit, l'intelligence*
a wit	*une personne d'esprit*
humour ['hju:mə]	*l'humour*
irony ['aiərəni]	*l'ironie*
a joke	*une plaisanterie*
a pun	*un jeu de mots*
stupidity	*la stupidité*
foolishness	*la bêtise*
a fool	*un imbécile, un sot*
a half-wit	*un nigaud*
an idiot, a nitwit	*un idiot*
nonsense	*des inepties, des sottises*
a prejudice ['predʒudis]	*un préjugé*
a bias [baiəs]	*un parti-pris*
memory	*la mémoire*
a memory	*un souvenir*
remembrance	*le souvenir*
a souvenir ['su:vəniə]	*un souvenir (objet)*
a blank	*un trou de mémoire*
imagination	*l'imagination*

an impression	*une impression*
intuition [,intju(:)'iʃən]	*l'intuition*
a guess	*une conjecture*
a fancy	*un caprice*
a fantasy ['fæntəsi]	*un fantasme*
a dream	*un rêve*
a nightmare ['naitmεə]	*un cauchemar*
insomnia	*l'insomnie*
a hallucination	*une hallucination*
insanity	*la folie, la démence*
an obsession [ɔb'zeʃən]	*une obsession*
a compulsion	*une compulsion*
an addiction	*une dépendance*
lunacy [lu:nəsi]	*l'aliénation mentale*
a lunatic, a madman	*un fou*
madness	*la folie*
a mania ['meinjə]	*une manie*
a maniac	*un maniaque*
paranoia	*la paranoïa*
schizophrenia	*la schizophrénie*
a psychiatrist [,sai'kaiətrist]	*un psychiatre*
a psychoanalyst	*un psychanalyste*
a shrink	*un psy*
thoughtful	*attentionné*
aware, conscious	*conscient*
relevant, pertinent	*pertinent*
mistaken	*erroné*
odd	*bizarre*
strange	*étrange*
weird [wiəd]	*bizarre, curieux*
surprising	*surprenant*
intelligent, smart	*intelligent*
clever	*astucieux, intelligent*
brilliant	*brillant*
gifted	*doué*
keen [ki:n]	*fin, aigu*
accurate ['ækjurit]	*précis*
logical	*logique*
broad-minded	*tolérant*
attentive	*attentif*
concentrated	*concentré*
careful	*soigneux*
bored [bɔ:d]	*qui s'ennuie*
boring	*ennuyeux*
inquisitive	*curieux*
curious ['kjuəriəs]	*curieux, bizarre*
absent-minded	*distrait*
wise [waiz]	*sage*
reasonable	*raisonnable*
prudent, cautious	*prudent*

sane	*sain d'esprit*
commonsense	*de bon sens*
sensible	*sensé*
indiscriminate	*manquant de discernement*
knowledgeable	*bien documenté*
well-informed	*bien informé*
educated	*instruit*
qualified	*qualifié*
well-read [red]	*cultivé*
certain ['sə:tn]	*certain*
sure [suə]	*sûr*
convinced	*convaincu*
confident	*confiant*
determined	*déterminé, décidé*
stubborn ['stʌbən]	*têtu*
doubtful ['dautful]	*indécis*
puzzled	*perplexe*
puzzling	*inexplicable*
enigmatic	*énigmatique*
predictable	*prévisible*
unpredictable	*imprévisible*
mysterious	*mystérieux*
intricate ['intrikit]	*complexe*
complicated	*compliqué*
suspicious	*méfiant, suspect*
wary ['wεəri]	*prudent, méfiant*
cautious ['kɔ:ʃəs]	*prudent*
witty	*spirituel*
humorous	*humoristique, amusant*
ironic(al)	*ironique*
stupid	*stupide, bête*
irrelevant [i'relivənt]	*hors-sujet*
foolish	*idiot*
dull [dʌl]	*peu intelligent*
thick	*bouché, borné*
absurd [əb'sə:d]	*absurde*
unintelligent	*inintelligent*
confused	*confus*
illogical	*illogique*
inept, inane [i'nein]	*inepte*
narrow-minded	*borné*
slow-witted	*lourdaud*
blank	*sans expression*
oblivious (to)	*inconscient (de)*
imaginative	*imaginatif*
intuitive	*intuitif*
fanciful	*fantasque*
insane [in'sein]	*fou*
obsessive	*obsédant ; obsessionnel*
compulsive	*compulsif*
addictive	*qui crée une dépendance*

lunatic, mad ['lu:nətik]	*fou*
neurotic	*névrosé*
delirious	*délirant*
paranoid	*paranoïaque*
psychological [,saikə'lɔdʒikəl]	*psychologique*
psychiatric [,saiki'ætrik]	*psychiatrique*
consciously	*consciemment*
knowingly	*sciemment*
mistakenly	*à tort*
curiously, strangely	*curieusement*
surprisingly	*étonnamment*
oddly	*bizarrement*
intelligently	*intelligemment*
cleverly	*astucieusement*
brilliantly	*brillamment*
accurately	*exactement*
logically	*logiquement*
deliberately	*délibérément*
unwittingly	*involontairement*
carefully	*soigneusement*
absent-mindedly	*distraitement*
wisely, sensibly	*sagement*
reasonably	*raisonnablement*
prudently, cautiously	*prudemment*
sensibly	*sagement*
indiscriminately	*sans discrimination*
certainly	*certainement, sans aucun doute*
probably	*probablement, sûrement*
confidently	*avec confiance*
stubbornly	*obstinément*
doubtfully	*d'un air de doute*
mysteriously	*mystérieusement*
suspiciously	*avec méfiance*
warily	*avec circonspection*
humorously	*avec humour*
ironically	*ironiquement*
stupidly, foolishly	*bêtement*
absurdly	*de manière absurde*
blankly	*d'un air absent*
intuitively	*intuitivement*
psychologically	*psychologiquement*
to think*	*penser*
to advise [əd'vaiz]	*conseiller*
to discover	*découvrir*
to estimate	*estimer*
to assess [ə'ses]	*évaluer*
to appreciate	*apprécier*

to expect	*s'attendre à*
to foresee*, to forecast*	*prévoir*
to foretell*	*prédire*
to understand*	*comprendre*
to grasp [gra:sp]	*saisir*
to mean*	*vouloir dire*
to intend (to)	*avoir l'intention (de)*
to hint	*insinuer, laisser entendre*
to misunderstand*	*comprendre de travers*
to mistake*	*confondre*
to judge, to deem	*juger*
to analyse [ænəlaiz]	*analyser*
to concentrate	*se concentrer*
to focus (on) ['fəukəs]	*se concentrer (sur)*
to ignore [ig'nɔ:]	*ne pas prêter attention à*
to notice	*remarquer*
to bore	*ennuyer*
to investigate	*examiner*
to inquire	*s'informer*
to study	*étudier*
to examine [ig'zæmin]	*examiner*
to reason	*raisonner*
to caution, to warn	*avertir*
to challenge	*défier*
to persuade [pə'sweid]	*persuader*
to inform	*informer*
to ascertain [,æsə'tein]	*établir*
to trust	*faire confiance à*
to rely on	*compter sur*
to doubt	*douter de*
to puzzle	*laisser perplexe*
to suspect	*soupçonner*
to hesitate	*hésiter*
to joke	*plaisanter*
to outwit someone	*se montrer plus malin que quelqu'un*
to fool	*duper*
to confuse	*troubler, confondre*
to mix up	*embrouiller*
to imagine [i'mædʒin]	*imaginer*
to guess	*deviner*
to fancy	*avoir envie de*
to dream*	*rêver*

Verbes : constructions délicates

to think

Think of the others!	*Pensez aux autres !*
What are you thinking about?	*À quoi pensez-vous ?*
Think it over!	*Réfléchissez-y !*
He is thought to be rich.	*Il passe pour être riche.*
I think he is a genius.	*Je pense que c'est un génie.*
I thought you were abroad.	*Je vous croyais à l'étranger.*
That's wishful thinking!	*C'est prendre ses désirs pour des réalités !*

to know

I've known him for years. (pas de forme progressive)	*Je le connais depuis des années.*
There's no knowing what people think.	*On ne peut pas savoir ce que pensent les gens.*
For all I know...	*Autant que je sache...*

to remember, to forget

He can't remember the accident.	*Il ne se souvient pas de l'accident.*
Remember (Don't forget) to go to the butcher's on your way home.	*Rappelle-toi (N'oublie pas) d'aller chez le boucher en rentrant.*
I remember meeting him years ago.	*Je me souviens l'avoir rencontré il y a des années.*
It's immaterial, forget about it.	*C'est sans importance, oublie cela.*

to remind

This song reminds me of my youth.	*Cette chanson me rappelle ma jeunesse.*
Remind him to come and see me.	*Faites-lui penser à venir me voir.*
Remind her that we have an appointment.	*Rappelez-lui que nous avons rendez-vous.*

to recall

What's the point of recalling painful memories?	*À quoi ça sert de se rappeler de mauvais souvenirs ?*

to occur

It occurred to me that...	*Il m'est venu à l'esprit que...*

to reckon

(US) = to think. I reckon you're right.	*Je pense que tu as raison.*
(GB) = to reckon with. It is a reality to be reckoned with.	*C'est une réalité avec laquelle il faudra compter.*
The time of reckoning has come.	*L'heure de vérité est arrivée.*

to mean

It means disaster.	*C'est la catastrophe à coup sûr.*
What do you mean?	*Que voulez-vous dire ?*
What do you mean to do?	*Qu'avez-vous l'intention de faire ?*

to intend

When do you intend to leave?	*Quand as-tu l'intention de partir ?*

to aim

He aims at (achieving) fame.	*Il aspire à la célébrité.*
He aims to get diplomas.	*Il vise à obtenir des diplômes.*

to look

The future looks bleak.	*L'avenir paraît sombre.*
She looks as if (as though) she's going to faint.	*Elle a l'air d'être sur le point de s'évanouir.*
We shall have to look for a solution.	*Il faudra que nous (re)cherchions une solution.*
to look into an intricate affair	*enquêter sur une affaire difficile*

to seem

The situation seems desperate.	*La situation semble désespérée.*
They seem to have reached an agreement.	*Ils semblent être arrivés à un accord.*

to prove

This proves nothing.	*Ceci ne prouve rien.*
His predictions proved (to be) right.	*Ses prédictions se sont révélées justes.*

to decide

He finally decided to come.	*Il s'est enfin décidé à venir.*
I've not yet decided on my partner.	*Je n'ai pas encore choisi mon partenaire.*
You'll have to decide what you're going to do.	*Il va falloir que tu décides (de) ce que tu vas faire.*

to search

The police searched the whole area for clues.	*La police a fouillé toute la région à la recherche d'indices.*

to seek*

to seek information	*chercher des renseignements*
This sort of data is widely sought after.	*Ce genre de données est très recherché.*

to consider

They consider him (to be) a fool.	*Ils le considèrent comme un imbécile.*
He is considering (contemplating) emigrating.	*Il envisage d'émigrer.*

to regard

I regard him as my son.	*Je le considère comme mon fils.*

to doubt

I doubt his sincerity.	*Je doute de sa sincérité.*
I very much doubt that he can succeed.	*Je doute fort qu'il puisse réussir.*

to trust

Trust him!	*Faites-lui confiance !*
I trust her judgment.	*Je me fie à son jugement.*
In God we trust.	*En Dieu nous mettons notre foi.*
Don't trust him with money.	*Ne lui confiez pas d'argent.*

Expressions

to think twice	*réfléchir sérieusement*
to have second thoughts	*revenir sur sa première décision*
to change one's mind	*changer d'avis*
to make up one's mind	*se décider*
to have a clear mind	*avoir les idées claires*
it's a weight off my mind	*c'est un gros souci de moins*
a sound mind in a healthy body	*un esprit sain dans un corps sain*
to be wise after the event	*se montrer informé après coup*
"Penny wise, pound foolish"	*faire des économies de bout de chandelle*
to make oneself understood	*se faire (bien) comprendre*
this is to the point	*ceci est pertinent*
that is beside the point	*cela n'a rien à voir*
to be prejudiced against	*avoir des préjugés contre*
to be biased	*avoir un parti-pris*
to be at a loss	*être perplexe*
to have a stroke of genius	*avoir un trait de génie*
to have a brilliant idea	*avoir une idée de génie*
to have brains	*être intelligent*
to be good at languages	*être bon en langues*
food for thought	*matière à réfléchir*
the brain drain	*l'émigration des chercheurs*
a brain trust	*un brain-trust (équipe d'experts)*
to have a brainwave	*avoir une idée géniale/une inspiration*
to pay attention to	*faire attention à*
to investigate a matter	*examiner une question/une affaire*
to inquire into a matter	*faire des recherches sur*
I haven't got a clue	*je n'en ai pas la moindre idée*
In all likelihood	*selon toute vraisemblance*
there is no evidence that...	*il n'y a rien qui prouve que...*
there is some evidence that...	*certains éléments prouvent que...*
it is (a) proof of his love	*c'est une preuve de son amour*
it is worth trying out/a try	*cela vaut la peine d'essayer*
it turned out to be true	*cela s'est révélé exact*
to speak/tell the truth	*dire la vérité*
to talk nonsense	*dire des absurdités*
to be positive about something	*être formel à propos de quelque chose*
to be ignorant of	*ignorer*
to be conscious/aware of	*être conscient de*
to become conscious of	*prendre conscience de*
it went unnoticed	*c'est passé inaperçu*
to be determined (to do something)	*être décidé (à faire quelque chose)*
to take a fact into account	*tenir compte d'un fait*
to be interested in a subject	*s'intéresser à un sujet*
to take no notice of	*ne pas prêter attention à*
to make/crack a joke	*faire une plaisanterie*
I seem to remember	*il me semble me rappeler*
within living memory	*de mémoire d'homme*
out of sight, out of mind	*loin des yeux, loin du cœur*

an absent-minded professor	*un professeur distrait*
a mad scientist	*un savant fou*
to drive like a maniac	*conduire comme un fou*
to be stark raving mad	*être fou à lier*
He was madly in love with Gertrude.	*Il était follement amoureux de Gertrude.*
it's sheer madness!	*c'est du délire !*

Exercices

I. Remettre en ordre les mots de manière à reconstituer des phrases correctes :

1. please / you / appointment / if / him / of / remind / meet / our / Paul
2. my / that / he / money / says / when / immaterial / banker / sincere / is / is / ?
3. grandmother / from / postcard / Miami / do / to / send / forget / a / not / your
4. him / was / guilt / everyone / evidence / no / suspected / his / there / of / but
5. Professor / was / that / discovery / Gissing / we / about / major / a / make / suspected / to
6. stroke / while / Archimedes / he / of / a / a / genius / was / had / bath / taking
7. think / mind / need / make / up / over / it / immediately / your / not / you
8. body / essential / thought / sound / was / that / he / mind / in / it / healthy / have / a / a / to
9. clue / as / haven't / murder / the / got / to / we / who / committed / a
10. wise / after / know / event / it / the / that / be / we / is / to / easy

II. Reformuler les phrases suivantes en utilisant les mots donnés entre parenthèses :

1. It is impossible to tell what Paul really intends to do. (knowing)
2. Korea is a country that will have to be taken into account in the future. (reckoned)
3. He was considered the greatest thinker of his time. (regarded)
4. Nobody can prove that he was the brain behind the crime. (evidence)
5. He suddenly realized that something was missing. (aware)
6. Until that event nobody had paid attention to his research. (unnoticed)
7. We shall have to examine this business carefully. (look)
8. Perhaps he has decided to give up after all. (may)
9. Everybody thought he was going to lose his temper. (looked)
10. He became paranoid and accused everybody of being unfair to him. (prejudiced)

III. **Apparier un élément de la colonne de droite avec un élément de la colonne de gauche pour former des ensembles cohérents :**

He bought himself a £100,000 sports car:	we could search the whole district for clues.
Some were convinced Dali was a genius,	but he seems determined.
I tried to explain my position to them	others thought he was stark raving mad.
He seems confident that he will succeed	I still find him totally unpredictable.
They are not yet convinced of the relevance of our policy,	we'll have to look into that matter closely.
He has not yet decided when he will make his next attempt	some people have more money than sense.
Should it prove necessary,	as soon as I have made up my mind.
I'm not sure he is telling the truth :	but, clever though he may be, I very much doubt it.
Although I have known Paul for years,	we shall have to try and persuade them.
I'll think it over and let you know my decision	but I did not manage to make myself understood.

4. Human life
La vie humaine

conception	*la conception*
heredity	*l'hérédité*
an embryo ['embriəu]	*un embryon*
a foetus ['fi:təs]	*un fœtus*
the womb [wu:m]	*l'utérus*
pregnancy	*la grossesse*
abortion	*l'avortement*
pregnancy termination	*l'IVG*
birth	*la naissance*
a baby	*un bébé*
an infant	*un petit enfant*
a child (children)	*un enfant*
infancy	*la petite enfance*
childhood ['tʃaildhud]	*l'enfance*
early youth	*la prime jeunesse*
a toddler	*un bambin*
a cradle ['kreidl]	*un berceau*
a nappy (GB), a diaper (US) ['daiəpə]	*une couche*
a lullaby ['lʌləbai]	*une berceuse*
a toy	*un jouet*
a game	*un jeu*
a pram	*un landau*
a pushchair	*une poussette*
growth	*la croissance*
adolescence	*l'adolescence*
an adolescent, a teenager	*un adolescent*
youth [ju:θ]	*la jeunesse*
a youth	*un jeune*
a youngster	*un jeune (garçon)*
the young	*les jeunes*
maturity	*la maturité*
an adult	*un adulte*
adulthood	*l'âge adulte*
a grown-up	*une grande personne*
experience	*l'expérience*
an experience	*une expérience*
wisdom	*la sagesse*
old age	*la vieillesse*

an old person	*un vieillard*
the old	*les vieux*
the elderly	*le troisième âge*
an elderly person, a senior citizen	*une personne âgée*
the very old	*le quatrième âge*
a veteran	*un ancien combattant*
a pensioner	*un retraité*
senility	*la sénilité*
loneliness	*la solitude*
death [deθ]	*la mort*
the dead [ded]	*les morts*
the deceased	*le(s) défunt(s)*
burial [ʻberiəl]	*l'enterrement*
mourning [ʻmɔ:niŋ]	*le deuil*
a funeral	*des obsèques*
cremation	*la crémation*
a crematorium	*un crématorium*
a coffin [ʻkɔfin]	*un cercueil*
ashes	*les cendres*
a tomb [tu:m]	*une tombe*
a cemetery	*un cimetière*
a graveyard	*un cimetière (d'église)*
a will	*un testament*
an heir [ɛə]	*un héritier*
an inheritance	*un héritage*
marriage [ʻmæridʒ]	*le mariage*
a husband	*un mari, un époux*
a wife	*une femme, une épouse*
wedlock	*le mariage (état)*
a wedding	*un mariage (cérémonie)*
the bride [braid]	*la mariée*
the bridegroom	*le marié*
engagement	*les fiançailles*
a fiancé(e) [fi'ã:nsei]	*un(e) fiancé(e)*
a bachelor [ʻbætʃələ]	*un célibataire*
a spinster	*une célibataire*
a widow	*une veuve*
a widower	*un veuf*
divorce	*le divorce*
a divorcee [di(:)ˌvɔ:'si:]	*un(e) divorcé(e)*
separation	*la séparation*
custody [ʻkʌstədi]	*la garde des enfants*
family	*la famille*
parents	*les parents (père et mère)*
relatives [ʻrelɔtivz]	*les parents*
a sibling	*un frère / une sœur*
a stepfather	*un beau-père (remariage)*

a stepmother	*une belle-mère (remariage)*
a father-in-law	*un beau-père*
a mother-in-law	*une belle-mère*
a son-in-law	*un gendre*
a daughter-in-law	*une belle-fille*
the in-laws	*la belle-famille*
grandparents	*les grands-parents*
a grandmother	*une grand-mère*
a grandfather	*un grand-père*
grandma, granny	*mamie*
grandpa, granddad	*papi*
a grandson	*un petit-fils*
a granddaughter	*une petite-fille*
great-grandparents	*les arrière-grands-parents*
an uncle	*un oncle*
an aunt [a:nt	*une tante*
a great uncle	*un grand-oncle*
forefathers	*les aïeux*
ancestors	*les ancêtres*
the offspring	*la progéniture*
an orphan [ʻɔ:fən]	*un(e) orphelin(e)*
unborn	*pas encore né*
living (épithète)	*vivant*
alive (attribut)	*vivant*
newborn	*nouveau-né*
young	*jeune*
childish	*puéril*
youthful	*jeune, juvénile*
childlike	*enfantin*
juvenile [ʻdʒu:vinail]	*juvénile*
adolescent, teenage	*adolescent*
ill-bred	*mal élevé*
well-bred	*bien élevé, de bonne famille*
dutiful	*obéissant*
adoptive	*adoptif*
adult	*adulte*
mature [mə'tjuə]	*mûr*
middle-aged	*d'un certain âge*
fit	*en forme*
lively [ʻlaivli]	*vif, vivant*
wise	*sage*
experienced	*expérimenté*
grey	*gris*
greying	*grisonnant*
bald [bɔ:ld]	*chauve*
white-haired	*aux cheveux blancs*
toothless	*édenté*
elderly	*assez âgé*
old	*vieux*
ageing	*vieillissant*
senile	*sénile*
alone (attribut)	*seul*

lonely	*seul, isolé*
single	*célibataire*
dying	*mourant*
dead	*mort*
beloved [bi’lʌvid]	*(bien)aimé*
late	*défunt, feu*
childishly	*comme un enfant*
wisely	*sagement*
mournfully	*tristement*
dutifully	*respectueusement*
to conceive	*concevoir*
to expect	*attendre*
to abort [ə’bɔ:t]	*avorter*
to breed*	*procréer, engendrer*
to bear* [bεə]	*porter*
to be born	*naître*
to christen [‘krisən]	*baptiser*
to scream	*hurler*
to cry	*pleurer*
to rock	*bercer*
to foster	*élever (sans adopter)*
to crawl	*marcher à quatre pattes*
to bring* up	*élever*
to grow* up	*grandir*
to educate	*éduquer*
to rebel [ri’bel]	*se rebeller*
to reject	*rejeter*
to mature	*mûrir*
to experience	*connaître*
to remain	*rester*
to become*	*devenir*
to retire [ri’taiə]	*prendre sa retraite*
to rest	*se reposer*
to age	*vieillir*
to die	*mourir*
to inherit	*hériter*
to bequeath [bi’kwi:θ]	*léguer*
to bury [‘beri]	*enterrer*
to cremate [kri’meit]	*incinérer*
to take* after	*tenir de*
to marry (tr.)	*épouser*
to divorce (tr.)	*divorcer de*
to adopt	*adopter*

Expressions

a living creature	*une créature vivante*
life expectancy	*l’espérance de vie*
life span	*la durée de vie*
the chance of a lifetime	*la chance de sa vie*
a baby boom	*une période de croissance démographique*
a test-tube baby	*un bébé éprouvette*
to be expecting a child	*attendre un enfant*
to have an abortion	*se faire avorter*
from the cradle (to the grave)	*du berceau (à la tombe)*
early in life	*tôt dans la vie*
to give birth (to)	*accoucher (de)*
a surrogate mother	*une mère porteuse*
he was born in 1948	*il est né en 1948*
a newborn child	*un nouveau-né*
to be born out of wedlock	*naître de parents non mariés*
an adopted child	*un enfant adoptif*
foster parents	*des parents nourriciers*
a 10-month-old baby	*un bébé de 10 mois*
juvenile delinquency	*la délinquance juvénile*
“Rebel without a cause”	*« La Fureur de Vivre »*
teenage rebellion	*la révolte de l’adolescence*
to come of age	*atteindre sa majorité*
to grow a beard	*se laisser pousser la barbe*
to settle down in life	*s’installer dans la vie*

to be in one's prime	*être dans la fleur de l'âge*
She is in her late thirties.	*Elle approche la quarantaine.*
He is in his early forties.	*Il a la quarantaine passée.*
to go bald	*devenir chauve*
to retire on a pension	*prendre sa retraite*
to be alive and kicking	*être plein de vie*
he is getting old	*il se fait vieux*
to have one foot in the grave	*avoir un pied dans la tombe*
old folks	*les vieux, les vieilles gens*
an old people's home	*une maison de retraite, un hospice*
an old-age pensioner	*un retraité*
an old fogey	*une vieille baderne*
late in life	*sur le tard, à un âge avancé*
to be 85 years old	*avoir 85 ans*
to be 85 years of age	*être âgé de 85 ans*
He died yesterday, aged 85.	*Il est mort hier, à l'âge de 85 ans.*
to attend a funeral	*assister à des obsèques*
her late husband	*son défunt mari*
"In loving memory of my husband"	*« En souvenir de mon cher époux »*
to inherit a fortune	*hériter d'une fortune*
to come into money	*faire un héritage*
an unmarried couple	*un couple non marié*
to get engaged	*se fiancer*
to get married	*se marier*
to marry into money	*épouser quelqu'un qui a de l'argent*
married life	*la vie conjugale*
to attend a wedding ceremony	*assister à un mariage*
a failed marriage	*un mariage qui finit en divorce*
to seek* a divorce	*demander le divorce*
to get divorced, to get a divorce (from)	*divorcer (de)*
joint custody	*la garde conjointe*

Phrases

She was born on 7 May 1943. [lire "on the seventh of May"]
Elle est née le 7 mai 1943.

She was born during the Second World War.
Elle est née pendant la Seconde Guerre Mondiale.

So she was 2 years old when the war ended.
Elle avait donc deux ans quand la guerre se termina.

Shakespeare died in 1616.
Shakespeare est mort (mourut) en 1616.

Shakespeare has been dead for about 400 years.
Il y a environ 400 ans que Shakespeare est mort.

She has worn deep mourning ever since her husband died.
Elle est en grand deuil depuis que son mari est mort.

Married life seems to agree with Philip, he looks younger every day.
Le mariage semble réussir à Philippe, il rajeunit de jour en jour.

John and Monica had been married (for) 30 years when they decided to get a divorce.
Jean et Monique étaient mariés depuis 30 ans quand ils ont décidé de divorcer.

Those craftsmen learn the trade of their forefathers from the cradle on.
Ces artisans apprennent le métier de leurs ancêtres dès le plus jeune âge.

I was not able to attend their wedding ceremony as they got married in Reno.
Comme ils se sont mariés à Reno, je n'ai pas pu assister à leur mariage.

On an average, single-parent families have lower incomes than two-parent ones.
Les familles monoparentales ont, en moyenne, des revenus moins élevés que les familles duoparentales.

Exercices

I. Apparier chaque mot de la colonne de gauche avec un mot de la colonne de droite :

senior	mother
deep	rebellion
a newborn	ceremony
foster	mourning
a single	soldiers
a wedding	citizens
adolescent	parents
a spinster	expectancy
veteran	aunt
life	baby

II. Traduire les expressions obtenues ci-dessus.

III. Compléter le texte en utilisant les verbes suivants à la forme appropriée :

to return / to bear / to be dead / to divorce / to marry / to retire / to be born / to settle / to live / to grow up

He ... in London in 1889. His parents being artists, his brother and himself ... in a music-hall environment.

He signed his first contract as a Hollywood film actor in 1913 and ... in the United States. He ... in the US for some 25 years when campaigns against him started, especially after he ... his second wife.

In 1943 he ... Oona O'Neill, his fourth wife who, over the years, ... him eight children. In 1947 the family fled McCarthy's America and ... to Europe. After ... in Switzerland, he virtually stopped making films.

He ... for several decades now but his films still have tremendous success all over the world.

Who was he?

5• Health and medicine
La santé et la médecine

Vocabulaire général

fitness	*la forme*
health [helθ]	*la santé*
the condition	*l'état*
a disease, an illness	*une maladie*
a fever ['fi:və]	*une fièvre*
the pulse [pʌls]	*le pouls*
an epidemic	*une épidémie*
a pandemic	*une pandémie*
a killer	*une maladie qui tue*
a cold	*un rhume*
the flu, influenza	*la grippe*
swine flu	*la grippe porcine*
a sore throat	*une angine*
a headache ['hedeik]	*un mal de tête*
pain, a pain	*la douleur, une douleur*
agony	*une douleur aiguë*
a check-up	*un bilan*
treatment	*un traitement, des soins*
comfort ['kʌmfət]	*le bien-être*
first aid	*les premiers soins*
contraception	*la contraception*
a condom	*un préservatif*
abortion	*l'avortement*
smoking	*le tabagisme*
a smoker	*un fumeur*
tobacco	*le tabac*
nicotine	*la nicotine*
tar	*le goudron*
alcohol ['ælkəhɔl]	*l'alcool*
an alcoholic	*un alcoolique*
a drunk, a drunkard	*un ivrogne*
drugs	*la drogue*
addiction	*la dépendance, l'accoutumance*
an addict	*un intoxiqué*
a trauma ['trɔ:mə]	*un traumatisme*
a wound [wu:nd]	*une plaie*
an injury ['indʒəri]	*une blessure*
a scar	*une cicatrice*
the injured,the wounded	*les blessés*
the dying	*les mourants*
starvation, famine	*la famine*
a famine ['fæmin]	*une famine*
malnutrition	*la malnutrition*
a doctor, a physician	*un médecin*
a patient ['peiʃənt]	*un malade, un patient*
a nurse	*un infirmier, une infirmière*
medical care	*les soins médicaux*
a prescription	*une ordonnance*
a medicine	*un médicament*
a drug	*une drogue, un médicament*
a pill	*une pilule*
a tablet	*un comprimé*
an injection, a shot	*une piqûre*
a diet [daiət]	*un régime*
an operation	*une intervention*
a vaccine ['væksi:n]	*un vaccin*
a transfusion	*une transfusion*
a therapy ['θerəpi]	*une thérapie*
euthanasia [,juθə'neizjə]	*l'euthanasie*
a life-support machine	*un appareil de réanimation*
madness	*la folie*
a fit	*une crise*
a diagnosis [,daiəg'nəusis]	*un diagnostic*
fit	*en forme*
ill (attr.), sick	*malade*
pregnant	*enceinte*
unborn	*à naître*
broken	*cassé*
short-sighted	*myope*
terminal	*en phase terminale*
deadly, lethal	*mortel*
plague-stricken	*frappé par la peste*
bed-ridden	*alité, grabataire*
addictive	*créant une dépendance*
viral ['vaiərəl]	*viral*
comfortable	*qui ne souffre pas*
paralyzed	*paralysé*

crippled	*estropié*
tobacco-related	*lié au tabac*
pollution-related	*lié à la pollution*
septic	*septique, infecté*
antiseptic	*antiseptique*
consumptive	*tuberculeux*
contaminated	*contaminé*
infected	*infecté*
HIV-positive	*séro-positif*
artificial	*artificiel*
pathological	*pathologique*
intestinal	*intestinal*
gynecological [,gainikə'lɔdʒikəl	*gynécologique*
painful	*douloureux*
traumatic	*traumatisant*
chronic	*chronique*
acute	*aigu*
unbearable	*insupportable*
drastic	*drastique, radical*
sane	*sain d'esprit*
insane	*fou*
compulsive	*compulsif*
insomniac	*insomniaque*
schizophrenic [,skitsəu'frenik]	*schizophrène*
paranoid	*paranoïaque*
seriously	*gravement*
severely	*sévèrement*
painfully	*douloureusement, péniblement*
terminally	*en phase terminale*
mentally	*mentalement*
comfortably	*sans souffrance*
fatally, mortally	*mortellement*
drastically	*radicalement*
to consult	*consulter*
to examine [ig'zæmin]	*examiner*
to test	*tester, analyser*
to look after, to care for	*soigner*
to operate on	*opérer*
to undergo*	*subir*
to cure	*guérir*
to heal	*se cicatriser*
to relieve	*soulager*
to recover	*se rétablir*
to abort	*avorter*
to detect	*dépister*
to X-ray ['eks'rei]	*radiographier*
to screen (trans.)	*faire un test de dépistage (sur)*
to spread* [spred]	*s'étendre*
to sterilize ['sterilaiz]	*stériliser*
to dress	*panser*
to stimulate	*stimuler*
to amputate	*amputer*
to transplant	*transplanter*
to pull out	*arracher, extraire*
to inject	*injecter*
to administer	*administrer*
to dispense	*préparer (pharmacie)*
to diagnose ['daiegnəuz]	*diagnostiquer*
to break* down	*s'effondrer, craquer*
to faint	*s'évanouir*
to suffer	*souffrir*
to hurt*	*faire mal*
to burn*	*brûler*
to swell*	*enfler*
to wound, to injure	*blesser*
to maim	*mutiler*
to drown [draun]	*(se) noyer*
to sneeze	*éternuer*
to cough [kɔf]	*tousser*
to asphyxiate	*asphyxier*
to choke	*s'étrangler, s'étouffer*
to contaminate	*contaminer*
to infect	*infecter*
to unplug	*débrancher*

Vocabulaire spécialisé

Disorders	***Les troubles***
sickness	*le malaise, la nausée*
seasickness	*le mal de mer*
appendicitis	*une appendicite*
a stomach upset	*un mal de ventre*
a stiff neck	*un torticolis*
a toothache	*un mal de dents*
tooth decay	*une carie*
backache	*le mal de dos*
blood pressure	*la tension artérielle*
measles	*la rougeole*
chicken pox	*la varicelle*
whooping cough	*la coqueluche*
scarlet fever	*la scarlatine*
mumps	*les oreillons*

a bruise [bru:z]	*une contusion*
a respiratory disease	*une maladie respiratoire*
asthma [‘æsmə]	*l’asthme*
concussion	*un traumatisme crânien*
a blister	*une ampoule*
sclerosis	*une sclérose*
thrombosis	*une embolie*
paralysis	*une paralysie*
angina [æn’dʒainə]	*l’angine de poitrine*
diabetes	*le diabète*
a heart attack	*un infarctus*
heart failure [‘feiljə]	*un arrêt cardiaque*
a stroke (TIA)	*une congestion cérébrale (AVC)*
a haemorrhage [‘hemərid3]	*une hémorragie*
haemophilia	*l’hémophilie*
a skin disease	*une maladie de peau*
hepatitis	*l’hépatite*
lung cancer	*le cancer du poumon*
breast cancer	*le cancer du sein*
leukaemia [lju(:)’ki:miə]	*la leucémie*
cholera	*le choléra*
malaria	*la malaria*
a bacteria	*une bactérie*
a microbe, a bug	*un microbe*
the plague	*la peste*
a venereal disease (VD) [vi’niəriəl]	*une maladie vénérienne (MST)*
Aids	*le sida*
hypochondria [,haipəu’kɔndriə]	*l’hypochondrie*
insomnia	*l’insomnie*
schizophrenia	*la schizophrénie*
paranoia	*la paranoïa*
a mania, an obsession	*une obsession*
an allergy [‘æləd3i]	*une allergie*
recovery	*la guérison*

Medical care — *Les soins médicaux*

a G.P. (General Practitioner)	*un généraliste*
surgery	*la chirurgie*
a surgery	*un cabinet médical*
a surgeon	*un chirurgien*
micro-surgery	*la microchirurgie*
brain surgery	*la neuro-chirurgie*
a specialist	*un spécialiste*
a therapist	*un thérapeute*
a heart specialist	*un cardiologue*
an eye specialist	*un oculiste*
a gynaecologist	*un gynécologue*
a paediatrician	*un pédiatre*
a psychiatrist [sai’ki-ətrist]	*un psychiatre*
a psychologist	*un psychologue*
a psychoanalyst	*un psychanalyste*
a shrink	*un psy*
a quack	*un charlatan*
a witch doctor	*un sorcier*
a dental surgeon	*un chirurgien-dentiste*
a dental surgery	*un cabinet dentaire*
hygiene	*l’hygiène*
sanitation	*l’hygiène publique*
a cough mixture	*un sirop pour la toux*
a pain killer	*un analgésique*
a sleeping tablet	*un somnifère*
a sedative	*un sédatif*
a tranquillizer	*un tranquillisant*
a potion	*une potion*
a placebo [plə’si:bəu]	*un placebo*
a syringe [‘sirind3]	*une seringue*
a needle	*une aiguille*
a blood test	*une analyse de sang*
a blood group	*un groupe sanguin*
a blood sample	*une prise de sang*
a drip	*une perfusion*
a breathalizer test	*un Alcotest*
an antidote	*un antidote*
a filling	*un plombage*
a denture [‘dent3ə]	*un appareil dentaire*
a hearing aid	*un appareil auditif*
a ward [wɔ:d]	*une salle (hôpital)*
a stretcher	*une civière*
an operating theatre	*une salle d’opération*
a stitch	*un point de suture*
a scan	*un scanner*
an X-ray [‘eks’rei]	*une radiographie*
chemotherapy	*la chimiothérapie*
a transplant	*une greffe*
a pacemaker	*un stimulateur cardiaque*
an anaesthetic [,ænis’θetik]	*une anesthésie*
a transfusion	*une transfusion*
a lunatic asylum [‘lu:nətik ə’sailəm]	*un asile d’aliénés*
a straitjacket	*une camisole de force*
group therapy	*une psychothérapie de groupe*

Expressions

to be ill	*être malade*
to be sick	*être malade, indisposé*
to feel sick	*avoir la nausée*
to be in hospital	*être à l'hôpital*
to be taken to hospital	*être hospitalisé*
He has been in hospital for a week.	*Il est hospitalisé depuis une semaine.*
to go to hospital	*aller à l'hôpital*
a sick person	*un malade*
the sick	*les malades*
a hospital for sick children	*un hôpital des enfants malades*
a dead person	*un mort*
the dead	*les morts*
an injured motorist	*un automobiliste blessé*
a serious injury	*une blessure grave*
severe burns	*de graves brûlures*
the casualty department	*le service des urgences*
a shot in the arm	*un stimulant, un coup de fouet*
a drug addict	*un toxicomane*
drug addiction	*la toxicomanie*
tobacco addiction	*la dépendance au tabac*
an alcohol-related disease	*une maladie liée à l'alcool*
a course of treatment	*un traitement, une cure*
a terminal illness	*une maladie terminale*
an intensive care unit	*un service de soins intensifs*
to have a (high) temperature	*avoir de la fièvre*
to have high blood pressure	*faire de la tension*
to have a sore throat	*avoir une angine, un mal de gorge*
to have a heart condition	*avoir une maladie de cœur*
to have a broken arm	*avoir le bras cassé*
to have a sprained ankle	*avoir une entorse à la cheville*
to have one's eyes tested	*se faire contrôler la vue*
to have an injection / a jab	*se faire faire une piqûre*
to give an injection / a jab	*faire une piqûre*
to have a scan	*passer un scanner*
to have an operation	*se faire opérer*
to have a course of chemotherapy	*faire une chimio(thérapie)*
to have an abortion	*se faire avorter*
to have a facelift	*se faire faire un lifting*
to go on a diet	*se mettre au régime*
a low-fat diet	*un régime pauvre en graisses*
to be on the pill	*prendre la pilule*
to be mentally ill	*être un malade mental*
to become / go mad	*devenir fou*
to be safe and sound	*être sain et sauf*
to be operated on	*être opéré*
to be in a critical condition	*être dans un état critique*
to be in a coma	*être dans le coma*
to be in agony	*souffrir le martyre*
to suffer from a heart disease	*souffrir d'une maladie cardiaque*

to die of pneumonia	*mourir d'une pneumonie*
to drop dead	*mourir subitement*
to undergo treatment for alcoholism	*suivre une cure de désintoxication*
to cure a disease	*guérir une maladie*
There is no cure for this disease	*Cette maladie est incurable*
Not all wounds heal naturally.	*Toutes les plaies ne guérissent pas naturellement.*
to resort to plastic surgery	*avoir recours à la chirurgie esthétique*
to catch a cold	*s'enrhumer*
to go septic	*s'infecter*
to determine the blood group	*déterminer le groupe sanguin*
infected blood	*le sang contaminé*
to unplug a life-support machine	*débrancher un appareil de réanimation*
kidney dialysis	*la dialyse rénale*
a blood donor	*un donneur de sang*
a bone-marrow donor	*un donneur de moelle osseuse*
in vitro fertilization	*la fécondation in vitro*
medically assisted procreation (MAP)	*la conception médicalement assistée*
drastic treatment	*un traitement de choc*
the WHO (World Health Organization)	*l'OMS (Organisation Mondiale de la Santé)*

Phrases

The remedy is sometimes worse than the disease.
Le remède est parfois pire que le mal.

Some physicians question the usefulness of slimming diets.
Certains médecins mettent en doute l'utilité des régimes d'amaigrissement.

Californian yuppies have become obsessed with fitness.
Les jeunes cadres californiens ont été gagnés par l'obsession de la forme physique.

During the famines of the 1840s the Irish died by the thousand.
Pendant les famines des années 1840 les Irlandais moururent par milliers.

The standards of sanitation were so low that epidemics developed.
Les conditions sanitaires étaient si mauvaises que des épidémies se propagèrent.

The sick and wounded were left to die on the battlefield.
On laissa les malades et les blessés mourir sur le champ de bataille.

Many more people died of heart disease than of cancer.
Beaucoup plus de gens mouraient de maladies cardiaques que du cancer.

You have quite a temperature, you must have caught the 'flu.
Tu as pas mal de température, tu dois avoir attrapé la grippe.

Should the terminally ill be given the means to end their lives?
Devrait-on fournir aux malades en phase terminale les moyens de mettre fin à leurs jours ?

The general use of condoms would put an end to the spread of AIDS.
L'utilisation généralisée des préservatifs mettrait fin à l'extension du Sida.

Exercices

I. Trouver les mots du chapitre correspondant aux définitions suivantes :

1. insane
2. an obsession
3. extremely or radically
4. pathologically suspicious
5. a continuous pain in the head
6. carrying the AIDS virus
7. struck by a contagious disease
8. induced by smoking
9. hypertension
10. without hope of recovery

II. Reformuler les phrases suivantes en utilisant les mots entre parenthèses :

1. He had to be operated on immediately. (operation)
2. He died quite suddenly after too good a meal. (to drop)
3. He badly needed to be stimulated. (a shot)
4. She wanted to abort on the grounds that she could not support a child. (abortion)
5. He suffered from a compulsive need of alcohol. (addicted)
6. Considering the violence of the crash it seems incredible that he escaped without a scar. (safe and sound)
7. People used to be terrified of tuberculosis because it was fatal. (cure)
8. She felt miserable for years until she decided to have an operation by a plastic surgeon. (surgery)
9. Some doctors accept to disconnect the machines that help a patient survive. (life-support)
10. But many refuse to administer to their dying patients doses of poison that would kill them. (lethal)

III. Compléter les phrases suivantes en employant des mots tirés du chapitre :

1. In spite of several ... the wrinkles still show on her carefully sun-tanned face.
2. In the 80s a new ... of malaria spread all over Africa, claiming millions of victims.
3. The government launched a campaign to advertise ... as a way to prevent AIDS from spreading.
4. He was ... wounded and died a few minutes later.
5. A growing number of Americans who suffer from ... diseases have their bodies frozen until new treatment is found.
6. Never before had so many scientists been working at finding an ... to this disease.
7. He was not seriously hurt in the accident but the ... was such that he forgot all that had happened.
8. AIDS and lung ..., although less widespread than heart disease, scare people more.
9. He was very brave, but the sight of the nurse holding the ... to give him an injection made him feel sick.
10. The footballer had to be carried off the pitch on a ... .

II. HUMAN ACTIVITIES

6. Work
Le travail

Vocabulaire général

a work (of art)	*une œuvre (d'art)*
a job	*un travail, un emploi*
an occupation, a trade	*un métier*
employment	*le travail, l'emploi*
unemployment	*le chômage*
a redundancy, a lay-off	*un licenciement*
a worker	*un travailleur*
a workman	*un ouvrier*
a workshop	*un atelier*
an apprentice	*un apprenti*
a temp	*un(e) intérimaire*
labour [‘leibə]	*la main d'œuvre/ le travail*
manpower, the labour force	*la main d'œuvre/ les effectifs*
a handyman	*un homme à tout faire*
a labourer	*un manœuvre*
moonlighting	*le travail au noir*
a moonlighter	*un travailleur au noir*
a slave	*un esclave*
slavery	*l'esclavage*
the grindstone	*le travail dur et monotone*
the workload	*la charge de travail*
a task	*une tâche*
a duty	*un devoir*
a chore [tʒɔ:]	*une corvée*
a routine	*une routine*
a time-table, a schedule	*un emploi du temps*
a commuter	*un banlieusard travaillant en ville*
skill	*l'habileté, la compétence*
ability	*l'aptitude*
talent	*le talent*
efficiency	*l'efficacité*
know-how	*le savoir-faire*
expertise	*la compétence*
an expert	*un expert, un spécialiste*
drive	*le dynamisme*
dedication	*le dévouement*
zeal [zi:l]	*le zèle*
a workaholic	*un bourreau de travail*
housework	*le ménage*
homework	*les devoirs*
an application	*une candidature*
an applicant	*un postulant*
a job seeker	*un demandeur d'emploi*
an interview	*un entretien*
training	*la formation*
retraining	*le recyclage*
further training	*la formation continue*
promotion	*l'avancement*
teleworking	*le télétravail*
hard	*dur*
hectic	*trépidant*
tiring	*fatigant*
boring	*ennuyeux*
repetitive	*répétitif*
tired	*fatigué*
exhausting	*épuisant*
exhausted	*épuisé*
overworked	*surmené*
dirty	*sale*
greasy [‘gri:si]	*couvert de cambouis*
menial [‘mi:niəl]	*subalterne*
manual	*manuel*
clerical	*de bureau*

secretarial	*de secrétariat*
(un)skilled	*(non) qualifié*
skilful	*habile*
official	*officiel*
junior	*subalterne, jeune*
senior	*supérieur*
gifted	*doué*
fit	*apte*
sophisticated	*perfectionné*
elaborate [i'læbərit]	*complexe*
outstanding	*exceptionnel*
shoddy	*de mauvaise qualité*
(un)safe	*(peu) sûr*
occasional	*intermittent*
vacant ['veikənt]	*vacant, libre*
temporary	*temporaire*
redundant	*licencié*
handy	*commode*
clever	*astucieux*
competent ['kɔmpitənt]	*compétent*
efficient	*efficace*
hard-working	*travailleur*
painstaking	*assidu, appliqué*
dedicated	*dévoué*
ambitious	*ambitieux*
casual	*intermittent, désinvolte*
offhand	*désinvolte*
slack	*négligent, peu sérieux*
smooth [smu:ð]	*lisse*
rough [rʌf]	*rugueux*
polished	*poli*
glossy	*brillant*
dull	*terne/ennuyeux*
mat	*mat*
hard (adj. ou adv.)	*dur*
manually	*à la main*
skilfully	*habilement*
elaborately	*minutieusement*
safely	*sûrement, sans danger*
occasionally	*occasionnellement*
efficiently	*efficacement*
competently	*avec compétence*
painstakingly	*assidûment*
casually	*irrégulièrement/ avec désinvolture*

to work	*travailler*
to toil	*peiner*
to labour	*travailler dur*
to botch	*bâcler, saboter*
to dodge	*se dérober à, esquiver*
to sweat [swet]	*transpirer/exploiter*
to exploit	*exploiter*
to master	*maîtriser*
to lack	*manquer de*
to clock in/out	*pointer à l'arrivée/ à la sortie*
to commute	*faire le trajet journalier*
to tackle	*s'attaquer à*
to apply (for)	*postuler*
to resign	*démissionner*
to take* on, to hire	*embaucher*
to appoint	*nommer*
to dismiss	*congédier, licencier*
to lay* off	*mettre au chômage*
to fire	*licencier, virer*
to hammer	*frapper au marteau*
to fit	*équiper, (s')ajuster*
to plane [plein]	*raboter*
to saw* [sɔ:]	*scier*
to nail	*clouer*
to screw [skru:]	*visser*
to varnish	*vernir*
to polish ['pɔliʃ]	*polir*
to repair, to mend	*réparer*
to fix	*arranger, réparer*
to service	*réviser*
to overhaul	*réviser complètement*
to (re)wire [ri'waiə]	*(re)faire l'installation électrique de*
to (dis)connect	*(dé)connecter*
to plug in	*brancher*
to unplug	*débrancher*
to blow* [bləu]	*faire sauter*
to plan	*concevoir*
to draft	*esquisser*
to design [di'zain]	*dessiner, concevoir*
to devise [di'vaiz]	*imaginer, concevoir*
to counsel, to advise	*conseiller*
to inform	*informer*
to assess	*estimer, évaluer*
to reckon	*compter, calculer*
to calculate	*calculer*

Les métiers

a craft	*un art, un métier*
a craftsman	*un artisan, un homme de métier*
craftsmanship	*la connaissance d'un métier*
DIY (do-it-yourself)	*le bricolage*
woodwork	***la menuiserie***
a joiner	*un menuisier*
a carpenter	*un charpentier*
a cabinet maker	*un ébéniste*
a lathe [leið]	*un tour*
a plane	*un rabot*
a saw	*une scie*
a hammer	*un marteau*
a nail	*un clou*
a screw	*une vis*
a screwdriver	*un tournevis*
a plank	*une planche*
insulation	*l'isolation*
double glazing	*le double vitrage*
mechanical engineering	***la mécanique***
car repairs	*la réparation automobile*
a mechanic, an engineer	*un mécanicien*
a garage ['gæra:dʒ]	*un garage*
an engine, a motor	*un moteur*
a cylinder	*un cylindre*
a valve	*une soupape*
the gearbox ['giəbɔks]	*la boîte de vitesses*
the clutch	*l'embrayage*
the brakes	*les freins*
the transmission	*la transmission*
the cooling system	*le système de refroidissement*
the radiator ['reidieitə]	*le radiateur*
a jack	*un cric*
a spanner	*une clé*
oil	*l'huile*
grease	*le cambouis*
overalls	*un bleu de travail*
servicing	*la révision*
a check-up	*une vérification*
an overhaul	*une révision complète*
the building industry	***l'industrie du bâtiment***
a building contractor, a builder	*un entrepreneur en bâtiment*
a stone mason	*un tailleur de pierres*
a bricklayer	*un maçon*
a plasterer	*un plâtrier*
a tiler	*un couvreur/un carreleur*
masonry ['meisnri]	*la maçonnerie*

a brick	*une brique*
mortar	*le mortier*
cement [si'ment]	*le ciment*
concrete ['kɔnkri:t]	*le béton*
sand	*le sable*
breeze block	*le parpaing*
a tile	*une tuile, un carreau (carrelage)*
a trowel ['trauəl]	*une truelle*
painting and decorating	***peinture et décoration***
a painter	*un peintre*
paint	*la peinture*
wallpaper	*le papier peint*
a brush	*un pinceau*
electrical engineering	***l'électrotechnique***
an electrician	*un électricien*
a circuit	*un circuit*
the wiring	*l'installation électrique*
a connection	*un raccordement*
a switch	*un commutateur*
a fuse [fju:z]	*un fusible*
a plug	*une prise*
pottery	***la poterie***
a potter	*un potier*
earthenware	*la faïence, la terre cuite*
clay	*l'argile*
(bone) china ['tʃainə]	*la porcelaine*
a kiln	*un four*
office work	***le travail de bureau***
a civil servant	*un fonctionnaire*
an official	*un responsable*
the management	*la direction*
the staff, the personnel	*le personnel*
the professions	*les professions libérales*
a lawyer ['lɔ:jə]	*un avocat*
a consultant	*un expert-conseil*
a draughtsman ['dra:ftsmən]	*un dessinateur industriel*
an architect ['a:kitkt]	*un architecte*
a surveyor [sə(:)'veiə]	*un géomètre*
accountancy	*la comptabilité*
a (chartered) accountant	*un (expert-) comptable*
the accounts	*les comptes*
an executive	*un cadre*
a secretary	*une secrétaire*
a personal assistant (PA)	*une secrétaire de direction*
a clerk [kla:k]	*un employé de bureau*
paperwork, red tape	*la paperasserie*
bureaucracy	*la bureaucratie*
an office	*un bureau*
the headquarters	*le siège (principal)*

Expressions

hard work	*un travail dur*
a hard worker	*un grand travailleur*
to work hard	*travailler dur*
a hectic working life	*une vie professionnelle trépidante*
to work overtime	*faire des heures supplémentaires*
to work long hours	*faire beaucoup d'heures*
long working hours	*de longues heures de travail*
slave labour	*la main d'œuvre asservie/un travail de forçat*
a sweated worker	*un travailleur exploité*
the workplace	*le lieu de travail*
to commute to work	*faire le trajet du domicile au travail*
to assign a task	*assigner une tâche*
to work from home	*travailler à domicile*
a work station	*un poste de travail*
to be on duty	*être de service*
to be off duty	*ne pas être de service, être en repos*
to seek employment	*chercher un emploi*
to look for a job	*chercher un travail*
situations vacant	*les offres d'emploi*
to apply for a job	*postuler pour un emploi*
a menial job	*un travail subalterne*
to know one's job	*connaître son affaire*
a white-/blue-collar worker	*un col blanc/bleu*
to work part-time	*travailler à temps partiel*
part-time work	*le travail à temps partiel*
full-time work	*le travail à plein temps*
a temporary job	*un travail temporaire*
an occasional worker	*un travailleur intermittent*
a skilled worker	*un ouvrier qualifié*
the rat race	*la foire d'empoigne*
the staff turnover	*le renouvellement du personnel*
the tools of the trade	*les outils de la profession*
to drive a nail (in)	*enfoncer un clou*
outstanding craftsmanship	*un/du travail remarquable*
to paint a room green	*peindre une pièce en vert*
a bull in a china shop	*un éléphant dans un magasin de porcelaine*
a clerical job	*un emploi de bureau*
a secretarial job	*un emploi de secrétariat*
a top civil servant / a government official	*un haut fonctionnaire*
to blow a fuse	*faire sauter les plombs*
to keep one's nose to the grindstone	*travailler sans répit*
to put a spanner in the works	*mettre des bâtons dans les roues*

Phrases

He was a joiner by trade.
Il était menuisier de son état.

It looks perfect – he's done a good job.
Cela semble parfait — il a fait du bon travail.

My holiday is over, I shall have to get back to the grindstone.
Mes vacances sont terminées, je vais devoir retourner au turbin.

He could no longer stand the rat race and resigned.
Il ne pouvait plus supporter la foire d'empoigne et a démissionné.

I wish he did not take his job so casually.
J'aimerais qu'il ne prenne pas son travail avec tant de désinvolture.

Some people would rather work from home.
Certaines personnes préféreraient travailler à domicile.

Others prefer to commute to the office daily.
D'autres préfèrent faire chaque jour le trajet jusqu'au bureau.

All applicants should master at least two foreign languages.
Tous les candidats devraient posséder au moins deux langues étrangères.

We had to hire a secretary to tackle all the red tape.
Nous avons dû embaucher une secrétaire pour faire face à toute la paperasserie.

Some youngsters prefer odd jobs to full-time employment.
Certains jeunes préfèrent des petits boulots à un emploi à plein temps.

The job market has been depressed for several months.
Il y a plusieurs mois que le marché de l'emploi est déprimé.

Exercices

I. Compléter les séquences suivantes en utilisant les équivalents anglais des noms français proposés dans le désordre :

1. a bank ... 2. office ... 3. the staff ... 4. a business ... 5. slave ... 6. a job ... 7. a six-cylinder ... 8. further ... 9. a sweated ... 10. a cabinet maker's ...

formation / demandeur / atelier / travail / employé / ouvrier / renouvellement / main d'œuvre / cadre / moteur

II. Compléter si nécessaire les phrases suivantes (in / on / into / to / for / as / from) :

I wish to apply (1)... the job advertised (2)... yesterday's Times.

He worked several years (3)... a consultant (4)... an international company.

They have just painted the whole house (5)... green.
She found commuting (6)... work every day extremely tiring.
The firm announced that it was about to take (7)... new clerical staff.
He never quite fitted (8)... his job and gradually came to hate it.
He finally resigned (9)... his post with Hargreaves and became a bricklayer.
He certainly has talent but he lacks (10)... enthusiasm.

III. Apparier un élément de la colonne de droite avec un élément de la colonne de gauche pour former des ensembles cohérents :

This modern piece of furniture looks shoddy	only a few weeks after being given promotion.
He may not have the competence of his predecessor	that left her time to look after the children.
We shall have to hire a new secretary	compared to what skilled craftsmen used to produce.
As a rule Lewis skilfully dodged schoolwork	so as to make it more comfortable.
We were astonished at John leaving the company	as he could no longer stand the same old routine.
He changed jobs	in order to tackle all this paperwork.
We had double glazing fitted in the living room	and is currently seeking employment.
He spends two hours a day at the wheel	but he certainly has more drive.
She was glad to find this part-time job	however, he managed to pass his exams in the end.
He left school a few months ago	commuting to and from work.

7• Leisure
Les loisirs

Vocabulaire général

rest	*le repos*	a party	*une fête, une soirée*
peace	*la paix*	a host, a hostess	*un hôte, une hôtesse*
quiet	*le calme*	a guest	*un invité*
a break	*un court repos*	a festival	*un festival, une fête*
a change	*un changement (de décor)*	a celebration	*des festivités, des fêtes*
entertainment	*les distractions*	a pastime	*un passe-temps*
laziness	*la paresse*	a hobby	*un passe-temps favori*
idleness	*l'oisiveté*	a game	*un jeu*
enjoyment	*le plaisir*	a contest	*un concours*

an opponent	*un adversaire*	to host [həust]	*accueillir*
a club	*un club*	to go* out	*sortir*
an enthusiast	*un passionné*	to celebrate	*fêter*
a fan, a fiend [fi:nd]	*un mordu*	to loaf [ləuf]	*traîner, traînasser*
a spoilsport	*un rabat-joie*	to play	*jouer*
free, spare (epith.)	*libre, disponible*	to deal* out	*donner, distribuer*
restful	*reposant*	to win*	*gagner*
peaceful(ly)	*paisible(ment)*	to lose*	*perdre*
quiet(ly), calm(ly)	*calme(ment)*	to cheat [tʃi:t]	*tricher*
entertaining	*distrayant*	to check	*faire échec à*
lazy (lazily)	*paresseux (-sement)*	to checkmate	*faire échec et mat à*
idle ['aidl]	*oisif*	to cast*	*jeter (des dés)*
enjoyable	*agréable*	to toss	*jeter (en l'air)*
(well-) deserved	*mérité*	to gamble	*jouer (de l'argent)*
keen	*ardent, enthousiaste*	to bet* (on)	*parier (sur)*
clever	*intelligent, astucieux*	to hitchhike ['hitʃhaik]	*faire de l'auto-stop*
cleverly	*astucieusement*	to camp	*camper*
awkward(ly)	*maladroit(ement)*	to swim*	*nager*
precise, accurate ['ækjurit]	*précis*	to dive	*plonger*
inaccurate	*inexact*	to bathe [beið]	*se baigner*
(in)accurately	*de manière (in)exacte*	to paddle	*barboter*
skilful(ly)	*habile(ment)*	to sunbathe	*prendre un bain de soleil*
crafty	*malin, astucieux*	to tan	*bronzer*
craftily	*astucieusement*	to bask	*se prélasser*
risky	*hasardeux*	to drown [draun]	*(se) noyer*
(un)lucky	*(mal)chanceux*	to row [rəu]	*ramer*
luckily	*par bonheur*	to sail	*faire de la voile*
fortunate	*heureux, chanceux*	to ride*	*monter, faire du cheval*
fortunately	*heureusement*	to mount	*enfourcher*
unfortunate(ly)	*malheureux (-sement)*	to dismount	*mettre pied à terre*
adventurous	*aventureux*	to gallop	*aller au galop*
determined	*décidé, résolu*	to canter	*aller au petit galop*
experienced	*expérimenté*	to trot	*aller au trot*
concentrated	*concentré*	to spur	*éperonner*
intent (on)	*attentif, absorbé*	to rear	*se cabrer*
patient(ly) ['peiʃənt]	*patient (-iemment)*	to throw*	*lancer ; désarçonner*
rare(ly)	*rare(ment)*	to load [ləud]	*charger*
colourful	*coloré, éclatant*	to download	*télécharger*
attractive	*attrayant*	to aim	*viser*
excited	*exalté, excité*	to fire	*tirer*
excitedly	*avec animation*	to tinker	*bricoler*
exciting	*passionnant*	to improve	*améliorer*
boring	*ennuyeux*	to collect	*collectionner*
picturesque	*pittoresque*	to devote	*consacrer*
pleasant(ly)	*agréable(ment)*	to film	*filmer*
gorgeous ['gɔ:dʒəs]	*somptueux, magnifique*	to photograph	*photographier*
lavish(ly)	*copieux (à profusion)*	to record	*enregistrer*
to rest	*se reposer*	to zoom (in on)	*faire un zoom (sur)*
to relax, to unwind* ['ʌn'waind]	*se détendre*	to focus (on)	*mettre au point (sur)*
to deserve	*mériter*	to process	*développer*
to entertain [ˌentə'tein]	*distraire ; recevoir*		

Vocabulaire spécialisé

1. Merrymaking — *Les réjouissances*

a (fun-) fair	*une fête foraine*	a circus ['sə:kəs]	*un cirque*
an amusement park	*un parc d'attractions*	a stall	*un stand*
an attraction	*une attraction*	a shooting range	*un stand de tir*
a roundabout	*un manège*	a dance	*une soirée dansante*
the dodgems	*les auto-tamponneuses*	a dance-hall	*un dancing*
		a ball	*un bal*
a puppet show	*un spectacle de marionnettes*	a night club	*une boîte de nuit*
		a pinball machine	*un flipper*
a puppet ['pʌpit]	*une marionnette*	hide-and-seek	*le cache-cache*

2. Games — *Les jeux*

cards	*les cartes*	a cue [kju:]	*une queue de billard*
a suit [sju:t]	*une suite*	bowling	*le jeu de boules*
a pack	*un jeu de cartes*	a pin	*une quille*
hearts [ha:ts]	*cœur*	a bowl [bəul]	*une boule*
diamonds ['daiəməndz]	*carreau*	a bowling alley	*un bowling*
		gambling	*les jeux d'argent*
spades	*pique*	a gambler	*un joueur*
clubs	*trèfle*	a bet	*un pari*
jack	*valet*	a tip	*un « tuyau »*
queen	*dame*	a horse race	*une course de chevaux*
king	*roi*		
ace [eis]	*as*	a racecourse	*un champ de course*
a trump	*un atout*	a greyhound race	*une course de lévriers*
a trick	*une levée, un pli*	a bookmaker	*un bookmaker*
a slam	*un chelem*	the odds	*la cote*
chess	*les échecs*	an outsider ['aut'saidə]	*un outsider*
a chess board	*un échiquier*		
a pawn [pɔ:n]	*un pion*	a favourite	*un favori*
a rook	*une tour*	the (football) pools	*le loto sportif*
a bishop	*un fou*	a lottery	*une loterie*
a knight	*un cavalier*	the jackpot	*le gros lot*
checkmate	*échec et mat*	the stakes	*l'enjeu*
stalemate	*pat*	the wheel	*la roue*
a move	*un coup*	a one-armed bandit, a fruit machine	*une machine à sous*
draughts [dra:fts]	*les dames*		
a piece	*un pion*	a coin [kɔin]	*une pièce de monnaie*
a die [dai] (dice)	*un dé*	heads	*face*
darts	*les fléchettes*	tails	*pile*
a dartboard	*une cible*	chance	*le hasard*
the bull's-eye	*le mille*	a chance	*une chance, une possibilité*
billiards ['biljədz]	*le billard*		
snooker/pool	*le billard américain*	luck [lʌk]	*la chance, la veine*

3. Open-air activities — *Les activités de plein air*

camping	*le camping*	an air mattress	*un matelas pneumatique*
a tent	*une tente*		
a sleeping bag	*un sac de couchage*		

a campsite	*un terrain de camping*
a caravan	*une caravane*
a camper van	*un camping-car*
a rucksack ['ruksæk], a backpack	*un sac à dos*
the open	*le plein air*
bathing ['beiðiŋ]	*la baignade*
sunbathing	*le bain de soleil*
a swimming-pool	*une piscine*
a swimsuit	*un maillot de bain*
a beach [biːtʃ]	*une plage*
skin diving	*la plongée sous-marine*
a snorkel, a tuba	*un tuba*
yachting ['jɔtiŋ]	*la navigation de plaisance*
boating	*le canotage*
sailing	*la voile*
a rowing boat	*une barque*
a punt	*un bateau à fond plat*
a canoe	*un canoë*
a sailing boat	*un bateau à voile*
a motor boat	*un bateau à moteur*
a mast	*un mât*
a sail	*une voile*
a rope	*un cordage*
an anchor [ænkə]	*une ancre*
a compass ['kʌmpəs]	*une boussole*
horse riding	*l'équitation*
a rider	*un cavalier*
a saddle	*une selle*
a bridle [braidl]	*une bride*
a spur	*un éperon*
a crop	*une cravache*
a stirrup	*un étrier*
hunting and shooting	*la chasse*
fox hunting	*la chasse au renard*
deer hunting	*la chasse au cerf*
a gun	*un fusil*
a rifle [raifl]	*une carabine*
a cartridge	*une cartouche*
a clay pigeon	*un pigeon d'argile*
game	*le gibier*
angling	*la pêche à la ligne*
an angler	*un pêcheur*
a rod	*une canne*
a (fishing-)line	*une ligne*
a hook [huk]	*un hameçon*
hang-gliding	*le deltaplane*
a hot air balloon	*une montgolfière*
ballooning	*faire de la montgolfière*
wind surfing	*la planche à voile*
cycling	*le cyclisme*
hiking ['haikiŋ]	*la randonnée*
bird-watching	*l'observation des oiseaux*
train-spotting	*l'observation des trains (types, etc.)*

4. Indoor hobbies — *Les activités d'intérieur*

DIY (do-it-yourself)	*le bricolage*
a DIY shop/store	*un magasin de bricolage*
an instruction leaflet	*un mode d'emploi*
stamp collecting	*la philatélie*
a stamp collection	*une collection de timbres*
photography [fə'tɔgrəfi]	*l'art photographique*
a photographer [fə'tɔgrəfə]	*un photographe*
a photograph, a picture	*une photographie*
a snapshot	*un instantané*
an exposure [iks'pəuʒə]	*un cliché*
a camera ['kæmərə]	*un appareil photo*
a movie camera	*une caméra*
a camcorder	*un caméscope*
a film	*un film, une pellicule*
a video system	*un équipement vidéo*
a video game	*un jeu vidéo*
a mobile phone	*un portable*

Expressions

spare time	*le temps libre*
to have time to spare/time on one's hands	*avoir du temps libre*
hard-won rest	*du repos bien mérité*
to take it easy	*se la couler douce*

to rest in the shade	*se reposer à l'ombre*
to have a coffee break	*faire une pause café*
to devote one's spare time to a hobby	*consacrer son temps libre à un passe-temps*
to have a party	*donner une soirée*
to have a good time/a whale of a time	*bien s'amuser*
to entertain friends	*recevoir des amis*
to spoil a party	*gâcher une soirée*
to join a club	*adhérer à un club*
to join in a celebration	*se joindre à une fête*
a game of skill	*un jeu d'adresse*
a game of chance	*un jeu de hasard*
to have a game of darts	*faire une partie de fléchettes*
to play hide and seek	*jouer à cache-cache*
the King of spades	*le roi de pique*
the Queen of diamonds	*la dame de carreau*
to take/win a trick	*prendre un pli*
grand slam	*grand chelem*
checkmate!	*échec et mat !*
to throw the dice	*jeter les dés*
to bet on a horse	*parier sur un cheval*
3 to 1 favourite	*favori à 3 contre 1*
the hot favourite	*le grand favori*
to have one chance in ten	*avoir une chance sur dix*
to toss a coin	*jouer à pile ou face*
the wheel of Fortune	*la roue de la Fortune*
to hit the jackpot	*gagner le gros lot*
to pitch a tent	*monter une tente*
to lose one's footing	*perdre pied*
to get a tan	*bronzer*
to get drowned	*se noyer*
to set sail	*hisser la voile*
on horseback	*à cheval*
to pull the trigger	*appuyer sur la détente*
to hit the bull's-eye	*mettre dans le mille*
a digital camera	*un appareil numérique*
a colour photograph	*une photo en couleur*
to take a picture	*prendre une photo*
to have a film processed	*faire développer une photo*
to download music	*télécharger de la musique*
to be clever with one's hands	*être adroit de ses mains*
third time lucky	*jamais deux sans trois*

Phrases

It's just beginner's luck.
Aux innocents les mains pleines.

The die is cast.
Les dés sont jetés.

Whose deal is it?
À qui est-ce de donner ?

It is your move.
C'est à vous de jouer.

What about (having) a game of billiards?
Et si nous faisions une partie de billard ?

He managed to win against the odds.
Il a réussi à gagner contre toute attente.

Kasparov's unpredictable moves perturbed his opponents.
Les coups imprévisibles de Kasparov déstabilisaient ses adversaires.

He is an inveterate gambler, there is no keeping him away from the races.
C'est un joueur invétéré, il n'y a pas moyen de le tenir à l'écart des courses.

They always showed us awfully boring films shot with their camcorder.
Ils nous montraient toujours des films affreusement ennuyeux tournés avec leur caméscope.

He took thousands of pictures with his state-of-the-art digital camera, but we've never seen any of them.
Il a pris des milliers de photos avec son appareil numérique ultra-perfectionné, mais nous n'en avons jamais vu une seule.

She was not keen on swimming, she only went to the beach to get a tan.
Elle n'était pas passionnée de natation, elle allait sur la plage juste pour bronzer.

You should have come, we had a whale of a time!
Tu aurais dû venir, on s'est éclatés !

She spends most of her spare time talking on her mobile phone.
Elle passe la plupart de ses loisirs à parler dans son portable.

Can the film industry survive if people go on downloading movies free of charge?
L'industrie cinématographique pourra-t-elle survivre si les gens continuent à télécharger les films gratuitement ?

Exercices

I. Trouver dans le chapitre les synonymes aux définitions suivantes :

1. a leisure activity : ...
2. a fan : ...
3. to travel by obtaining free lifts in motor vehicles : ...
4. turn to play (noun) : ...
5. a kill-joy : ...
6. attractive and colourful : ...
7. to become a member (of a club) : ...
8. a competition : ...
9. to achieve great success : ...
10. to lie in the sun : ...

II. Reformuler les phrases suivantes en utilisant les mots donnés entre parenthèses :

1. You should relax for a short while (a break).
2. The odds against his winning are 20 to 1 (one chance).
3. Take it easy my boy and try to have a good time (enjoy).
4. He was lucky enough to succeed at his first attempt (beginner).
5. Would you like to play cards? (game)
6. This horse has an excellent chance of winning (hot).
7. We enjoyed ourselves enormously (whale).
8. She likes golf a lot (keen).
9. The irrevocable move has been made (cast).
10. His first shot was right in the centre of the target (bull).

III. Compléter les phrases suivantes au moyen des mots figurant dans le chapitre :

1. As we could not reach a decision, we ... a coin.
2. Only an Englishman could ... his leisure time to such a hobby as train-spotting.
3. I have no time to ... for that sort of entertainment.
4. He spends all his weekends reading papers to decide what horses he will ... money on.
5. He took a well ... rest in his seaside cottage.
6. U...ly, Aunt Mary lost her fortune at the races.
7. He was a s... snooker player, yet he never won a major contest.
8. He enjoys basking l... in the sun.
9. She enjoyed entertaining celebrities at her l... parties in Beverley Hills.
10. Since you are such a k... bridge player you should join our club

8• Sport
Le sport

Vocabulaire général

a game	*un jeu, une partie*	a draw [drɔ:]	*un match nul*
a match	*un match*	a defeat	*une défaite*
a win, a victory ['viktəri]	*une victoire*	a winner	*un vainqueur*
		a loser	*un perdant*
a title	*un titre*	a lead	*une avance*

practice, training	*l'entraînement*
a coach	*un entraîneur*
a warm-up	*un échauffement*
fitness	*la forme*
an effort	*un effort*
strength	*la force*
stamina	*l'endurance*
a challenge	*un défi ; un challenge*
a challenger	*un prétendant*
a competition	*une compétition*
a tournament	*un tournoi*
a league	*une ligue*
heats	*des éliminatoires*
a quarter-final	*un quart de finale*
a semi-final	*une demi-finale*
a final ['fainl]	*une finale*
a cup	*une coupe*
a championship	*un championnat*
a trial ['traiəl]	*une épreuve de sélection*
an achievement	*une réussite, un exploit*
a record	*un record*
a medal	*une médaille*
a player	*un joueur*
a substitute	*un remplaçant*
an opponent	*un adversaire*
a contestant	*un concurrent*
a rival	*un rival*
rivalry	*la rivalité*
an amateur	*un amateur*
a professional	*un professionnel*
a team, a side	*une équipe*
a referee, a ref	*un arbitre*
a whistle	*un sifflet*
a sportsman	*un sportif*
fair play, fairness	*la sportivité*
fairness, fair play	*l'équité, le fair-play*
a tracksuit	*un survêtement*
sports gear [giə]	*la tenue, l'équipement sportif*
trainers	*des chaussures de sport*
a jersey ['dʒə:zi]	*un maillot*
a cap	*une casquette ; une sélection*
a stadium ['steidjəm]	*un stade*
a field, a pitch	*un terrain*
the venue ['venju:]	*le lieu (d'une rencontre)*
a track	*une piste*
a lap	*un tour (de piste)*
a grandstand	*une tribune*
the terraces ['terəsiz]	*les gradins*

the crowd	*la foule, les spectateurs*
a season ticket	*un abonnement*
excitement	*l'enthousiasme*
a climax ['klaimæks]	*un paroxysme*
athletic [æθ'letik]	*athlétique*
fit	*en forme*
muscular	*musclé*
fast, quick	*rapide*
supple	*souple*
agile ['ædʒail]	*agile*
resilient [ri'ziliənt]	*résistant*
breathless	*essoufflé*
victorious	*victorieux*
unbeaten	*invaincu*
unbeatable	*imbattable*
exciting	*passionnant*
boring	*ennuyeux*
breathtaking	*époustouflant*
dramatic	*spectaculaire*
professional	*professionnel*
amateur	*amateur*
(un)fair	*(in)juste*
foul	*irrégulier, interdit*
tough [tʌf]	*rude, viril*
violent	*violent*
rough [rʌf]	*brutal*
vicious	*méchant, brutal*
chauvinistic	*chauvin*
panic-stricken	*pris de panique*
to win*	*gagner*
to lose* [ləuz]	*perdre*
to draw* [drɔ:]	*faire match nul*
to challenge	*défier*
to beat*	*battre*
to qualify	*se qualifier*
to lead*	*mener*
to rank	*se classer*
to practise	*s'entraîner*
to train	*(s') entraîner*
to warm up	*s'échauffer*
to jog	*faire du jogging*
to aim	*viser*
to hit*	*frapper, atteindre*
to miss	*manquer*
to kick	*donner un coup de pied (dans)*
to catch*	*attraper*
to throw*	*lancer*
to score	*marquer*
to tackle	*plaquer*
to trip	*(faire) trébucher*
to strike*	*frapper*
to knock out	*mettre KO*
to cycle	*faire du vélo*

to ski [ski:]	*skier*	to wreck [rek]	*démolir*
to skate	*patiner*	to trample	*piétiner*
to slide*	*glisser*	to caution [ˈkɔ:ʃən]	*avertir, mettre en garde*
to climb	*grimper*		
to run*	*courir*	to send* off	*expulser*
to sprint	*sprinter*	to control	*maîtriser*
to leap*, to jump	*sauter*	to check	*contrôler*
to dive [daiv]	*plonger*	to ban	*interdire*
to swim*	*nager*	to administer	*administrer*
to pass, to overtake*	*doubler*	to inject	*injecter*
to accelerate	*accélérer*	to disqualify	*disqualifier*
to catch* up with	*rattraper*	to rig	*truquer*
to retire [ri'taiə]	*abandonner*	to sponsor	*patronner*
to rip up	*déchirer*	to endorse	*apposer sa griffe à*
to smash	*briser*	to recruit [ri'ku:t]	*recruter*
to hurl [hə:l]	*lancer (violemment)*	to sign (on)	*engager*
to yell	*hurler*		

Vocabulaire spécialisé

football, soccer ***le football***

a forward [ˈfɔ:wəd]	*un avant*	a header	*une tête*
a fullback	*un arrière*	a foul	*une faute*
a winger	*un ailier*	a goal	*un but*
a striker [ˈstraikə]	*un buteur*	a goalkeeper	*un gardien*
a linesman	*un arbitre de touche*	midfield	*le milieu de terrain*
the kick-off	*le coup d'envoi*	a corner kick	*un corner*
half-time	*la mi-temps*	a free kick	*un coup franc*
a shot	*un tir*	a penalty kick	*un penalty*
a pass	*une passe*		

rugby football ***le rugby***

Rugby Union	*le jeu à 15*	a scrum	*une mêlée*
Rugby League	*le jeu à 13*	a ruck	*une mêlée ouverte*
a prop	*un pilier*	a line-out	*une touche*
a hooker	*un talonneur*	a tackle	*un plaquage*
the front row	*la ligne d'avants*	a try	*un essai*
a three-quarter	*un trois-quarts*	a conversion	*une transformation*
a winger	*un ailier*	a drop-goal	*un drop*
a fly half	*un demi d'ouverture*	a penalty kick	*une pénalité*
a scrum half	*un demi de mêlée*		

tennis ***le tennis***

a racket	*une raquette*	a backhand	*un revers*
a net	*un filet*	the spin	*l'effet*
a volley	*une volée*	singles	*le simple*
a serve / service	*un service*	doubles	*le double*
a forehand	*un coup droit*		

athletics — ***l'athlétisme***

an event [i'vent]	*une épreuve*	the host country	*le pays organisateur*
the 100 metres	*le 100 mètres plat*	a gold medallist	*un(e) médaillé(e) d'or*
the 400 metre hurdles	*le 400 mètres haies*	the opening (closing) ceremony	*la cérémonie d'ouverture (de clôture)*
the high jump	*le saut en hauteur*	an awards ceremony	*une remise de médailles*
the long jump	*le saut en longueur*	a national anthem	*un hymne national*
the pole vault	*le saut à la perche*	swimming	*la natation*
the javelin	*le javelot*	a swimmer	*un(e) nageur(se)*
the discus ['diskəs]	*le disque*	free style	*la nage libre*
the shot	*le poids*	breast stroke	*la brasse*
the pace	*le rythme*	crawl	*le crawl*
a stride	*une foulée*	backstroke	*le dos crawlé*
a relay	*une course de relais*	butterfly stroke	*la brasse papillon*
gymnastics	*la gymnastique*		
the Olympics (the Olympic Games)	*les Jeux olympiques*		

golf — ***le golf***

a golfer	*un golfeur*	the green	*le green*
a golf course	*un terrain de golf*	a hole	*un trou*

racing — ***la course, les courses***

cycling ['saikliŋ]	*le cyclisme*	formula 1	*la formule 1*
a cyclist, a rider	*un cycliste*	a starting grid	*une grille de départ*
a stage	*une étape*	the pole position	*la pole position*
a timed trial ['traiəl]	*un contre la montre*	the pits	*les stands*
motor racing	*la course automobile*	a bend	*un virage*
a racing car	*une voiture de course*	horse racing	*la course hippique*
a sports car	*une voiture de sport*	a racehorse	*un cheval de course*
a Grand Prix	*un Grand Prix*	a thoroughbred	*un pur-sang*

winter sports — ***les sports d'hiver***

skiing ['ski:iŋ]	*le ski*	a ski run	*une piste*
Nordic skiing	*le ski de fond*	a sledge	*une luge*
a skier	*un skieur*	ice-skating	*le patinage sur glace*
downhill	*la descente*	a skater	*un patineur*
a slalom	*un slalom*	a skating rink, an ice rink	*une patinoire*
Alpine skiing	*le ski alpin*		
cross-country skiing	*le ski de fond*	speed skating	*le patinage de vitesse*
a ski	*un ski*	figure skating	*le patinage artistique*
a stick, a pole	*un bâton*	ice hockey	*le hockey sur glace*

boxing — ***la boxe***

a boxer	*un boxeur*	a straight	*un direct*
a punch	*un coup*	an uppercut	*un uppercut*
a lightweight	*un poids léger*	wrestling	*le catch*
a middleweight	*un poids moyen*	a wrestler	*un catcheur*
a heavyweight	*un poids lourd*	a hold	*une prise*
a hook	*un crochet*		

mountaineering — ***l'alpinisme***

an alpinist, a climber	*un alpiniste*	an ice axe	*un piolet*
to abseil	*descendre en rappel*	a rope	*une corde*

other sports	***autres sports***
martial arts	*les arts martiaux*
riding	*l'équitation*
weightlifting	*l'haltérophilie*
fencing	*l'escrime*
water-skiing	*le ski nautique*
surfing	*le surf*
windsurfing	*la planche à voile*
(a surfboard)	*une planche de surf*
sail-carting	*le char à voile*
flying	*l'aviation*
gliding	*le vol à voile*
hang-gliding	*le deltaplane*

Sport in question / Le sport en question

violence	*la violence*
a hooligan	*un voyou, un vandale*
hooliganism	*le vandalisme*
chauvinism ['ʃəuvinizm]	*le chauvinisme*
crowd control	*le contrôle des foules*
surveillance	*la surveillance*
CCTV	*la télévision en circuit fermé*
a fine [fain]	*une amende*
a ban	*une interdiction*
disgrace	*la disgrâce*
a fence	*une barrière, une clôture*
a warning	*un avertissement*
an injury ['indʒəri]	*une blessure*
a stampede	*une débandade*
a tragedy	*un drame*
doping ['dəupiŋ]	*le dopage*
amphetamines	*les amphétamines*
anabolic steroids	*les anabolisants*
growth hormones	*les hormones de croissance*
pain killers	*les analgésiques*
a cheat	*un tricheur*
abuse	*l'abus*
exclusion	*l'exclusion*
sport and money	*le sport et l'argent*
the earnings	*les gains*
a fee	*un cachet*
a lure [ljuə]	*un appât*
a prize [praiz]	*un prix*
a bribe [braib]	*un pot de vin*
bribery	*la corruption*
a transfer	*un transfert*

Expressions

to be a keen sportsman	*être un passionné de sport*
to be keen on sport	*avoir la passion du sport*
to practise a sport	*pratiquer un sport*
to do a lot of sport	*faire beaucoup de sport*
to take exercise	*faire de l'exercice*
to go jogging	*faire du jogging*
to be athletic	*être sportif*
to be in good shape	*être en (bonne) forme*
a fast runner	*un coureur rapide*
a quick pace	*un rythme rapide*
to put to the test	*mettre à l'épreuve*
to be short of practice	*manquer d'entraînement*
to be out of breath	*être essoufflé*
to burn oneself out	*s'user*
a major sporting event	*une épreuve sportive importante*

a home (away) match	*un match à domicile (à l'extérieur)*
to meet one's match	*trouver un adversaire à sa taille*
to challenge an opponent	*mettre un adversaire au défi*
to take up the challenge	*relever le défi*
a narrow victory	*une victoire remportée de justesse*
a crushing victory	*une victoire écrasante*
the winning side / team	*l'équipe victorieuse*
to be on top	*dominer*
to be outclassed	*être surclassé*
an unbeaten series	*une série de victoires*
to rank among the top ten	*se classer parmi les dix meilleurs*
a cup final	*une finale de coupe*
to lead from start to finish	*mener du début à la fin*
to draw the crowds	*attirer les foules*
the fighting spirit	*la détermination, le cran*
kick-off time	*l'heure du coup d'envoi*
to score a goal (a try)	*marquer un but (un essai)*
a converted try	*un essai transformé*
to play a waiting game	*attendre son heure*
to play for time	*jouer la montre*
injury time	*les arrêts de jeu*
a three-nil victory	*une victoire par 3 à 0*
the Champions' League	*la Ligue des Champions*
love-15	*zéro-quinze*
30 all	*30 partout*
deuce	*égalité*
game, set and match Miss Williams	*jeu, set et match Mlle Williams*
to break serve	*prendre le service*
a 7-foot-tall American basketball player	*un joueur de basket américain de 2m10*
to deal blows	*asséner des coups*
to inflict injuries on one's opponent	*blesser son adversaire*
to throw in the towel	*jeter l'éponge*
to break a world record	*battre un record du monde*
track and field events	*les courses et concours (athlétisme)*
a middle-distance runner	*un coureur de demi-fond*
a long-distance runner	*un coureur de fond*
to lead the field	*être en tête*
to clear a hurdle (a bar)	*franchir une haie (une barre)*
to be in the running	*avoir une chance de réussir, de gagner*
to be out of the running	*n'avoir aucune chance*
to harvest medals	*engranger des médailles*
gender verification	*la vérification du sexe*
to go on a skiing holiday	*aller aux sports d'hiver*
an 18-hole golf course	*un golf de 18 trous*
to make a lightning start	*faire un départ fulgurant*
to set a new track record	*établir un nouveau record de la piste*
a late tackle	*un plaquage (tackle) à retardement*
foul play	*le jeu irrégulier*
to be cautioned	*recevoir un avertissement*
to be sent off	*être expulsé*

to be sent to the sin bin	*être expulsé temporairement*
unsportsmanlike (disgraceful) conduct	*un comportement déloyal (scandaleux)*
a season-ticket holder	*un (supporter) abonné*
to hurl beer bottles	*lancer des canettes*
to wreck a stadium	*démolir un stade*
stadium surveillance	*la surveillance des stades*
to check hooliganism	*contrôler le vandalisme*
to go on the rampage	*se déchaîner*
a banned substance	*une substance interdite*
to increase muscle capacity	*accroître la capacité musculaire*
performance-enhancing drugs	*des substances visant à améliorer les performances*
drug abuse	*l'abus des substances dopantes*
a sham amateur	*un faux amateur*
the Olympic Committee	*le Comité Olympique*
to host the Olympics	*être le pays organisateur des J.O.*
the lure of money	*l'attrait de l'argent*
richly-endowed tournaments	*des tournois richement dotés*
prize money	*des gains*
rigged matches	*des matches truqués*
huge transfer fees	*des primes de transfert énormes*
to endorse sports equipment	*mettre sa griffe sur des équipements sportifs*
an endorsement contract	*un contrat commercial*
to cash in on one's success	*tirer un parti financier de son succès*

Phrases

Slow and steady wins the race.
Doucement va loin.

Get your skates on!
Dépêche-toi ! (Mets tes patins !)

That was a great shot by Bobby Charlton!
Un tir magnifique de Bobby Charlton !

Three laps to go and Hamilton is still in the lead.
Il reste trois tours et Hamilton est toujours en tête.

He led the field from start to finish.
Il a mené de bout en bout.

Manchester United beat Arsenal 3-nil.
Manchester United bat Arsenal trois à zéro.

Cricket: second Test Match in Delhi. A crushing defeat for England.
Cricket : deuxième Test Match à Delhi. Écrasante défaite de l'Angleterre.

His victory at Wimbledon netted him £200,000.
Sa victoire à Wimbledon lui a rapporté 200 000 livres.

They are on a skiing holiday in the Alps.
Ils sont aux sports d'hiver dans les Alpes.

In Liverpool, hooliganism reached a climax in the 1980s.
À Liverpool, la violence dans les stades a atteint son paroxysme dans les années 80.

He is suspected of using second-generation EPO to win the Tour de France.
On le suspecte d'avoir utilisé de l'EPO de deuxième génération pour gagner le Tour.

Exercices

I. Traduire en français les titres suivants :

Athletics: Women jump at last gender bars.
Britons harvest Olympic medals!
Soccer: Liverpool badly need home win.
Stadium security services decline responsibility.
World Cup: Host country gets a sinking feeling.
Rugby football: England's unbeaten series comes to an end.
Tennis stars lose their shine.
Squash: Britons score singles double.
Motor racing: Lightning start disqualifies Prost.
Cycling: Timed trial settles the Tour.

II. Traduire en anglais les phrases suivantes :

Ce fut un match viril mais correct.
L'Angleterre menait 1 à 0 à la mi-temps.
Il avait gagné plusieurs étapes avant d'abandonner.
Il vient de battre le record du monde pour la dixième fois !
Les vrais amateurs ne peuvent pas vraiment concurrencer des professionnels bien entraînés.
L'essai gagnant a été marqué par la ligne d'avants galloise.
Cantona venait d'écoper d'un carton rouge.
Les athlètes sont souvent accusés d'être des amateurs marrons.
Une fois encore les supporters se sont déchaînés après le match.

III. Réécrire les phrases suivantes en intercalant un complément pertinent introduit par la préposition appropriée :

Jesse Owens won four events in 1936.
He was disqualified and never allowed to compete again in an official event.
The US relay team beat the other contenders.
They now screen all supporters before they are allowed to enter the stadium.
Most of the people who were trampled were Italian supporters.
Professional tennis players tend to prefer richly endowed tournaments.
At last Chelsea scored the equalizer.

A brilliant try and Wales beat Scotland.
The whistle went and a boring match ended.
Each time he beat the pole vault record he received £ 50,000.
Compléments : *nearly a second / drug abuse / weapons / death / the Berlin Olympics / a goalless draw / hard competition / injury time / Barry John / prize money*
Prépositions : *for / to / during / by / in / on / at*

9. Food and drink
La nourriture et la boisson

cooking	***la cuisine***		
a cook [kuk]	*un(e) cuisinier(ère)*	a frying pan	*une poêle*
a chef [ʃef]	*un chef de cuisine*	a pot	*une marmite*
a kitchen	*une cuisine*	a cast iron casserole	*une cocotte en fonte*
a cooker	*une cuisinière (à gaz, etc.)*	a pressure cooker	*un autocuiseur*
		a kettle	*une bouilloire*
an oven [ʻʌvn]	*un four*	a skewer [skjuə]	*une brochette*
a microwave (oven)	*un micro-ondes*	a rolling pin	*un rouleau à pâtisserie*
a toaster	*un grille-pain*		
a food processor	*un robot (culinaire)*	a brush	*un pinceau, une brosse*
a coffee maker	*une cafetière électr.*		
a deep-fat fryer	*une friteuse électr.*	(tin) foil	*du papier aluminium*
cooking utensils	*la batterie de cuisine*	cling film	*du film étirable*
a saucepan [ʻsɔ:spən]	*une casserole*		

ingredients	***les ingrédients***		
meat	*la viande*	pickles	*des petits légumes au vinaigre*
mutton [ʻmʌtn]	*le mouton*		
pork	*le porc*	parsley [ʻpa:sli]	*le persil*
beef	*le bœuf*	garlic	*l'ail*
veal	*le veau*	onion	*l'oignon*
lamb [læm]	*l'agneau*	curry powder	*la poudre de cari*
poultry [ʻpəultri]	*la volaille*	seasoning	*l'assaisonnement*
fish	*le poisson*	milk	*le lait*
seafood	*les fruits de mer*	butter	*le beurre*
shellfish	*les crustacés*	an egg	*un oeuf*
vegetables	*les légumes*	flour [ʻflauə]	*la farine*
salt	*le sel*	pastry [ʻpeistri]	*la pâte (brisée, etc.)*
pepper	*le poivre*		
oil	*l'huile*	dough [dɔ:]	*la pâte (à pain, etc.)*
vinegar	*le vinaigre*	a crumb [krʌm]	*une miette*
salad dressing	*la vinaigrette*	yeast	*la levure*
mustard [ʻmʌstəd]	*la moutarde*	baking powder	*la levure (chimique)*
		cream	*la crème (fraîche)*

coffee	*le café*	granulated sugar	*le sucre cristallisé*
chocolate	*le chocolat*	caster sugar	*le sucre en poudre*
raisins	*les raisins secs*	brown sugar	*le sucre roux*
a lump of sugar	*un morceau de sucre*		

meals — ***les repas***

breakfast	*le petit déjeuner*	a starter	*un hors d'œuvre*
lunch	*le déjeuner*	a dessert [di'zə:t]	*un dessert*
dinner	*le dîner*	the main course	*le plat principal*
supper	*le souper*	a treat	*une gâterie, un régal*
teatime	*l'heure du thé*	a snack [snæk]	*un en-cas*
a helping	*une part, une portion*	cereal ['siəriəl]	*des céréales*
a spoonful	*une cuillerée*	a cold spread	*un buffet froid*
a slice [slais]	*une tranche*	a barbecue ['ba:bikju:]	*un barbecue*
a course [kɔ:s]	*un plat*	a kebab	*une brochette*
an appetizer ['æpitaizə]	*un amuse-gueule*	a fast [fa:st]	*un jeûne*

dishes — ***les plats***

flavour ['fleivə]	*la saveur*	smoked haddock	*du haddock*
taste	*le goût*	steak and kidney pie	*de la tourte au bœuf et aux rognons*
a recipe ['resipi]	*une recette*		
soup	*la soupe*	shepherd's pie	*du hachis Parmentier*
broth [brɔθ]	*le bouillon*	a shoulder of lamb	*une épaule d'agneau*
a salad	*une salade composée*	a leg of lamb	*un gigot*
boiled eggs	*des œufs à la coque*	roast turkey	*de la dinde rôtie*
scrambled eggs	*des œufs brouillés*	a stew [stju:]	*un ragoût*
bacon and eggs	*des œufs au bacon*	a casserole	*un ragoût en cocotte*
boiled potatoes	*des pommes de terre à l'eau*	ice cream	*la crème glacée*
		a cake	*un gâteau, un cake*
mashed potatoes	*de la purée*	pastry	*la pâtisserie*
fish and chips	*du poisson avec des frites*	a fruit pie	*une tourte aux fruits*
		a tart	*une tarte*
fish fingers	*des bâtonnets de poisson*	cheese and biscuits	*fromage et biscuits salés*
		cottage cheese	*du fromage blanc*

accompaniments — ***les accompagnements***

sliced bread	*du pain en tranches*	crisps	*des chips*
a loaf [ləuf]	*un pain*	chips	*des frites*
a roll [rəul]	*un petit pain*	sauce	*de la sauce*
toast	*du pain grillé*	gravy ['greivi]	*de la sauce (de viande)*
a biscuit ['biskit]	*un biscuit*		

table service — ***le service à table***

a tray	*un plateau*	a salt-cellar	*une salière*
a plate	*une assiette*	a pepper pot	*un poivrier*
a side plate	*une petite assiette*	a pepper mill	*un moulin à poivre*
crockery	*la vaisselle*	a sugar basin ['beisn]	*un sucrier*
china ['tʃainə]	*la porcelaine*	cutlery	*les couverts*
a teaset	*un service à thé*	a knife (knives)	*un couteau*
a cup	*une tasse*	a fork	*une fourchette*
a saucer ['sɔ:sə]	*une soucoupe*	a spoon	*une cuillère*
a wine glass	*un verre à vin*	a table-cloth	*une nappe*
a decanter	*une carafe (vin)*	a table mat	*un dessous-de-plat*
a jug [dʒʌg]	*un pichet, une carafe*	a napkin/serviette	*une serviette*

a restaurant [‘restərɔ̃ŋ]	*un restaurant*
an inn	*une auberge*
a waiter, a waitress	*un serveur, une serveuse*
a tip	*un pourboire*
drinks	***les boissons***
a beverage	*une boisson*
a pub	*un pub*
a pint	*une pinte (0,565 ,l.)*
a (beer) mug	*une chope*
beer, ale [eil]	*la bière*
draught [dra:ft] beer	*la bière pression*
lager [‘la:gə]	*la bière blonde*
bitter (GB)	*la bière anglaise*
cider [‘saidə]	*le cidre*
soft drinks	*les boissons non alcoolisées*
fruit juice	*le jus de fruits*
gin-and-tonic	*le gin-tonic*
whisky and soda	*le whisky-soda*
claret	*le bordeaux*
burgundy [‘bə:gəndi]	*le bourgogne*
a vintage	*un millésime*
sherry	*le jerez*
port	*le porto*
brandy	*le cognac, la fine*
plum brandy	*l'eau de vie de prune*
alcohol [‘ælkɔhəl]	*l'alcool*
liquor [‘likə] (US)	*les boissons alcoolisées*
a liqueur [li’kjuə]	*une liqueur*
a cork	*un bouchon*
a corkscrew	*un tire-bouchon*
a round	*une tournée*
tasty	*savoureux*
delicious(ly) [di’liʃəs]	*délicieux (-sement)*
delicate(ly)	*délicat(ement)*
refined	*raffiné*
spiced [‘spaist]	*aux épices, épicé*
hot	*chaud, épicé*
spicy	*épicé, très relevé*
salty	*salé*
light(ly)	*léger(ement)*
crisp	*croustillant*
heavy(-vily)	*lourd(ement)*
stodgy	*bourratif*
substantial(ly)	*copieux (-sement)*
frugal [‘fru:gəl]	*frugal, simple*
plentiful(ly)	*copieux (-sement)*
lavish	*copieux, plantureux*
lavishly	*généreusement*
lean	*maigre*
fat	*gras, gros*

the bill	*l'addition*
a caterer [‘keitərə]	*un traiteur*
catering	*la restauration*
a guest	*un invité, un hôte*
a host [həust]	*un hôte (celui qui reçoit)*
greedy	*gourmand*
greedily	*voracement*
ravenous [‘rævənəs]	*affamé, vorace*
overfed	*trop bien nourri*
underdone, rare	*saignant*
medium	*à point*
well done	*bien cuit*
overdone	*trop cuit*
fresh(ly)	*frais (fraîchement)*
stale [steil]	*rassis*
tender	*tendre*
tough [tʌf]	*dur*
to feed*	*nourrir*
to hull	*décortiquer, écosser*
to peel	*peler, éplucher*
to cook	*cuisiner, faire cuire*
to chop	*hacher (au couteau)*
to mince [mins]	*hacher (au hachoir)*
to grind* [graind]	*moudre*
to roast	*rôtir*
to bake	*cuire au four*
to toast	*griller (pain, etc.)*
to butter	*beurrer*
to spread*	*tartiner, répartir*
to barbecue	*griller au charbon de bois*
to stew [stju:]	*cuire en ragoût*
to boil	*(faire) bouillir*
to simmer	*mijoter*
to fry [frai]	*faire frire/revenir*
to mix	*mélanger*
to rub in, to fold	*incorporer*
to stir [stə:]	*remuer, agiter*
to beat*	*battre*
to whip	*fouetter*
to knead	*pétrir*
to dress	*accommoder*
to season	*assaisonner*
to slice	*trancher (couper en rondelles)*
to carve [ka:v]	*découper (viande)*
to serve	*servir*
to share (out)	*partager, répartir*
to picnic	*faire un pique-nique*
to brew [bru:]	*faire infuser (thé) ; brasser (bière)*
to fill	*remplir*

to pour [pɔ:]	*verser*	to drink*	*boire*
to hand round	*(faire) passer*	to swallow	*avaler*
to wait (on)	*servir*	to chew [tʃu:]	*mâcher*
to cater (for)	*préparer un repas (pour)*	to guzzle	*s'empiffrer/boire goulûment*
to order	*commander*	to gulp down	*engloutir*
to tip	*donner un pourboire*	to taste	*goûter*
to treat	*régaler*	to lick	*lécher*
to entertain	*recevoir*	to savour ['seivə]	*savourer*
to eat*	*manger*	to sip	*boire à petites gorgées*
to eat* up	*tout manger, finir*	to fast	*jeûner*

Expressions

to lay the table	*mettre la table*
to have a second helping	*reprendre*
to help oneself to meat	*se servir de viande*
to have breakfast	*prendre le petit déjeuner*
to have haddock for breakfast	*prendre du haddock au petit déjeuner*
to invite someone to lunch	*inviter quelqu'un à déjeuner*
a light meal	*un repas léger*
to be teetotal	*ne jamais boire d'alcool*
to be hungry/thirsty	*avoir faim/soif*
to have an appetite	*avoir de l'appétit*
to be parched	*mourir de soif*
to be starving	*avoir une faim de loup*
to stand someone a drink	*payer à boire à quelqu'un*
a ravenous eater	*un mangeur vorace*
tips (not) included	*service (non) compris*
a posh restaurant	*un restaurant huppé*
a fast food place	*un «fast food»*
a pizza parlour	*une pizzeria*
a cookery book	*un livre de cuisine*
Cheers!	*À la vôtre !*
Just a drop!	*Juste une goutte, une larme*
Half a pint of lager, please.	*Un demi de bière blonde, SVP.*
This round is on me.	*C'est ma tournée.*
To jump out of the frying pan into the fire.	*Tomber de Charybde en Scylla.*
What's cooking?	*Qu'est-ce qui se mijote ?*
How many pieces of toast?	*Combien de tartines ?*
What's your poison?	*Qu'est-ce que vous buvez ?*

Phrases

He's got other fish to fry.
Il a d'autres chats à fouetter.

That's not my cup of tea.
Ce n'est vraiment pas mon genre.

As a rule Christine doesn't mince her words.
En règle générale, Christine ne mâche pas ses mots.

She knows on which side her bread is buttered.
Elle sait où est son intérêt.

It's the pot calling the kettle black.
C'est la Pitié qui se moque de la Charité.

That's a fine kettle of fish.
Nous voilà dans de beaux draps.

Would you like some more meat?
Voulez-vous encore un peu de viande ?

Help yourself to some cheese.
Prenez du fromage.

What would you like to drink?
Qu'est-ce que je vous sers ?

He's had one too many!
Il a bu un coup de trop !

Leave it to simmer for two hours.
Laissez mijoter deux heures.

Exercices

I. Traduire en français les mots en gras (8pts) :

A recipe for Strawberry Scones.
Ingredients: 225g (8 ounces) flour / 4 **teaspoonfuls baking powder** / a **pinch ground ginger** / 40g (11 1/2 oz) butter / 1 **egg yolk** / - about 120ml (4 fluid ounces) milk, plus extra for brushing
Filling: 200ml (7 fl.oz) **double cream** / 250g (9 oz) strawberries, **hulled**

II. Remettre en ordre les phases successives de la recette (12pts) :

1. Roll it out on a lightly floured board to a thickness of 2.5 cm (1 inch).
2. Bake the scones in the oven preheated to 230°C (450°F) for 10 minutes, until they are well risen and golden brown.
3. Rub in the butter with the fingertips until the mixture is like fine crumbs, then stir in the sugar.
4. First mix together the flour, baking powder, salt and ginger.
5. Place the rounds of dough on a baking sheet and brush the tops with milk which will make them look shiny when baked.
6. Serve the scones filled with strawberry cream.
7. Beat the egg yolk and milk, then add just enough to the flour mixture to make a light dough.
8. Whip the cream to make the filling.
9. Cut the dough into rounds with a 5 cm (2 inch) cutter.

10. Leave them to cool.
11. Slice the strawberries and fold them into the cream.
12. Knead the dough gently.

1-	2-	3-	4-	5-	6-
7-	8-	9-	10-	11-	12-

III. A recipe for Rhubarb Crumble (10pts)

Ingredients: 450g (1lb) rhubarb (preferably young and pink stems) / 170g (6oz) flour / 1 teaspoonful baking powder / 85g (3oz) butter / 110g (4oz) vanilla sugar or soft brown sugar / a tiny pinch ground ginger

Compléter la recette en choisissant les verbes appropriés dans la liste suivante : "to peel", "to spread", to serve", to bake", "to add", to mix", to press", to rub", "to cut".

--- the rhubarb into one-inch pieces (Do not --- it, as you would lose the delicate pink colour). Put it into a fireproof dish with two tablespoonfuls water. --- the flour, ginger and baking powder together in a bowl. Cut the butter into small pieces, then cut these into the flour with a knife until as well --- as possible. --- the sugar and --- this lightly into the flour and butter with the fingertips till the mixture forms crumbs. --- the crumbs lightly over the rhubarb but do not --- them down. --- in a fairly hot oven (205°C, 400°F) for 30 to 40 minutes, until the crumble is crisp on top. --- hot, warm or cold with cream.

10. The arts
Les arts

Vocabulaire général

an artist — *un artiste*
realism ['riəlizəm] — *le réalisme*
classicism — *le classicisme*
romanticism — *le romantisme*
lyricism — *le lyrisme*
a melodrama — *un mélodrame*
a comedy — *une comédie*
an epic — *une épopée*
a tragedy — *une tragédie*
pathos ['peiθɔs] — *le pathétique*
wit — *l'esprit*
a satire ['sætaiə] — *une satire*
a satirist ['sætərist] — *un écrivain satirique*
irony ['aiəni] — *l'ironie*
humour ['hju:mə] — *l'humour*
the moral — *la morale*
a moralist — *un moraliste*
a critic — *un critique*
a parody — *une parodie*
a character — *un personnage*
a caricature [ˌkærikə'tjuə] — *une caricature*
the hero — *le héros*
the villain — *le méchant*
the atmosphere — *l'atmosphère*
the structure — *la structure*
the outline — *les grandes lignes*
the story — *l'histoire*
the plot — *l'intrigue*
the climax ['klaimæks] — *le paroxysme, l'apogée*
an anticlimax — *une chute*
a theme [θi:m] — *un thème*
a development — *un rebondissement*
the meaning — *le sens*

the ending	*la fin*
a show	*un spectacle*
a performance	*une représentation, une interprétation*
the foreground	*l'avant-scène*
the background	*l'arrière-plan*
artistic(ally)	*artistique(ment)*
aesthetic(ally) [i:s'θetikəli]	*esthétique(ment)*
classic(al)	*classique*
realistic(ally)	*réaliste (d'une manière réaliste)*
romantic	*romantique*
lyrical	*lyrique*
sentimental(ly)	*sentimentale(ment)*
dramatic	*spectaculaire*
pathetic(ally)	*pathétique(ment)*
satirical	*satirique*
ironical(ly)	*ironique(ment)*
sarcastic(ally)	*sarcastique(ment)*
humorous	*humoristique*
comic(al)	*comique*
tragic(ally)	*tragique(ment)*
poetic, poetical(ly)	*poétique(ment)*
(un)rhymed	*(non) rimé*
epic	*épique*
critical	*critique*
funny	*drôle*
witty	*spirituel*
hilarious [hi'lεəriəs]	*hilarant*
sensitive	*sensible*
(non-) figurative	*(non) figuratif*
abstract	*abstrait*
concrete [kən'kri:t]	*concret*
delightful(ly)	*délicieux (-sement)*
brilliant(ly)	*brillant (-amment)*
breathtaking	*époustouflant*
majestic	*majestueux*
impressive	*impressionnant*
graceful(ly)	*gracieux (-sement)*
light	*léger, clair*
ugly ['ʌgli]	*laid*
clumsy ['klʌmzi]	*gauche*
pejorative	*péjoratif*
imposing	*imposant*
glamorous	*brillant, prestigieux*
heavy (-vily)	*lourd(ement)*
solemn(ly)	*solennel(lement)*
deep(ly), profound(ly)	*profond(ément)*
shallow, superficial	*peu profond, superficiel*
vulgar	*vulgaire*
coarse [kɔ:s]	*grossier*
subtle [sʌtl] (-btly)	*subtil(ement)*

refined	*raffiné*
affected	*maniéré*
didactic [di'dæktik]	*didactique*
dull	*terne*
tedious ['ti:diəs]	*ennuyeux*
lively ['laivli]	*vivant*
vivid	*vif, frappant*
expressive	*expressif*
picturesque	*pittoresque*
gaudy ['gɔ:di]	*tapageur, criard*
exciting	*passionnant*
striking	*saisissant*
moving	*émouvant*
touching	*touchant*
lengthy	*(très) long, interminable*
intricate, elaborate	*compliqué, complexe*
ornate [ɔ:'neit]	*très orné*
bare	*dépouillé*
hackneyed	*rebattu, galvaudé*
melodious	*mélodieux*
harmonious(ly)	*harmonieux (-sement)*
high-pitched	*aigu*
jarring	*discordant*
live [laiv]	*en direct, en public*
ancient	*ancien, antique*
Roman	*romain*
medieval	*médiéval*
Romanesque	*roman*
Gothic ['gɔθik]	*gothique*
Tudor	*Tudor*
Elizabethan	*élisabéthain*
mock Gothic	*faux gothique*
to describe	*décrire*
to depict	*dépeindre*
to portray	*représenter*
to sketch	*esquisser, faire un croquis*
to evoke	*évoquer*
to convey	*communiquer, faire sentir*
to relate	*relater*
to criticize	*critiquer*
to stress	*insister sur*
to enhance	*mettre en valeur*
to set* off	*rehausser*
to stand* out	*ressortir*
to drag on	*traîner en longueur*
to perform	*jouer, exécuter*
to act	*jouer (acteur)*
to rehearse [ri'hə:s]	*répéter*
to prompt	*souffler*
to applaud [ə'plɔ:d]	*applaudir*
to boo [bu:]	*huer*
to hiss	*siffler*

to encore	*bisser*
to cheer	*acclamer*
to listen to	*écouter*
to conduct [kən'dʌkt]	*diriger*
to record [ri'kɔ:d]	*enregistrer*
to release	*sortir, faire paraître*
to publish	*publier*
to attend	*assister à*
to practise (trans.)	*pratiquer, s'exercer*
to tune [tju:n]	*accorder*
to carve	*ciseler, sculpter*
to draw*	*dessiner*
to paint	*peindre*
to sculpt	*sculpter*
to mould [mɔ:ld]	*mouler*
to draft	*esquisser, préparer*
to design	*dessiner, créer*
to plan	*concevoir*
to cast*	*distribuer les rôles (cinéma) ; mouler (statue)*
to dub	*doubler*
to direct	*diriger, mettre en scène*
to feature (in)	*jouer (dans)*
to star (in)	*être la vedette (dans)*
to sit*	*poser*
to clash	*jurer, détonner*
to match	*s'assortir à*
to tone down	*adoucir, atténuer*
to exhibit	*exposer*

Vocabulaire spécialisé

1. Literature — *La littérature*

poetry — *la poésie*

a poet	*un poète*
a rhyme [raim]	*une rime*
a line	*un vers*
a sonnet ['sɔnit]	*un sonnet*
a stanza ['stænzə]	*une strophe*
a nursery rhyme	*une comptine*
a ballad	*une ballade, une romance*
scanning	*la scansion*
the stress	*l'accentuation*

prose — *la prose*

a novel(ist)	*un roman(cier)*
the narrator	*le narrateur*
fiction	*la fiction*
a short story	*une nouvelle*
a (fairy) tale	*un conte (de fée)*
a detective story	*un roman policier*
a romance	*un roman à l'eau de rose*
an essay	*un essai*
a biography	*une biographie*
a diary ['daiəri]	*un journal*
the style	*le style*

drama/theatre — *le théâtre*

the stage [steidʒ]	*la scène*
a playwright ['pleirait]	*un dramaturge*
a play	*une pièce*
an act	*un acte*
a scene	*une scène*
an actor/actress	*un(e) comédien(ne)*
a comedian	*un comique*
a role, a part	*un rôle*
the leading role	*le rôle principal*
the cast	*la distribution*
a dialogue	*un dialogue*
a cue	*une réplique*
a soliloquy	*un soliloque*
the set	*le décor*
the props	*les accessoires*
the backdrop	*la toile de fond*
the dress rehearsal	*la répétition générale*
the audience	*le public*
the curtain	*le rideau*
the wings	*les coulisses*
the box office	*le bureau de location*

2. Cinema — *Le cinéma*

a picture, a movie	*un film*
the screen	*l'écran*
a film star	*une vedette de cinéma*

an extra	*un figurant*
a director	*un metteur en scène*
a producer	*un producteur*
a script writer	*un scénariste*
a silent film	*un film muet*
an animated cartoon	*un dessin animé*
a western	*un western*
a musical (comedy)	*une comédie musicale*
a thriller	*un film à suspense*
a full-length film	*un long métrage*
a short film	*un court métrage*
a screenplay	*un scénario*
the shooting	*le tournage*
a shot	*une prise*
the soundtrack	*la bande son*
a subtitle	*un sous-titre*
a close-up	*un plan rapproché, un gros plan*
a clip	*un extrait*
special effects	*les effets spéciaux*
a stunt	*une cascade*
a stunt man	*un cascadeur*

3. Music — *La musique*

classical music	*la musique classique*
a symphony	*une symphonie*
a concerto [kən'tʃə:təu]	*un concerto*
chamber music	*la musique de chambre*
a quartet	*un quatuor*
an opera	*un opéra*
jazz	*le jazz*
Negro spirituals	*des negro spirituals*
folk music	*la musique folklorique*
pop music	*la musique pop*
singing	*le chant*
a (Christmas) carol	*un chant de Noël*
a concert	*un concert*
a concert hall	*une salle de concert*
an opera house	*un opéra (lieu)*
a musician	*un musicien*
a composer	*un compositeur*
a conductor	*un chef d'orchestre*
a singer	*un(e) chanteur (-se)*
a prima donna	*une prima donna*
a pop star	*une vedette (de variété)*
a soloist	*un soliste*
a virtuoso [,və:tju'əuzəu]	*un virtuose*
an orchestra	*un orchestre*
a choir ['kwaiə]	*une chorale*
a band	*un orchestre (jazz)*
a pianist	*un pianiste*
a violinist ['vaiəlinist]	*un violoniste*
a music lover	*un mélomane*
a musical instrument	*un instrument de musique*
a violin ['vaiəlin]	*un violon*
a viola	*un alto*
a cello ['tʃeləu]	*un violoncelle*
a (double) bass [beis]	*une contrebasse*
a (bass) guitar	*une guitare (basse)*
a harpsichord	*un clavecin*
an organ	*un orgue*
a synthesizer	*un synthétiseur*
a horn	*un cor*
a clarinet	*une clarinette*
a flute [flu:t]	*une flûte*
an oboe	*un hautbois*
a trumpet	*une trompette*
a bugle ['bju:gl]	*un clairon*
an accordion	*un accordéon*
a string	*une corde*
a keyboard ['ki:bɔ:d]	*un clavier*
a drum	*un tambour*
the drums	*la batterie*
acoustics [ə'ku:stiks]	*l'acoustique*
rhythm [riðm]	*le rythme*
harmony	*l'harmonie*
a tune [tju:n]	*un air*
the lyrics	*les paroles*
a chorus ['kɔ:rəs]	*un refrain*
a note	*une note*
a chord [kɔ:d]	*un accord*
a scale	*une gamme*
a record ['rekɔ:d]	*un disque*
an album	*un album*
a compact disc (CD)	*un disque compact*
a tape	*une bande magnétique*
black vinyl ['vainil]	*le vinyle*
a studio	*un studio*
dance	*la danse*
a ballet dancer	*un(e) danseur (-se)*
tap dancing	*les claquettes*
a dance floor	*une piste de danse*
a folk dance	*une danse folklorique*

4. Painting — *La peinture*

a painter	*un peintre*
a painting	*une peinture*
a picture	*un tableau*
a drawing	*un dessin*
a sketch	*un croquis*
a masterpiece	*un chef d'œuvre*

a daub [dɔ:b]	*une croûte*	a brush	*un pinceau*
a water-colour	*une aquarelle*	an easel	*un chevalet*
a pastel [pæstl]	*un pastel*	a colour	*une couleur*
a print	*une estampe, une gravure*	a shade	*un ton, une nuance*
		the spectrum	*le spectre, la gamme*
a fresco	*une fresque*	red	*rouge*
an exhibit	*un objet exposé*	yellow	*jaune*
an exhibition	*une exposition*	green	*vert*
a museum [mju(:)'ziəm]	*un musée*	blue	*bleu*
		indigo	*indigo*
an art gallery	*une galerie d'art*	purple	*violet*
a portrait	*un portrait*	brown	*marron, brun*
a nude	*un nu*	orange	*orange*
a landscape	*un paysage*	grey	*gris*
a seascape	*une marine*	white	*blanc*
a still life	*une nature morte*	black	*noir*
a model	*un modèle*	golden	*doré*
a canvas ['kænvəs]	*une toile*	pink	*rose*
a frame	*un cadre*		

5. Architecture — *L'architecture*

an architect ['a:kitekt]	*un architecte*	a façade [fə'sa:d]	*une façade*
a town planner	*un urbaniste*	a porch	*un porche, un narthex*
a monument	*un monument*		
a mansion	*un hôtel particulier*	a nave	*une nef*
a manor ['mænə]	*un manoir*	a vault	*une voûte*
a palace	*un palais*	an altar	*un autel*
a castle	*un château*	a choir	*un chœur*
a tower	*une tour*	a stained-glass window	*un vitrail*
a keep	*un donjon*		
battlements	*des créneaux*	a steeple	*un clocher*
a drawbridge	*un pont-levis*	a spire ['spaiə]	*une flèche*
a temple	*un temple*	a gargoyle ['ga:gɔil]	*une gargouille*
a column	*une colonne*	a sculptor	*un sculpteur*
a pillar	*un pilier*	a statue	*une statue*
a capital	*un chapiteau*	a sculpture, a carving	*une sculpture*
an arch	*un arc, une arche*		
an arcade	*une arcade*	bronze	*le bronze*
a church	*une église*	marble	*le marbre*
an abbey ['æbi]	*une abbaye*	plaster	*le plâtre*
a chapel	*une chapelle*	a mould [mɔ:ld]	*un moule*
a cloister	*un cloître*	a cast	*un moulage*
a cathedral	*une cathédrale*		

Expressions

Art for Art's sake	*l'art pour l'art*
a work of art	*une œuvre d'art*
an outstanding achievement	*une réussite exceptionnelle*
an unexpected development	*un rebondissement inattendu*
the underlying theme	*le thème sous-jacent*
blank verse	*vers blancs (pentamètres iambiques non rimés)*
to get an insight into a subject	*être éclairé sur un sujet*
a brilliant performance	*une interprétation brillante*

a novel by Dickens	*un roman de Dickens*
to put on an act	*jouer la comédie*
to top the bill	*être en tête d'affiche*
to level criticism at	*adresser des critiques à*
behind the scene/in the wings	*en coulisses*
to play to the gallery	*jouer pour la galerie*
to be in the limelight	*être sous les feux de la rampe*
to book one's seat	*réserver sa place*
a box-office hit	*un film (une pièce) qui fait recette*
to go to the pictures/movies	*aller au cinéma*
to shoot a film	*tourner un film*
on location	*en extérieur, en décor naturel*
just released	*qui vient de sortir*
a blue film	*un film porno*
(non)figurative art	*l'art (non) figuratif*
matching colours	*des couleurs assorties*
navy blue	*bleu marine*
dark brown	*marron foncé*
to play a musical instrument	*jouer d'un instrument de musique*
to play the piano / the guitar / etc.	*jouer du piano / de la guitare / etc.*
canned/recorded music	*de la musique enregistrée*
a stringed/wind instrument	*un instrument à cordes/à vent*
a recording studio	*un studio d'enregistrement*
a gospel song	*un chant religieux noir*
to sing in tune/out of tune	*chanter juste/faux*
a symphony by Beethoven	*une symphonie de Beethoven*
Beethoven's 9th symphony	*la 9e symphonie de Beethoven*

Phrases

He who pays the piper calls the tune.
Qui paie les violons choisit la musique. (« the piper » : le joueur de cornemuse)

"A thing of Beauty is a joy for ever." (J. Keats)
Une chose belle est une joie à jamais.

Laurence Olivier starred in most of Shakespeare's plays.
Laurence Olivier a joué les premiers rôles dans la plupart des pièces de Shakespeare.

His next film is to be released early next year.
Il est prévu que son prochain film sorte au début de l'année prochaine.

Dirk Bogarde was better known as an actor than as a novelist.
Dirk Bogarde était davantage connu comme acteur que comme romancier.

West Side Story remained a box office hit for many years.
West Side Story *demeura de longues années un grand succès populaire.*

His latest recording of Schubert's ballads is a brilliant performance.
Son dernier (en date) enregistrement des ballades de Schubert est une interprétation brillante.

As a guitarist Gabriel accompanied many famous singers.
Gabriel a accompagné comme guitariste beaucoup de chanteurs célèbres.

This brooch sets your dress off well.
Cette broche met bien ta robe en valeur.

Somerset Maugham's short stories marvellously depict the middle-class mores.
Les nouvelles de Somerset Maugham sont une merveilleuse peinture des mœurs des classes moyennes.

Exercices

I. Compléter les titres en utilisant les termes appropriés dans la liste suivante : a film, a novel, an opera, a play, a poem (by, starring). Donner ensuite la traduction.

1. The Picture of Dorian Gray: ... Oscar Wilde.
2. Limelight: ... Charlie Chaplin.
3. The Magic Flute: ... Mozart.
4. A Night at the Opera: ... the Marx Brothers.
5. The River of no Return: ... Marilyn Monroe.
6. All's Well that Ends Well: ... William Shakespeare.
7. Gone with the Wind: ... M. Mitchell.
8. The Dirty Dozen: ... Lee Marvin.
9. Shadow of a Doubt: ... Hitchcock.
10. The Canterbury Tales: ... Chaucer.

II. La phrase suivante est un moyen de retenir une séquence de mots du chapitre "The Arts" ; trouver les 6 mots et le terme qui les résume.

Richard of York gave battle in vain.

III. Traduire en anglais :

1. *un vitrail gothique.*
2. *une église en faux roman.*
3. *un écrivain de romans policiers.*
4. *John Wayne était la vedette de* Rio Bravo.
5. *Elle chante faux.*
6. *Clara est très musicienne.*
7. *C'était un remarquable danseur de claquettes.*
8. *Un concert en plein air.*

IV. Compléter les phrases suivantes à l'aide de mots tirés du chapitre.

1. Many of the fans said that John wrote the best ... while Paul composed the best tunes.
2. He could no longer bear to be in the ... and retired to his mock Tudor manor in Beverly Hills.
3. His colours never seem to ... and yet the effect is strikingly harmonious.
4. To make a joke and laugh at it is near the lowest form of ... .
5. Films shot ... ... often look more realistic than those made in studios.
6. Before ... the British Chamber Orchestra, he used to play the cello.
7. His last play ... a feeling of bitterness and despair.
8. This piano needs ... ; it is dreadfully out of tune.
9. She starred in some 25 films and ... in countless others.
10. I would rather read subtitles than watch badly ... films.

III. IDEAS

11• Commenting on a text
Le commentaire de texte

Vocabulaire général

a writer	*un écrivain*
an author ['ɔ:θə]	*un auteur*
a journalist	*un journaliste*
a text	*un texte*
a passage	*un passage*
an extract, an excerpt	*un extrait*
an account	*un compte-rendu*
an essay	*un essai*
a summary	*un résumé*
a topic	*un sujet*
a means	*un moyen*
a device [di'vais]	*un procédé*
an issue ['iʃu:]	*un sujet, un problème*
the scope	*la portée, l'étendue*
a controversy	*une controverse, une polémique*
a contrast ['kɔntra:st]	*un contraste*
a discrepancy	*une contradiction, une divergence*
a thesis (theses)	*une thèse*
an antithesis [æn'tiθisis]	*une antithèse*
a synthesis ['sinθisis]	*une synthèse*
the stress, the emphasis	*l'insistance, l'accent*
an analysis	*une analyse*
an examination	*un examen*
an allusion, a hint	*une allusion*
a criticism	*une critique*
a point	*un point essentiel, un argument*
a viewpoint	*un point de vue*
a paradox	*un paradoxe*
an objection	*une objection*
a prejudice	*un préjugé*
a bias	*un parti pris, un préjugé*

an assumption	*une supposition, une hypothèse*
an aim	*un but, un objectif*
a target ['ta:git]	*un objectif, une cible*
an argument	*un argument, une dispute*
a statement	*une déclaration*
an understatement	*une litote*
a comment	*un commentaire*
an image ['imidʒ]	*une image*
a comparison [kəm'pærisn]	*une comparaison*
an assumption	*une hypothèse*
a quotation	*une citation*
a witticism	*un mot d'esprit*
an innuendo	*une insinuation*
a line	*une ligne, un vers*
a phrase	*une expression*
a transition	*une transition*
a cliché ['kli:ʃe]	*un cliché*
a stereotype	*un stéréotype*
an outlook (on)	*une vue, une perspective (sur)*
an ideology [,aidi'ɔldʒi]	*une idéologie*
a philosophy	*une philosophie*
(un)interesting	*(in)intéressant*
exciting	*passionnant*
commonplace	*banal, ordinaire*
hackneyed	*rebattu, galvaudé*
far-fetched	*forcé, tiré par les cheveux*
formal	*formal*
high-brow [brau]	*guindé*
bombastic	*grandiloquent*
subtle ['sʌtl]	*subtil*
informal, colloquial	*familier*
convincing	*convaincant*

convincingly	*de manière convaincante*
misleading	*trompeur*
obvious	*évident*
obviously	*de manière évidente*
spurious ['spjuəriəs]	*faux, apocryphe*
fallacious [[fə'leiʃəs]	*fallacieux*
clear(ly)	*clair(ement)*
straightforward	*honnête, franc / simple*
logical(ly)	*logique(ment)*
consistent (with)	*logique, compatible (avec)*
relevant ['relivənt]	*pertinent*
irrelevant, beside the point	*sans rapport avec le sujet*
paradoxica(ly)	*paradoxal(ement)*
contradictory	*contradictoire*
controversial	*controversé*
unquestionable (bly)	*indubitable(ment)*
concise [kən'sais]	*concis*
concisely	*avec concision*
exhaustive [ig'zɔ:stiv]	*exhaustif, complet*
exhaustively	*complètement*
close [kləus]	*proche, voisin*
outspoken	*franc, carré*
disparaging	*désobligeant, méprisant*
scathing ['skeiðiŋ]	*acerbe*
uncompromising	*intransigeant*
uncompromisingly	*en se refusant à toute concession*
non-committal	*réservé, sans se compromettre*
committed	*engagé*
(un)biased	*(im)partial*
paradoxical(ly)	*paradoxal(ement)*
humorous(ly)	*humoristique (avec humour)*
ironical(ly)	*ironique(ment)*
sharp	*cinglant, acerbe*
acute [ə'kju:t]	*perspicace, aigu*
literal(ly)	*littéral(ement)*
mere(ly)	*pur(ement) et simple(ment)*
striking	*frappant*
evocative	*évocateur*
witty	*spirituel*
melancholy	*mélancolique*
romantic	*romantique*
idealistic	*idéaliste*
utopian	*utopique*
to state	*déclarer*
to claim	*prétendre*
to express	*exprimer*

to convey	*communiquer, faire passer*
to reveal	*révéler*
to expose	*dévoiler*
to expound	*exposer, expliquer*
to analyse	*analyser*
to examine	*examiner*
to demonstrate	*démontrer*
to account for	*justifier, expliquer*
to develop	*développer*
to comment on	*commenter*
to convince	*convaincre*
to illustrate	*illustrer*
to quote	*citer*
to refer to	*faire référence à*
to allude to,	*faire allusion à*
to hint at	
to imply	*laisser entendre, impliquer*
to note (a fact)	*noter, remarquer (un fait)*
to notice (a detail)	*remarquer (un détail)*
to focus on ['fəukəs]	*(se) concentrer sur*
to dwell* on	*s'arrêter, s'étendre sur*
to stress, to emphasize	*mettre l'accent sur*
to enlarge on	*développer*
to explain	*expliquer*
to discuss (trans.)	*discuter de*
to digress	*faire une digression*
to define	*définir*
to sum up	*résumer, récapituler*
to infer	*déduire, conclure*
to imply [im'plai]	*impliquer*
to suggest	*suggérer*
to reconcile	*concilier*
to stem from	*découler de*
to result in	*aboutir à*
to result from	*résulter de*
to entail	*entraîner, comporter*
to aim (at + nom ou gérondif)	*viser, aspirer à*
to aim (to + inf.)	*même sens*
to examine	*examiner*
to consider	*considérer, envisager*
to overlook	*oublier, négliger*
to omit	*omettre*
to elude, to evade	*éluder, éviter*
to advocate	*préconiser*
to extol, to praise	*faire l'éloge de*
to criticize	*critiquer*
to object (to)	*élever une objection (contre)*
to (dis)approve (of)	*(dés)approuver*

to suggest	*suggérer*	to evoke,	*évoquer, rappeler*
to suppose	*supposer*	to conjure up	
to caricature	*caricaturer*	to contrast (with)	*contraster (avec)*

Vocabulaire spécialisé

Literary production	***La production littéraire***		
a novelist	*un romancier*	a fairy tale	*un conte de fée*
a short story writer	*un nouvelliste*	a detective story	*un roman policier*
a poet (f. poetess)	*un(e) poète(sse)*	a thriller	*un roman de série noire*
a playwright, a dramatist	*un dramaturge*	a comic (book)	*une bande dessinée*
an art critic	*un critique d'art*	a science-fiction novel	*un roman de science-fiction*
a reviewer	*un critique (journaliste)*	a Gothic novel	*un roman noir (ou gothique)*
a comic writer	*un auteur de bandes dessinées*	poetry, verse (ind.)	*la poésie*
a ghost writer	*un nègre*	a poem	*un poème*
fiction (sing. inden.)	*les œuvres romanesques*	a sonnet	*un sonnet*
		a nursery rhyme	*une comptine*
a novel	*un roman*	a collection of poems	*une anthologie*
a short story	*une nouvelle*	drama	*le théâtre*
a biography [bai'ɔgrəfi]	*une biographie*	a play	*une pièce de théâtre*
		a comedy	*une comédie*
a diary ['daiəri]	*un journal intime*	a tragedy	*une tragédie*
a tale	*un récit, un conte*	a translation	*une traduction*

Analysing a text	***L'analyse de texte***		
a literary genre	*un genre littéraire*	sound patterns	*les jeux de sonorités*
a classic	*un classique*	an alliteration	*une allitération*
classicism	*le classicisme*	an assonance	*une assonance*
romanticism	*le romantisme*	an echo ['ekəu]	*un écho*
realism	*le réalisme*	a metaphor	*une métaphore*
naturalism	*le naturalisme*	an extended metaphor	*une métaphore filée*
a legend	*une légende*		
a myth [miθ]	*un mythe*	a symbol	*un symbole*
an anecdote	*une anecdote*	the narrative ['nærətiv]	*la narration (récit)*
a vignette	*un (court) tableau*		
(literary) criticism	*la critique (litéraire)*	the narrator [næ'reitə]	*le narrateur*
a satire ['sætaiə]	*une satire*		
a depiction	*une peinture, une description*	a character	*un personnage*
		the hero (f. heroine)	*le héros (héroine)*
a caricature [,kærikə'tjuə]	*une caricature*	the point of view	*le point de vue*
		a first-person narrative	*un récit à la 1re personne*
a parody	*une parodie*		
plagiarism	*le plagiat*	an interior monologue	*un monologue intérieur*
a rhyme [raim]	*une rime*		
the rhyme pattern	*l'agencement des rimes*	the plot	*l'intrigue*
		the setting	*le décor*
a stanza ['stænzə]	*une strophe*	an episode	*une péripétie*

a development	*un rebondissement*	indirect / reported speech	*le discours indirect*
suspense (ind.)	*le suspense*	the register	*le niveau de langue*
a climax	*un paroxysme*	slang	*l'argot*
an anticlimax	*une chute*	a synonym	*un synonyme*
the ending	*la fin*	a double-entendre	*un mot à double sens*
a link	*un lien*	a pun	*un jeu de mots*
a feature	*un trait particulier*		
direct speech	*le discours direct*		

Expressions

This is an article from ... dated ...	*C'est un article tiré de ... et daté du*
This text dates back to...	*Ce texte remonte à...*
The text deals with the question of...	*Le texte traite de la question de...*
The text bears upon / on the issue of...	*Le texte porte sur la question de...*
The document we have to comment on...	*Le document que nous devons commenter...*
The author is mainly concerned with...	*L'auteur s'intéresse surtout à...*
This text is an extract / excerpt from...	*Ce texte est un extrait de...*
To sum up the text we can say...	*Pour résumer le texte nous pouvons dire que...*
As the author says...	*Comme le dit l'auteur...*
As the recording stresses...	*Comme l'enregistrement le souligne...*
to lay the emphasis on	*mettre l'accent sur, souligner*
to level criticism at	*adresser des critiques à*
to be critical of	*se montrer critique à l'égard de*
the case for / against	*les arguments pour / contre*
to put forward an opinion	*exprimer une opinion, un avis*
à bare statement of facts	*un simple énoncé des faits*
to commit oneself to something	*s'engager à quelque chose*
to support an opinion	*soutenir / appuyer une opinion*
to be prejudiced / biased against	*avoir des préjugés / un parti-pris contre*
the crux / heart of the matter	*le nœud de l'affaire*
that is not the point	*là n'est pas le problème*
that is a moot point	*c'est un point discutable*
on the face of it	*à première vue*
to raise objections	*soulever des objections*
a burning issue	*un sujet brûlant*
a topical question	*une question d'actualité*
to take into consideration	*prendre en considération*
all things considered	*tout bien considéré*
to draw the reader's attention to	*attirer l'attention du lecteur sur*
to be related to	*être lié à*
paradoxically enough	*aussi paradoxal que cela puisse paraître*
strangely enough	*aussi étrange que cela puisse paraître*
the moral of the story	*la morale de l'histoire*

Phrases

This article was published in *The Times* on 12 June 2008.
Cet article a été publié dans le Times *le 12 juin 2008.*

This excerpt deals with (bears on) the consequences of devaluation.
Cet extrait traite des conséquences de la dévaluation.

In this text, the author tackles a burning issue.
Dans ce texte, l'auteur aborde une question brûlante.

This text is a sharp criticism of modern trends.
Ce texte est une critique sévère des tendances actuelles.

The author advocates a totally different approach to the problem.
L'auteur préconise une façon totalement différente d'aborder le problème.

What the writer predicted turned out (proved) to be right.
Ce que l'auteur a prédit s'est avéré juste.

The whole argument boils down to two main questions.
Tout le débat se résume en deux questions principales.

Several points stand out in this passage.
Plusieurs points se détachent dans ce passage.

There is more to this statement than meets the eye.
Cette déclaration a une autre signification moins évidente.

This remark is not to be taken literally.
Cette remarque n'est pas à prendre au pied de la lettre.

The text falls into three main parts.
Le texte se divise en trois parties principales.

The author arouses the reader's interest by means of several devices.
L'auteur suscite l'intérêt du lecteur en utilisant plusieurs procédés.

The events in this passage are seen from the narrator's point of view.
Les évènements de ce passage sont perçus du point de vue du narrateur.

The narrator's ironical tone makes the passage something of a caricature.
Le ton ironique du narrateur fait de ce passage une sorte de caricature.

There is a gradual building up to a climax.
La tension monte progressivement jusqu'à un paroxysme.

Exercices

I. Donner les mots du chapitre correspondant aux définitions suivantes :

1. pertinent 2. too often repeated 3. far from obvious 4. a contradiction 5. an allusion 6. to concentrate on 7. to stress 8. a debatable topic 9. fallacious, deceiving 10. to recommend

II. Compléter les phrases suivantes au moyen de mots tirés du chapitre et en tenant compte des indices donnés :

1. This short text is an -----p- from the US President's inauguration speech.
2. The subtitle is a q-------- from Shakespeare.
3. The essay is a sharp c-------- of contemporary customs.
4. Far from taking sides, the journalist remains n---c--------.
5. To i--------- the point let us take the example of the Watergate scandal.
6. As a rule Anglo-Saxon journalists are more apt to --p--- scandals than their French counterparts.
7. He tries to give an --b----- account of the two opposite theses.
8. The author's v-------- significantly differs from the opinion generally accepted.
9. Ironically -----h, the writer was to take a few years later the very decision he had criticized.
10. But let us not d---- on this painful subject.
11. However sincere the journalist may be, there is one detail he ---t- and which I want to stress.
12. We could describe the third part as a s-------- in which the author tries to reconcile the two antithetic points of view.
13. The Prime Minister's bitter remark is not c--------- with the government's European policy.
14. Saying that getting involved in Iraq was a slight mistake sounds like an u------------- to me.
15. It must be n---- that more and more people now disagree with the government on this point.
16. According to him the problem mainly ---m- from the fact that we have lost confidence in our abilities.
17. Without explicitly saying it the minister seems to i---- that he would not object to a complete withdrawal.
18. He e----- the virtues of hard work and patience.
19. I am afraid it will be hard to -------l- the two antagonistic outlooks.
20. At first sight the argument is pretty convincing ; on closer -x--------- however, there are a few flaws in the reasoning.

12. Time
Le temps

a second ['sekənd]	*une seconde*	a moment	*un instant*
a minute ['minit]	*une minute*	a while	*un moment*
an hour [auə]	*une heure*	a spell	*une (courte) période*

a day	*un jour*
the date	*la date*
a night	*une nuit*
sunrise	*le lever du soleil*
dawn, daybreak	*le lever du jour*
daylight	*la lumière du jour*
the morning	*le matin*
midday, noon	*midi*
the afternoon	*l'après-midi*
the evening	*le soir*
dusk [dʌsk]	*le crépuscule*
sunset	*le coucher du soleil*
midnight	*minuit*
a week	*une semaine*
a weekday	*un jour de semaine*
Monday	*lundi*
Tuesday	*mardi*
Wednesday ['wenzdi]	*mercredi*
Thursday	*jeudi*
Friday	*vendredi*
the weekend	*le week-end*
Saturday	*samedi*
Sunday	*dimanche*
a fortnight	*une quinzaine, deux semaines*
a month	*un mois*
January	*janvier*
February	*février*
March	*mars*
April	*avril*
May	*mai*
June	*juin*
July [dʒu(:)'lai]	*juillet*
August	*août*
September	*septembre*
October	*octobre*
November	*novembre*
December	*décembre*
a season	*une saison*
spring	*le printemps*
summer	*l'été*
autumn, the fall (US)	*l'automne*
winter	*l'hiver*
a quarter, a term	*un trimestre*
a semester	*un semestre*
a year	*une année*
a decade	*une décennie*
a period	*une période*
a stage	*une étape*
circumstances	*les circonstances*
an era ['iərə]	*une ère*
an age	*un âge, une époque*
a cycle ['saikl]	*un cycle*
a century ['sentʃuri]	*un siècle*
eternity	*l'éternité*

the time	*l'heure*
a clock	*une horloge*
a watch	*une montre*
a wrist-watch	*une montre-bracelet*
an alarm-clock	*un réveil*
a dial ['daiəl]	*un cadran*
a sundial	*un cadran solaire*
the hands	*les aiguilles*
a time-bomb	*une bombe à retardement*
the past	*le passé*
memory	*la mémoire*
a memory, a recollection	*un souvenir*
experience [iks'piəriəns]	*l'expérience*
a reminder [ri'maində]	*un pense-bête, un rappel*
an antique	*une antiquité*
a diary [['daiəri]	*un agenda*
a delay	*un retard*
the future	*l'avenir*
an evolution	*une évolution*
a change	*un changement*
a prospect, an outlook	*une perspective*
a forecast	*une prévision*
a projection	*une projection*
an expectation	*une attente, une espérance*
fate, destiny	*le destin, le sort*
doom	*le destin (funeste)*
a fortune-teller	*une diseuse de bonne aventure*
a prophet	*un prophète*
a soothsayer	*un devin*
antediluvian	*antédiluvien*
prehistoric, primeval	*préhistorique*
ancient ['einʃənt]	*ancien, de vieille date*
extinct	*éteint, disparu*
antique [æn'ti:]	*antique*
antiquated, obsolete	*désuet, suranné*
old-fashioned, outmoded	*démodé*
outdated	*périmé*
old	*vieux*
former, previous, prior	*précédent*
recent	*récent*
contemporary	*contemporain*
modern	*moderne*
current ['kʌrənt] present-day	*actuel*
young	*jeune*
existing	*existant*

immediate	*immédiat*
instant	*instantané*
momentary	*passager*
fleeting	*fugace, éphémère*
new	*nouveau*
updated	*mis à jour, modernisé*
well-timed	*opportun*
punctual	*ponctuel*
seasonable	*de saison / opportun*
next	*prochain*
novel	*nouveau, original*
expected	*attendu, espéré*
impending	*imminent*
prospective	*en perspective, futur*
(forth)coming	*à venir*
approaching	*approchant*
subsequent	*ultérieur*
fatal ['feitl]	*fatal, inévitable*
fated	*destiné, condamné*
ultimate	*ultime*
short, brief	*court, bref*
short-lived	*sans lendemain*
quick	*rapide*
sudden	*soudain*
prompt	*prompt, diligent*
slow	*lent*
delayed	*retardé*
overdue	*en retard / en souffrance*
belated	*attardé / tardif*
remote	*lointain*
persistent	*persistant*
lasting	*durable*
eternal, everlasting	*éternel*
timeless	*éternel / intemporel*

Frequency — *La fréquence*

hourly	*toutes les heures*
daily (adj. ou adv.)	*quotidien(nement)*
twice a day	*deux fois par jour*
every other day	*tous les deux jours*
monthly (adj. ou adv.)	*mensuel, par mois*
weekly (adj. ou adv.)	*hebdomadaire, par semaine*
once a year	*une fois par an*
yearly	*annuel, par année*
never	*jamais*
hardly ever	*presque jamais*
seldom, rarely	*rarement*
at times	*par moments*
occasionally	*occasionnellement*
once in a while	*une fois en passant*
on and off, intermittently	*par intermittence*
sporadically	*sporadiquement*
infrequently	*peu fréquemment*
from time to time	*de temps en temps*
now and then, now and again	*de temps en temps, par moments*
sometimes	*quelquefois, parfois*
more often than not	*assez souvent*
often	*souvent*
usually, customarily	*habituellement*
as a rule, generally	*en général*
regularly	*régulièrement*
normally	*normalement*
most often	*le plus souvent*
almost always	*presque toujours*
invariably	*invariablement*
inevitably	*fatalement*
every time, on every occasion without exception, unfailingly	*chaque fois sans exception*
perpetually	*perpétuellement*
continually, unceasingly	*sans arrêt*
always	*toujours*

The passing of time — *L'écoulement du temps*

from time immemorial	*depuis le début des temps*
BC (before Christ)	*avant Jésus-Christ*
AD (Anno Domini)	*après Jésus-Christ*
ages ago	*il y a une éternité*
long ago	*il y a longtemps*
in past times, in times past	*autrefois*
in the past	*dans le temps*
in those days	*à cette époque(-là)*
in the old days	*au temps jadis*
in the good old days	*au bon vieux temps*
in the days of...	*à l'époque de...*
at one time	*à une certaine époque*
formerly	*dans le temps, précédemment*
previously	*antérieurement*
this day last year	*il y a aujourd'hui un an*
not long ago	*il n'y a pas longtemps*
a fortnight ago	*il y a quinze jours*
last week	*la semaine dernière*

this day last week	*il y a aujourd'hui huit jours*
for some time past	*depuis quelque temps*
recently	*récemment*
lately	*dernièrement*
a while ago	*il y a quelque temps*
the day before	*la veille*
the day after	*le lendemain*
the day before yesterday	*avant-hier*
yesterday	*hier*
yesterday afternoon	*hier après-midi*
last night	*hier soir, cette nuit*
now	*maintenant*
up to now, so far	*jusqu'à maintenant*
from now on, henceforth	*à partir de maintenant*
in future	*dorénavant*
currently	*actuellement*
nowadays, these days	*de nos jours*
today	*aujourd'hui*
at the present time	*à l'heure actuelle*
as times go	*par les temps qui courent*
at the moment	*en ce moment*
for the time being	*pour l'instant*
in the meantime, meanwhile	*pendant ce temps*
temporarily	*temporairement*
provisionally	*provisoirement*
already	*déjà*
immediately, at once,	*immédiatement*
straightaway	*sur l'instant*
presently	*tout de suite*
in a minute	*dans une seconde*
in a short while	*dans un petit moment*
tomorrow	*demain*
the day after tomorrow	*après-demain*
in three days' time	*dans trois jours*
within a week	*dans la semaine qui vient*
by the weekend	*d'ici au week-end*
soon	*bientôt*
as soon as possible	*dès que possible*
in the shortest possible time	*dans les plus brefs délais*
in the short run / term	*à court terme*
later on	*plus tard*
afterwards (adv.)	*après, ensuite*

in the near future	*dans un avenir proche*
this day next year	*dans un an jour pour jour*
in years to come	*dans les années à venir*
in the long run / term	*à long terme*
one day	*un jour*
sooner or later	*tôt ou tard*
in the course of time	*avec le temps*
in the end	*à la fin*
eventually, ultimately	*en fin de compte*
in the distant future	*dans un avenir lointain*
forever	*pour toujours*
eternally	*éternellement*
to last [la:st]	*durer*
to forget*	*oublier*
to remember	*se rappeler*
to bear* in mind	*ne pas oublier*
to recollect, to recall	*se souvenir de*
to remind	*rappeler*
to look back	*se tourner vers le passé*
to anticipate	*anticiper*
to precede	*précéder*
to predict	*prédire*
to forecast*	*prévoir*
to expect	*s'attendre à, espérer*
to wait for	*attendre*
to long for	*souhaiter vivement*
to look forward to	*attendre avec impatience*
to look ahead	*penser à l'avenir*
to draw* near	*approcher (date)*
to spend*	*passer (du temps)*
to waste	*perdre (son temps)*
to pass, to elapse	*passer, s'écouler*
to span	*couvrir une période*
to drag on	*traîner en longueur*
to gain, to save	*gagner (du temps)*
to outlast	*durer plus longtemps que*
to delay	*retarder*
to postpone, to put* off	*remettre à plus tard*
to hurry, to hasten	*se hâter*
to tick	*faire tic-tac*
to wind* up [waind]	*remonter*
to ring*	*sonner*
to strike*	*sonner (horloge)*
to chime [tʃaim]	*carillonner*

Expressions

a quarter of an hour	*un quart d'heure*
half an hour	*une demi-heure*
an hour and a half	*une heure et demie*
two and a half hours	*deux heures et demie*
8 o'clock	*8 heures*
8 a.m.	*huit heures du matin*
8 p.m.	*vingt heures*
8 o'clock sharp	*8 heures précises*
about 8	*environ 8 heures*
twenty past seven	*sept heures vingt*
half past seven, seven thirty	*sept heures et demie, sept heures trente*
twenty to eight	*huit heures moins vingt*
Greenwich Mean Time (GMT)	*l'heure de Greenwich*
daylight-saving time	*l'heure d'été*
on the last Tuesday of January	*le dernier mardi de janvier*
Christmas Eve	*la veille de Noël*
Christmas Day	*le jour de Noël*
Boxing Day	*le lendemain de Noël*
New Year's Eve	*la veille du nouvel an*
New Year's Day	*le jour du nouvel an*
Twelfth Night	*l'Épiphanie*
Easter Day	*le jour de Pâques*
in Victorian times	*à l'époque victorienne*
in the early seventies	*au début des années 70*
in the mid-eighteenth century	*au milieu du XVIIIe siècle*
in the mists of time	*dans la nuit des temps*
in late February	*à la fin du mois de février*
to take one's time	*prendre son temps*
a race against time	*une course contre la montre*
to be on time	*être à l'heure*
to be dead on time	*être pile à l'heure*
to come in time (for)	*arriver à temps*
in no time	*en un instant*
to be late, behind time	*être en retard*
early in the morning	*tôt le matin*
late at night	*tard le soir*
to work from dawn to dusk	*travailler du matin au soir*
to run short of time	*manquer de temps*
to be ahead of one's time	*avoir des idées avancées*
at a given time	*à un moment donné*
in due time, in due course	*en temps voulu*
just in time	*juste à temps*
once upon a time...	*il était une fois*
spare time	*le temps libre*
at any time	*à toute heure*
lunch time	*l'heure du déjeuner*
holiday time	*l'époque des vacances*
to have time off	*se reposer, prendre des congés*

to have a day off	*prendre un jour de congé*
a fortnight's holiday	*quinze jours de vacances*
to have a good time	*bien s'amuser*
for the first time	*pour la première fois*
first, firstly	*dans un premier temps, premièrement*
ten times running	*dix fois de suite*
at a time	*d'un seul coup, à la fois*
day in, day out	*jour après jour*
to work by the day	*travailler à la journée*
ten days' notice	*un préavis de dix jours*
in a day or so	*dans un jour ou deux*
in my young days	*du temps de ma jeunesse*
a three-month-old baby	*un bébé de trois mois*
a five-year-old child	*un enfant de cinq ans*
century-old traditions	*des traditions séculaires*

Phrases

So far, so good.
Jusqu'ici, tout va bien.

The day when pigs will fly.
Le jour où les poules auront des dents.

It is ages since we last saw him.
Cela fait une éternité que nous l'avons vu pour la dernière fois.

It is high time you started working!
Il est grand temps que vous vous mettiez au travail.

He spends most of his time watching TV.
Il passe le plus clair de son temps à regarder la télé.

I wish you would not waste your time playing cards.
Je souhaiterais que tu ne perdes pas ton temps à jouer aux cartes.

What time is it by your watch?
Quelle heure est-il à ta montre ?

He should arrive any minute now.
Il devrait arriver d'une minute à l'autre.

Things are no longer what they used to be.
Les choses ne sont plus ce qu'elles étaient.

There is no telling what the future holds in store.
On ne peut pas dire ce que l'avenir nous réserve.

Time lost cannot be won again (Time past cannot be recalled).
Le temps perdu ne se rattrape jamais.

Time was when people would walk or cycle to work...
Il fut un temps où les gens allaient au travail à pied ou à vélo...

Will that time ever come back?
Ce temps-là reviendra-t-il jamais ?

Exercices

I. Remplacer le mot ou le groupe de mots en italiques par un mot ou une expression équivalent :

1. They are due to come in *two weeks' time.*
2. This should be done *in the shortest possible time.*
3. This review is published every *three months.*
4. He works from *morning till night.*
5. I'll see you in a *moment.*
6. The meeting had to be *put off.*
7. They met on *December 24th.*
8. You should have come *immediately.*
9. They arrived at *7.40.*
10. I *rarely* go and visit them these days.

II. Compléter par la préposition qui convient :

1. He was dead ... time, as usual.
2. ... a rule, I never drink coffee so late at night.
3. Once ... a time, there was a beautiful princess...
4. You can't work and watch TV ... the same time.
5. I am looking forward ... meeting them.
6. These workers are paid ... the hour.
7. They arrived just in time ... the match.
8. You can sleep here ... the time being.
9. I want this work to be finished ... the next three days.
10. He has a glass of whisky once ... a while.

III. Traduire :

1. *Je l'ai rencontrée il y a quinze jours.*
2. *C'était la veille de Pâques.*
3. *Le printemps est ma saison préférée.*
4. *Il se lève toujours à l'aube.*
5. *As-tu terminé ton devoir en temps voulu ?*
6. *Nous n'allons presque jamais au cinéma.*
7. *Leur amour fut sans lendemain.*
8. *Le facteur ne passe que tous les deux jours.*
9. *Il me faut souvent travailler tard le soir.*
10. *Est-ce que vous vous êtes bien amusés pendant vos quinze jours de vacances?*

13· Religion and ethics
La religion et la morale

faith [feiθ]	*la foi*
a creed, a belief	*un credo, une croyance*
a cult	*un culte*
a sect	*une secte*
Christianity	*le christianisme*
(Roman) Catholicism	*le catholicisme (romain)*
a Catholic ['kæθəlik]	*un catholique*
Protestantism	*le protestantisme*
a Protestant ['prɔtistənt]	*un protestant*
an evangelist	*un évangélisateur*
Buddhism	*le bouddhisme*
a Buddhist	*un bouddhiste*
Hinduism	*l'hindouisme*
a Hindu	*un hindou*
Islam	*l'Islam*
a Moslem, a Muslim	*un musulman*
Judaism	*le judaïsme*
a Jew, a Jewess	*un juif, une juive*
a god, a goddess	*un dieu, une déesse*
God	*Dieu*
Christ	*le Christ*
the Lord	*le Seigneur*
an idol ['aidl]	*une idole*
a prophet	*un prophète*
a prophecy	*une prophétie*
an angel	*un ange*
the Devil	*le Diable*
glory	*la gloire*
a miracle	*un miracle*
salvation	*le salut*
heaven ['hevn]	*le ciel*
paradise	*le paradis*
hell	*l'enfer*
Doomsday	*le jour du Jugement Dernier*
the gospel ['gɔspəl]	*l'évangile*
a prayer	*une prière*
a hymn	*un cantique*
a sermon	*un sermon*
a blessing	*une bénédiction*
mass	*la messe*
christening	*le baptême*
a festival	*une fête*
Christmas	*Noël*
Easter	*Pâques*
Whitsun	*la Pentecôte*

Halloween	*la veille de la Toussaint*
All Saints' Day	*la Toussaint*
a church	*une église*
a cathedral [kə'θi:drəl]	*une cathédrale*
an abbey ['æbi]	*une abbaye*
a monastery ['mɔnəstəri]	*un monastère*
a convent	*un couvent*
a temple	*un temple*
a mosque [mɔsk]	*une mosquée*
a synagogue	*une synagogue*
a shrine	*un sanctuaire*
a parish	*une paroisse*
a see	*un évêché, un archevêché*
the clergy	*le clergé*
a priest	*un prêtre*
a parson	*un pasteur*
a vicar ['vikə]	*un pasteur anglican*
a nun [nʌn]	*une religieuse*
a monk	*un moine*
a bishop	*un évêque*
an archbishop	*un archevêque*
a cardinal	*un cardinal*
the Pope [pəup]	*le Pape*
a preacher	*un prédicateur*
a saint	*un saint*
a martyr ['ma:tə]	*un martyr*
martyrdom	*le martyre*
a crusade [kru'seid]	*une croisade*
a pilgrimage	*un pèlerinage*
a pilgrim	*un pèlerin*
zeal [zi:l]	*le zèle, la ferveur*
a zealot ['zelət], a fanatic	*un fanatique*
fundamentalism	*l'intégrisme*
a fundamentalist	*un intégriste*
creationism	*le créationisme*
a creationist	*un créationiste*
a scapegoat	*un bouc émissaire*
a believer	*un croyant*
a missionary	*un missionnaire*
a congregation	*une assemblée de fidèles*
the flock	*les ouailles*
fervour	*la ferveur*
fanaticism	*le fanatisme*

a (non) conformist	*un (non) conformiste*
atheism	*l'athéisme*
an atheist [‘eiθiist]	*un athée*
agnosticism [æg’nɔstisizəm]	*l'agnosticisme*
an agnostic	*un agnostique*
a heathen [‘hi:ðən]	*un païen*
a freethinker	*un libre-penseur*
a Freemason	*un franc-maçon*
sorcery, witchcraft	*la sorcellerie*
a witch	*une sorcière*
a witch-hunt	*une chasse aux sorcières*
a ghost [gəust]	*un esprit*
a soul	*une âme*
morals, morality	*la moralité*
ethics [‘eθiks]	*la morale*
an ethic	*une déontologie*
charity	*la charité*
conscience	*la conscience*
a sin	*un péché*
a sinner	*un pécheur*
temptation	*la tentation*
forgiveness	*le pardon*
Good	*le Bien*
Evil [‘i:vl]	*le Mal*
manicheism [‘mæniki:izm]	*le manichéisme*
a vice	*un vice*
a virtue	*une vertu*
a principle	*un principe*
Evolution	*la théorie de l'évolution des espèces*
an oath [əuθ]	*un serment*
a criterion [krai’tiəriən](pl. criteria)	*un critère*
a scruple [‘skru:pl]	*un scrupule*
harm	*un mal, un tort*
remorse	*le remords*
malice	*la méchanceté, la malveillance*
a lie	*un mensonge*
a liar [‘laiə]	*un menteur*
treachery [‘tretʃəri]	*la traîtrise*
a hypocrite [‘hipəkrit]	*un hypocrite*
hypocrisy [hi’pɔkrəsi]	*l'hypocrisie*
a coward [‘kauəd]	*un lâche*
frankness	*la franchise*
esteem	*l'estime*
the truth [tru:θ]	*la vérité*
religious(ly)	*religieux (-sement)*
devout [di’vaut]	*dévot, pieux*
puritanical	*puritain*
Christian	*chrétien*

Catholic	*catholique*
Protestant	*protestant*
Anglican	*anglican*
Moslem, Muslim	*musulman*
Jewish	*juif*
prophetic(ally)	*prophétique(ment)*
sacred [‘seikrid]	*sacré*
holy [‘həuli]	*saint, bénit*
right(ly)	*juste(ment)*
righteous	*vertueux*
wrong(ly)	*mal, injuste(ment)*
evil	*mauvais, malveillant*
wicked [‘wikid]	*méchant, malfaisant*
faithful(ly)	*fidèle(ment)*
strict(ly)	*strict(ement)*
pagan [‘peigən]	*païen*
agnostic	*agnostique*
sectarian	*sectaire*
evangelical	*évangélique*
fanatic	*fanatique*
intolerant	*intolérant*
ecumenical	*œcuménique*
parochial [pə’rəukjəl]	*paroissial, de clocher*
virtuous	*vertueux*
deserving	*méritant*
scrupulous(ly)	*scrupuleux (-sement)*
frankly	*franc(hement)*
(un)worthy	*(in)digne*
cowardly (adj.)	*lâche*
wicked(ly)	*vilain(ement)*
sinful	*inavouable, honteux*
diabolical [ˌdaiə’bɔlikəl]	*diabolique*
heinous [‘heinəs]	*abominable*
depraved	*dépravé*
treacherous	*traître, déloyal*
hypocritical(ly)	*hypocrite(ment)*
remorseful	*plein de remords*
remorsefully	*avec remords*
to believe (in)	*croire (en)*
to worship	*faire ses dévotions (intr.), adorer, vénérer (tr.)*
to practise	*pratiquer*
to pray	*prier*
to kneel*	*s'agenouiller*
to obey (trans.)	*obéir (à)*
to abide* by	*se conformer à*
to preach	*prêcher*
to convert	*convertir*
to bless	*bénir*
to christen [‘krisn]	*baptiser*
to swear* [swɛə]	*jurer, blasphémer*
to vow [vau]	*jurer de*
to sin	*pécher*

to tempt	*tenter*	to deserve	*mériter*
to repent (of)	*se repentir (de)*	to condone	*fermer les yeux sur*
to confess	*(se) confesser*	to forgive*	*pardonner*
to lie [lai]	*mentir*	to reprove	*réprouver*
to conceal	*cacher, tenir secret*	to persecute	*persécuter*
to betray	*trahir*		

Expressions

to say one's prayers	*dire/faire ses prières*
to go to church	*aller à l'église, à la messe*
to attend mass	*assister à la messe*
the Church of England	*l'église anglicane*
God willing...	*si Dieu le veut*
for God's sake	*pour l'amour du ciel*
God bless you	*Dieu te/vous bénisse*
Thank God!	*Dieu merci*
vice and virtue	*le vice et la vertu*
Good versus Evil	*le Bien contre le Mal*
Talk of the devil!	*Quand on parle du loup...*
a heinous crime	*un crime abominable*
a fallen angel	*un ange déchu*
a patron saint	*un saint patron*
to do good / harm	*faire le bien / le mal*
to perform miracles	*accomplir des miracles*
to have loose morals	*être d'une moralité relâchée*
high moral standards	*des critères moraux très stricts*
to take an oath	*prêter serment*
to stick to one's principles	*rester fidèle à ses principes*
to cast a spell	*jeter un sort*
to do something out of malice	*faire qqch par malveillance*
to feel remorse	*avoir des remords*
to confess (to) a crime	*avouer un délit*
doomed to failure	*voué à l'échec*

Phrases

God helps those who help themselves.
Aide-toi, le ciel t'aidera.

Charity begins at home.
Charité bien ordonnée commence par soi-même.

Religion is the opium of the people. (Karl Marx)
La religion, c'est l'opium du peuple.

A religion is but a successful sect.
Une religion n'est jamais qu'une secte qui a réussi.

He confessed to committing many deadly sins.
Il a avoué avoir commis maints péchés mortels.

The new President must swear on the Bible to serve his country.
Le nouveau Président doit jurer sur la Bible de servir son pays.

God forbid that such wicked acts should be committed.
Dieu fasse que des actes aussi vils ne soient pas commis.

Considering his evil actions he got what he deserved.
Étant donné ses vilenies il a eu ce qu'il méritait.

She was charged with witchcraft and burnt to death.
Elle fut accusée de sorcellerie et brûlée vive.

Crusades were undertaken supposedly to recapture the Holy Land.
En théorie les croisades furent entreprises pour reconquérir la Terre Sainte.

After blessing the crowd the Pope preached against abortion.
Après avoir béni la foule le pape prêcha contre l'avortement.

Is it not amazing that some American schools should teach creationism rather than Evolution?
N'est-il pas stupéfiant que certaines écoles américaines enseignent le créationnisme plutôt que la théorie de l'évolution des espèces ?

Exercices

I. Compléter chaque élément de phrase de la colonne de gauche en choisissant la proposition appropriée dans la colonne de droite.

1. His efforts were doomed from the start;	A. he can go to the devil.
2. The crusaders believed there was no harm	B. to have them burnt as heretics.
3. Tortured by the Inquisition	C. to helping the poor in Calcutta.
4. His high moral principles prevented him	D. whom they considered a prophet.
5. After all the harm he has done	E. from condoning such hypocrisy.
6. Accusing people of sorcery was enough	F. he didn't have a ghost of a chance.
7. Some thought King Edward had too loose morals	G. in massacring the infidel.
8. She devoted all her energy	H. perform miracles live on television.
9. Every Sunday in the US you can watch preachers	I. they confessed sins they had never committed.
10. The Cult members worshipped their leader	J. to be the head of the Church of England.

II. Trouver les mots du chapitre correspondant aux définitions suivantes :

sufferings and death:
to give a benediction:
morally bad:
day of the Last Judgement:
to venerate:
the dominant religion of India:
deeply religious:
journey to a sacred place:
(not always holy) spirit
to cause someone to change their belief:

III. Thème. Traduire les expressions suivantes :

les fidèles :
un temple bouddhiste :
être tenté du démon :
se repentir de ses péchés :
des critères moraux très stricts :
il l'a fait par fanatisme religieux :
les bons et les méchants :
obéir aux règles :
une attitude hypocrite :
la conscience morale :

IV. SCIENCE AND TECHNOLOGY

14. Science and research
La science et la recherche

a laboratory, a lab	*un laboratoire*
an institute	*un institut*
a lab assistant	*un laborantin*
a technique	*une technique*
a field	*un domaine*
a patent	*un brevet*
an engineer [,endʒi'niə]	*un ingénieur, un technicien*
an experiment	*une expérience*
an observation	*une observation*
a sample	*un échantillon*
an extract	*un extrait*
an event [i'vent]	*un événement, une manifestation*
a phenomenon (phenomena)	*un phénomène*
a process	*un processus*
a mechanism	*un mécanisme*
a study	*une étude*
a record	*un fait enregistré*
a measure	*une mesure*
a chart	*un graphique*
accuracy ['ækjurəsi]	*la précision*
synthesis	*la synthèse*
analysis	*l'analyse*
a possibility	*une possibilité*
a hypothesis, an assumption	*une hypothèse*
a flaw [flɔ:]	*un défaut, un point faible*
a purpose	*un but*
a thinker	*un penseur*
a panel	*un comité, une commission*
a thinktank	*un groupe d'experts, de savants*
a brain	*un cerveau*
an expert	*un expert*
a layman	*un profane*
a researcher, a research worker	*un chercheur*
a scholar	*un érudit*
a scientist	*un savant*
a pioneer [,paiə'niə]	*un pionnier*
an innovator	*un innovateur*
a genius	*un génie*
a whiz(z) kid	*un petit génie*
a wizard	*un sorcier, un magicien*
a visionary	*un visionnaire*
progress	*le progrès*
an advance	*un progrès*
a challenge	*un défi*
a prospect, an outlook	*une perspective*
a basis (bases)	*une base, un fondement*
a principle	*un principe*
a formula	*une formule*
a theory	*une théorie*
a law	*une loi*
a dilemma	*un dilemme*
a clue	*un indice*
a proof	*une preuve*
a hurdle	*un obstacle (à franchir)*
a finding, a discovery	*une découverte*
an inroad (into)	*une percée*
a breakthrough	*une découverte de grande portée*
a benefit	*un bienfait*
an upheaval [ʌp'hi:vəl]	*un bouleversement*
a mistake	*une erreur*
intuition	*l'intuition*
creativity	*la créativité*
inventiveness	*l'esprit d'invention*
ingenuity [,indʒi'nju:iti]	*l'ingéniosité*
a topic	*un sujet*
a talk	*une discussion, un débat*
a lecture ['lektʃə]	*une conférence*
a mathematician	*un mathématicien*
a chemist ['kemist]	*un chimiste*
a biochemist	*un biochimiste*
a physicist	*un physicien*

a geophysicist	*un géophysicien*
an astrophysicist	*un astrophysicien*
a geneticist	*un généticien*
mechanics	*la mécanique*
acoustics	*l'acoustique*
optics	*l'optique*
a robot	*un robot*
robotics	*la robotique*
electricity	*l'électricité*
electrolysis	*l'électrolyse*
hydraulics	*l'hydraulique*
relativity	*la relativité*
matter	*la matière*
vacuum ['vækjuəm]	*le vide*
a solid	*un solide*
a liquid	*un liquide*
a fluid	*un fluide*
a salt	*un sel*
an acid	*un acide*
a base	*une base*
a chemical ['kemikəl]	*un produit chimique*
equipment	*le matériel*
a microscope	*un microscope*
a lens	*une lentille*
a magnet	*un aimant*
a magnetic field	*un champ magnétique*
a battery	*une pile*
scales	*une balance*
a crucible ['kru'sibl]	*un creuset*
a furnace	*un four*
a test tube	*une éprouvette*
a balloon	*un ballon*
a Bunsen burner	*un bec Bunsen*
an accelerator	*un accélérateur*
light	*la lumière*
a ray, a beam	*un rayon*
a photon	*un photon*
a neutron	*un neutron*
an electron	*un électron*
a proton	*un proton*
a cell	*une cellule*
a nucleus ['nju:kliəs]	*un noyau*
a molecule	*une molécule*
an atom	*un atome*
a quark	*un quark*
a particle	*une particule*
a protein	*une protéine*
a gene [dʒi:n]	*un gène*
a chromosome	*un chromosome*
a hormone	*une hormone*
a clone	*un clone*
cloning	*le clonage*
a mutant ['mju:tənt]	*un mutant*
a germ, a microbe	*un microbe*
a virus	*un virus*
a bacillus [bə'siləs]	*une bacille*
an antibody	*un anticorps*
a vaccine ['væksin]	*un vaccin*
scientific	*scientifique*
learned ['lə:nid]	*instruit, savant*
ingenious [in'dʒi:njəs]	*ingénieux*
accurate	*précis, exact*
rational	*rationnel*
empirical	*empirique*
random	*aléatoire, au hasard*
undocumented	*non documenté*
intuitive	*intuitif*
inventive	*inventif*
innovative	*novateur*
far-reaching	*d'une grande portée*
traditional	*traditionnel*
basic	*de base, élémentaire*
theoretical [θiə'retikl]	*théorique*
problematic(al)	*problématique*
efficient	*efficace*
reliable [ri'laiəbl]	*fiable*
faulty	*défectueux*
unknown	*inconnu*
bewildering	*déroutant*
ethical	*moral, éthique*
unethical	*contraire à l'éthique*
questionable	*discutable*
genetic	*génétique*
hereditary	*héréditaire*
artificial	*artificiel*
foreign ['fɔrin]	*étranger*
surrogate	*de remplacement, de substitution*
incurable	*incurable*
immune	*immunisé*
sterile	*stérile*
hazardous ['hæzədəs]	*dangereux*
lethal	*mortel*
optical	*microscopique*
aqueous ['eikwiəs]	*aqueux*
dense	*dense*
rarefied	*raréfié*
solid	*solide*
liquid	*liquide*
fluid	*fluide*
colourless	*incolore*
tasteless	*insipide*
inodorous	*inodore*
flammable, inflammable	*inflammable*
uninflammable	*ininflammable*
living	*vivant*
inanimate	*inanimé*
tangible	*tangible*

elusive [i'lu:siv]	*insaisissable, intangible*	to invent	*inventer*
infinitesimal	*infinitésimal*	to innovate	*innover*
subatomic	*subatomique*	to spearhead	*être à l'avant-garde de*
to search for	*chercher*	to pioneer	*ouvrir la voie, être le premier*
to assume	*supposer*	to revolutionize [,revə'lu:ʃənaiz]	*révolutionner*
to study	*étudier*	to lag behind	*être à la traîne*
to delve into	*étudier dans le détail, fouiller*	to catch* up (with)	*rattraper, combler son retard*
to hunt down, to track	*traquer*	to puzzle	*laisser perplexe*
to focus on ['fəukəs]	*se concentrer sur*	to analyse	*analyser*
to experiment	*expérimenter*	to test	*tester, essayer*
to create	*créer*	to magnify ['mægnifai]	*grossir, amplifier*
to predict	*prédire*	to magnetize	*aimanter*
to foresee*	*prévoir*	to rarefy	*raréfier*
to detect	*détecter*	to vanish	*disparaître*
to estimate	*estimer*	to materialize	*se matérialiser*
to measure ['meʒə]	*mesurer*	to heat	*chauffer*
to ponder	*réfléchir, méditer*	to cool	*faire refroidir*
to deduce	*déduire*	to stir [stə:]	*agiter*
to discover, to find* out	*découvrir*	to dissolve	*dissoudre*
to improve	*améliorer*	to melt	*fondre*
to solve	*résoudre*	to dilute	*diluer*
to work out, to figure out	*trouver la solution*	to weigh [wei]	*peser*
to fall short (of)	*ne pas atteindre son but*	to compare	*comparer*
to design	*concevoir*	to occur	*se produire*
to devise	*mettre au point*	to isolate	*isoler*
to develop	*développer, mettre au point*	to tamper with	*manipuler*
to perfect	*perfectionner*	to clone	*cloner*
to harness	*maîtriser*	to break* out	*se déclarer, éclater*
to confirm	*confirmer*	to annihilate	*anéantir*
to prove	*prouver*	to violate ['vai-əleit]	*violer*
		to ban	*interdire*
		to boycott	*boycotter*
		to fund	*financer*

Expressions

to do research	*faire des recherches*
to carry out research into a subject	*faire des recherches sur un sujet*
a field of research	*un domaine de recherche*
a research-and-development laboratory (an R&D lab)	*un laboratoire de développement et de recherche*
a research team	*une équipe de chercheurs*
laboratory equipment	*du matériel de laboratoire*
lab experiments	*des expériences en laboratoire*
animal experiments	*des expériences sur des animaux*
cruelty-free	*non testé sur les animaux*

to carry out an experiment	*effectuer une expérience*
industrial research	*recherche appliquée*
experimental research	*recherche expérimentale*
to collect information	*rassembler des informations*
raw data	*des données brutes*
scientific data	*des données scientifiques*
a serendipitous discovery	*une découverte heureuse (faite par hasard)*
a scientific bombshell	*une découverte scientifique révolutionnaire*
a Nobel prizewinner	*un lauréat du prix Nobel*
a scientific puzzle	*une énigme scientifique*
a missing link	*un lien manquant*
the genetic coding	*le code génétique*
a genetically modified organism (GMO)	*un OGM*
genetic fingerprinting	*l'identification par les gènes*
DNA	*l'ADN*
RNA	*l'ARN*
a sorcerer's apprentice	*un apprenti sorcier*
to be on the brink of	*être sur le point de*
to have an /the edge on	*avoir un avantage sur, avoir un temps d'avance*
to make headway, to make progress	*progresser*
to make great strides	*avancer à grands pas*
to be in the vanguard	*être à l'avant-garde*
to turn a process around	*inverser un processus*
to be on the trail of	*être sur la piste de*
a science park	*un parc scientifique*
applied sciences	*les sciences appliquées*
pure science	*la science pure*
the space race	*la course à l'espace*
nuclear physics	*la physique nucléaire*
the atomic theory	*la théorie atomique*
the splitting of the atom	*la séparation de l'atome*
the atomic weight	*le poids atomique*
the atom bomb	*la bombe atomique*
lethal radiation	*la radiation mortelle*
ultraviolet radiation	*la radiation ultraviolette*
X rays	*des rayons X*
the speed of light	*la vitesse de la lumière*
a space lab, a skylab	*un laboratoire spatial*
artificial intelligence	*l'intelligence artificielle*
hi-tech medicine	*la médecine de pointe*
a test-tube baby	*un bébé éprouvette*
a spark of life	*une étincelle de vie*
a living cell	*une cellule vivante*
complex organic compounds	*des composés organiques complexes*
a chicken-and-egg problem	*comment savoir quelle est la cause et quel est l'effet ?*

Phrases

To invent is to choose.
Inventer, c'est choisir.

If not truth, then what are scientists after?
Si ce n'est la vérité, alors quel est l'objet de la quête des scientifiques ?

Science opens new windows on the human mind.
La science ouvre de nouveaux horizons sur l'esprit humain.

The experimenter, more and more as knowledge develops, must be able to think with instruments.
De plus en plus, au fur et à mesure que les connaissances s'enrichissent, l'expérimentateur doit penser avec des instruments.

Science researchers face profound moral questions.
Les chercheurs scientifiques sont confrontés à des questions morales d'une grande portée.

Much of these biologists' speculation has yet to be verified in the lab.
Une grande partie des hypothèses de ces biologistes n'ont pas encore été vérifiées en laboratoire.

This new drug is being experimented on guinea pigs.
Ce nouveau médicament est en cours d'expérimentation sur des cobayes.

Many people strongly oppose animal experiments.
Beaucoup de gens sont fermement opposés à l'expérimentation sur des animaux.

Despite numerous lab experiments, no one has yet managed to develop a vaccine to fight the AIDS virus.
Malgré de nombreuses expériences en laboratoire, personne n'a encore réussi à mettre au point un vaccin pour lutter contre le SIDA.

The current research in the field of cloning is leading more and more people to think that scientists are tampering with nature.
Les recherches actuelles dans le domaine du clonage amènent de plus en plus de gens à penser que les scientifiques manipulent la nature.

Exercices

I. Retrouver les expressions en combinant des éléments des deux colonnes (en commençant par celle de gauche) :

a field	discovery
to split	sciences
to carry out	intelligence
applied	kid
a research	fluid
a colourless	data
a far-reaching	the atom
a whizz	of research
scientific	an experiment
artificial	worker

II. Quels sont les adjectifs correspondant aux définitions suivantes :

1. having no flavour:
2. that may be trusted:
3. that cannot be cured:
4. in accordance with or based on reason:
5. lifeless:
6. having much knowledge:
7. producing a desired result:
8. based on theory:
9. able to resist infection:
10. defective:

III. Former des paires d'éléments ayant des sens proches :

a sample	innovative
a fluid	hazardous
a ray	an innovator
a cell	to melt
to devise	a liquid
to experiment	an extract
to dissolve	a beam
dangerous	a nucleus
a pioneer	to develop
inventive	to test

15. Electronics and computer science
L'électronique et l'informatique

computing	*l'informatique (pratique)*
computerization	*l'informatisation*
data ['deitə]	*les données*
data processing	*le traitement des données*
hardware	*le matériel informatique*
a computer	*un ordinateur*
a personal computer (PC)	*un ordinateur individuel*
a laptop, a notebook	*un portable*
a microcomputer	*un micro-ordinateur*
a package	*un ensemble, une configuration*
a monitor	*un moniteur*
a switch	*un interrupteur*
a circuit	*un circuit*
a transistor	*un transistor*
a semiconductor	*un semi-conducteur*
a fuse [fju:z]	*un fusible*
a chip	*une puce*
a microprocessor	*un microprocesseur*
a cell	*une cellule*
a signal	*un signal*
a wavelength	*une longueur d'onde*
a frequency ['fri:kwənsi]	*une fréquence*
a slot	*une fente, un connecteur*
a socket	*une prise femelle, un connecteur*
a jack	*une fiche*
a cable	*un câble*
a battery	*une pile, une batterie*
a screen	*un écran*

the homepage	*la page d'accueil*
a password	*un mot de passe*
the menu	*le menu*
a pull-down menu	*un menu déroulant*
the toolbar	*la barre d'outils*
an icon ['aikɔn]	*une icône*
the control panel	*le tableau de commande*
a shortcut	*un raccourci*
a window	*une fenêtre*
a cursor	*un curseur*
an arrow	*une flèche*
a keyboard	*un clavier*
a key [ki:]	*une touche*
a digit ['didʒit]	*un chiffre*
a mouse	*une souris*
a mouse-pad	*un tapis*
a joystick	*une manette de jeu*
a videogame	*un jeu vidéo*
a headset	*des écouteurs*
a speaker	*un haut-parleur*
a peripheral	*un périphérique*
compatibility	*la compatibilité*
interactivity	*l'interactivité*
a drive	*un lecteur*
a microdisk	*une disquette (3,5")*
a scanner	*un scanner*
a printer	*une imprimante*
a hard copy	*une sortie papier*
a listing	*un listage, un listing*
a ribbon	*un ruban*
a cartridge	*une cartouche*
a network	*un réseau*
a gadget, a gizmo (US)	*un gadget*
a calculator	*une calculatrice*
a photocopier, a copier	*un photocopieur*
a teleprinter, a telewriter	*un téléscripteur*
a fax machine	*un télécopieur*
a videotex	*un minitel*
maintenance	*l'entretien, la maintenance*
troubleshooting	*recherche de la panne*
software	*Les logiciels*
a program	*un programme*
the operating system	*le système d'exploitation*
a virus	*un virus*
a worm [wə:m]	*un ver*
a hacker	*un pirate*
a bug [bʌg	*un défaut, un bogue*
programming	*la programmation*
a programmer	*un programmeur*
a user ['ju:zə]	*un utilisateur*

a software application	*un logiciel*
a freeware program	*un graticiel*
a shareware program	*un partagiciel*
a utility [ju:'tiliti]	*un utilitaire*
a language	*un langage*
a standard	*une norme*
a bit	*un bit*
a byte [bait]	*un octet*
a megabyte	*un méga-octet*
memory	*la mémoire*
storage	*le stockage*
a data base	*une base de données*
a data bank	*une banque de données*
a data file	*un fichier de données*
the directory	*le catalogue*
electronic mail	*messagerie, courrier électronique*
a network	*un réseau*
a website	*un site web*
an address [ə'dres]	*une adresse*
an address book	*un carnet d'adresses*
a chat room	*un salon virtuel (un site de chat)*
an access code	*un code d'accès*
a search engine	*un moteur de recherche*
computer graphics	*l'infographie*
a word processor	*un traitement de texte*
a font	*une police*
a spell-checker	*un correcteur orthographique*
a spreadsheet program	*un tableur*
graphics	*le graphisme*
a chart	*un diagramme, un graphique*
input	*entrée*
output	*sortie*
digital	*numérique*
analog	*analogique*
faulty, balky	*défectueux*
built-in	*intégré*
interactive	*interactif*
compatible	*compatible*
user-friendly	*convivial, facile d'utilisation*
computerized	*informatisé*
computer-aided / assisted	*assisté par ordinateur*
sophisticated	*perfectionné*
state-of-the-art	*dernier cri, à la pointe du progrès*
top-of-the-line	*haut de gamme*
elaborate [i'læbəreit]	*compliqué*

customized, custom-made	*personnalisé, sur mesure*
innovative	*innovant*
multitask	*multitâche*
multifunction	*multifonctions*
expandable	*extensible*
tedious ['ti:diəs]	*fastidieux*
repetitive	*répétitif*
boring	*ennuyeux*
time-consuming	*qui prend beaucoup de temps*
time-saving	*qui économise du temps*
convenient	*pratique*
ubiquitous	*omniprésent*
tiny [taini]	*minuscule*
huge [[hju:dʒ]	*énorme*
infallible	*infaillible*
vulnerable	*vulnérable*
portable	*portable*
light	*léger*
versatile	*polyvalent*
to compute	*calculer*
to plug (into)	*(se) brancher (sur)*
to power	*alimenter, mettre sous tension*
to switch on	*mettre en route*
to switch off	*éteindre*
to connect	*brancher, relier*
to chat	*chatter*
to access	*accéder à*
to click	*cliquer*
to activate	*activer*
to install	*installer*
to uninstall	*désinstaller*
to format ['fɔ:mæt]	*formater*
to start	*démarrer*
to run*	*faire tourner*

to select	*sélectionner*
to load [ləud]	*charger*
to overflow	*dépasser la capacité*
to save	*enregistrer*
to back up	*faire une copie de sauvegarde*
to duplicate	*dupliquer*
to read*	*lire*
to lock	*verrouiller*
to process	*traiter*
to type	*taper*
to press	*appuyer*
to display	*afficher*
to scroll down	*dérouler*
to edit	*mettre en forme*
to debug	*éliminer les erreurs*
to cut* and paste	*couper-coller*
to erase, to delete [di'li:t]	*effacer*
to cancel	*annuler*
to clear	*effacer (mémoire)*
to retrieve	*récupérer*
to sort	*trier*
to scan	*scanner*
to file	*classer*
to label ['leibl]	*étiqueter*
to gather	*rassembler*
to provide	*fournir*
to wire [waiə]	*câbler*
to update	*actualiser*
to upgrade	*améliorer, perfectionner*
to computerize	*informatiser*
to supersede [ˌsju:pə'si:d]	*remplacer, détrôner*
to photocopy, to xerox	*photocopier*

Expressions

office technology, office automation	*la bureautique*
communications technology	*la télématique*
a fiber-optic cable	*un câble à fibre optique*
a cordless phone	*un téléphone sans fil*
a portable phone	*un téléphone portable*
information technology	*les technologies de l'information*
the global village	*le village planétaire*
a communications satellite (com-sat)	*un satellite de communication*
a weather satellite	*un satellite météo*
a satellite dish	*une antenne parabolique*
the computer age	*l'ère de l'informatique*
a home-shopping network	*un réseau d'achat à domicile*

consumer electronics	*l'électronique grand public*
the computer industry	*l'industrie de l'informatique*
computer equipment	*le matériel informatique*
the computer department	*le service informatique*
computer crime	*la criminalité informatique*
software piracy	*le piratage des logiciels*
computer piracy	*le piratage informatique*
operating costs	*les coûts de fonctionnement*
a light pen / pencil	*un crayon optique*
a control device	*un dispositif de contrôle*
a remote control	*une télécommande*
a laser beam	*un faisceau laser*
a video-display unit (VDU)	*une console vidéo*
a video-touch screen	*un écran tactile*
digital display	*l'affichage numérique*
a software engineer	*un ingénieur en programmation*
a software maker	*un fabricant de logiciels*
a computer expert, a computer scientist	*un informaticien*
a speech / voice synthesizer	*un synthétiseur vocal*
a speech-recognition program	*un programme de reconnaissance vocale*
digital sound recording	*enregistrement numérique du son*
a flight simulator	*un simulateur de vol*
virtual reality	*la réalité virtuelle*
a desktop computer	*un ordinateur de bureau*
a portable PC	*un portable*
a laptop PC	*un compact*
a palmtop PC	*un ordinateur de poche*
a pocket calculator	*une calculatrice de poche*
an electronic organizer	*un agenda électronique*
a dot-matrix printer	*une imprimante matricielle*
an ink-jet / bubble-jet printer	*une imprimante à jet d'encre*
a laser printer	*une imprimante laser*
a CD-ROM player	*un lecteur CD-ROM*
a CD / DVD burner	*un graveur de CD / DVD*
a software library	*une bibliothèque de logiciels*
RAM (Random Access Memory)	*mémoire vive*
ROM (Read Only Memory)	*mémoire morte*
BASIC (Beginners' All-purpose Symbolic Instruction Code)	*le BASIC*
computer-aided design (CAD)	*la conception assistée par ordinateur*
computer-aided translation	*la traduction automatique*
interactive technology	*la technologie interactive*

Phrases

Software is the Achilles' heel of the computer revolution.
Les logiciels sont le talon d'Achille de la révolution informatique.

Software applications are getting more and more user-friendly, which means computing is now accessible to almost everyone.
Les logiciels deviennent de plus en plus conviviaux, ce qui signifie que l'informatique est désormais à la portée de pratiquement tout le monde.

About 27 percent of America's 92 million households have home computers.
Environ 27 pour cent des 92 millions de foyers américains possèdent un ordinateur familial.

An increasing number of people think that shopping on the Net is cheaper and more convenient.
De plus en plus de gens pensent qu'il est plus économique et pratique de faire ses achats sur internet.

The revolution in consumer electronics will change the way you live and work.
La révolution de l'électronique grand public changera la façon dont vous vivez et travaillez.

A single failure of a computer-software program could have serious consequences.
Une seule défaillance d'un logiciel pourrait avoir des conséquences graves.

Many teenagers spend too much time playing videogames on their computers.
Beaucoup d'adolescents passent trop de temps à jouer à des jeux vidéo sur leur ordinateur.

More and more executives are seen feeding data into their portable computers while commuting.
On voit de plus en plus de cadres entrer des données sur leur ordinateur portable dans les trains de banlieue.

There will never be a computer model that can mimic the things the brain can do.
Il n'existera jamais un modèle d'ordinateur capable d'imiter les choses que le cerveau peut faire.

Computer scientists are aware of the dangers of hacking and computer viruses.
Les informaticiens sont conscients des dangers du piratage et des virus informatiques.

Exercices

I. Trouver les réponses aux définitions suivantes :

1. a device to turn electric apparatus on or off.
2. a complete set of keys, on a typewriter for example.
3. this is where data are displayed.
4. it is made up of eight bits.
5. easy to use.
6. that can do various tasks.
7. a type of phone which you can use anywhere.
8. provides power, even if there is a power cut.
9. what is inserted into a drive.
10. your program will not work if it contains one.

II. Quels sont les noms correspondant aux verbes suivants (il peut y avoir plus d'une seule réponse) :

1. to store 2. to compute 3. to computerize 4. to process 5. to program

III. A quoi correspondent les sigles suivants :

1. a PC 2. a CD-ROM 3. RAM 4. BASIC 5.CAD

IV. Compléter :

1. A word ... is a utility that enables you to type in and print out text.
2. The French Minitel is an on-line data ... .
3. It uses the phone ... to communicate data.
4. Press the ... to power your computer.
5. He keeps all his appointments recorded in an electronic ... .
6. Don't forget to switch ... your computer when you have finished with it.
7. Most people don't write their own programs ; they buy software ... .
8. BASIC is the most common computer ... .
9. 54 is a two- ... number.
10. You move your ... to reach the various menus

16· Industry and industrial relations
L'industrie et les relations industrielles

Vocabulaire général

an industry	*une industrie*
an industrialist	*un industriel*
a manufacturer	*un fabricant*
heavy industry	*l'industrie lourde*
light industry	*l'industrie légère*
an industrial sector	*un secteur industriel*
work	*le travail*
a job	*un travail, emploi*
a task	*une tâche*
a factory, a plant	*une usine*
a workshop	*un atelier*
a work station	*un poste de travail*
a sweatshop ['swetʃɔp]	*un atelier clandestin*
a warehouse	*un entrepôt*
labour, manpower	*la main d'œuvre*
the workforce	*la main d'œuvre (effectifs)*
the staff, the personnel[ˌpə:sə'nel]	*le personnel*
a worker	*un travailleur, ouvrier*
a workman	*un ouvrier, travailleur manuel*
a skilled worker	*un ouvrier qualifié*
a semi-skilled worker *(OS)*	*un ouvrier spécialisé*
an unskilled worker	*un manœuvre*
a blue-collar (worker)	*un col bleu*
a white-collar worker	*un col blanc*
a temp	*un intérimaire*
a foreman	*un contremaître*
an engineer [ˌendʒi'niə]	*un technicien, un ingénieur*
a draughtsman, draftsman	*un dessinateur, un concepteur*
a manual worker	*un travailleur manuel*
a mechanic	*un mécanicien*
a craftsman	*un artisan*
a craft	*un art, métier (artisanal)*
a trade	*un métier*
a skill	*une compétence*
the know-how	*le savoir-faire*
training	*la formation*
further training	*la formation continue*
retraining	*le recyclage*
a training course	*un stage de formation*
goods	*les marchandises, articles*
a product	*un produit*
an item ['aitəm]	*un article*
a standard	*une norme, un niveau*
a process	*un procédé*
production	*la production*
the output	*la production, le rendement*

assembly	*le montage*
mass-production	*la production de grande série*
an assembly line	*une chaîne de montage*
a (conveyor) belt	*un tapis roulant, une chaîne*
the pace	*le rythme*
a break	*une pause*
safety	*la sécurité*
efficiency	*l'efficacité*
a safety standard	*une norme de sécurité*
mobility	*la mobilité*
flexibility	*la flexibilité, souplesse*
the yield	*le rendement*
staff turnover	*le renouvellement du personnel*
a shift	*une période de travail, équipe*
flexitime	*les horaires mobiles*
a machine	*une machine*
machinery	*l'ensemble des machines*
an employer	*un employeur*
an employee [ˌemplɔiˈi]	*un employé*
job hunting	*la recherche de travail*
unemployment	*le chômage*
the unemployed, the jobless	*les chômeurs*
an unemployed worker, a jobless worker	*un chômeur*
streamlining	*le dégraissage*
delocation	*la délocalisation*
moonlighting	*le travail au noir*
a moonlighter	*un travailleur au noir*
automation	*l'automatisation*
mechanization	*la mécanisation*
a robot [ˈrəubɔt]	*un robot*
an automaton	*un automate*
robotics	*la robotique*
industrial	*industriel*
manual	*manuel*
mechanical	*mécanique*
efficient [iˈfiʃənt]	*efficace*
effective [iˈfektiv]	*efficace, qui a des résultats*
mechanized	*mécanisé*
automated	*automatisé*
miniaturized	*miniaturisé*
sophisticated	*hautement perfectionné*
remote-controlled	*télécommandé*
good-quality	*de bonne qualité*

hi-tech	*de haute technologie de pointe*
advanced	*avancé*
versatile	*souple*
flawless, perfect	*parfait*
safe	*sûr*
streamlined	*profilé, aérodynamique*
well-oiled	*bien huilé*
shoddy	*bâclé, mal fini*
faulty	*défectueux*
bad-quality	*de mauvaise qualité*
greasy [ˈgri:si]	*gras, maculé de cambouis*
unsafe	*peu sûr, dangereux*
obsolete [ˈɔbsəli:t]	*obsolète, dépassé*
outdated	*démodé*
ailing	*en mauvaise posture*
time-consuming	*chronophage, qui prend du temps*
wooden	*en bois*
woollen	*en laine*
stainless	*inoxydable*
synthetic	*synthétique*
gold-plated	*plaqué or*
hard-working	*travailleur*
skilled	*qualifié*
unskilled	*non qualifié*
rewarding	*gratifiant*
boring, dull	*ennuyeux*
tedious [ˈti:djəs]	*assommant*
unrewarding	*ingrat*
underpaid	*sous-payé*
understaffed	*à court de personnel*
well-paid	*bien payé*
ill-paid	*mal payé*
idle [aidl]	*paresseux*
redundant	*au chômage, qui a été licencié*
unemployed	*au chômage*
to make*	*faire, fabriquer*
to manufacture	*fabriquer*
to assemble	*monter*
to dismantle	*démonter*
to produce	*produire*
to turn out	*produire, fabriquer*
to process	*traiter, transformer*
to design [diˈzain]	*dessiner, créer*
to devise [diˈvaiz]	*imaginer, inventer, concevoir*
to develop [diˈveləp]	*développer, mettre au point*
to mass-produce	*fabriquer en série*
to operate [ˈɔpəreit]	*faire fonctionner*

to test	*essayer, mettre à l'essai*	to hammer	*marteler*
to simulate	*simuler*	to tighten up	*resserrer*
to streamline	*rationaliser*	to screw [skru:]	*visser*
to automate	*automatiser*	to train	*former*
to mechanize	*mécaniser*	to retrain	*recycler*
to standardize	*standardiser*	to take* on, to hire	*embaucher*
to improve	*améliorer*	to fire, to dismiss	*renvoyer*
to evolve [i'vɔlv]	*évoluer (intr.) ; élaborer (tr.)*	to lay* off	*licencier, débaucher*
to sabotage	*saboter*	to trim	*écrémer (le personnel restructurer*
to refine	*raffiner*	to close down	*fermer (définitivement)*
to extract	*extraire*	to strike*	*faire grève*
to cast*	*couler, fondre*	to protest	*protester*
to melt	*fondre*	to claim	*revendiquer*
to smelt	*fondre, extraire par fusion*	to demand	*réclamer, revendiquer*
to lubricate	*lubrifier*	to resume [ri'zju:m]	*reprendre, recommencer*
to spin*	*filer*	to exploit	*exploiter*
to weave*	*tisser*	to sweat [swet]	*(faire) transpirer, exploiter*
to saw* [sɔ:]	*scier*		

Vocabulaire spécialisé

1. Factories

the iron and steel industry	*l'industrie sidérurgique*	the timber industry	*l'industrie du bois*
an iron works	*une usine sidérurgique*	a sawmill	*une scierie*
a steel works (plant)	*une aciérie*	shipbuilding	*la construction navale*
a foundry ['faundri]	*une fonderie*	a shipyard	*un chantier naval*
a blast furnace	*un haut-fourneau*	the textile industry	*l'industrie textile*
the oil industry	*l'industrie pétrolière*	a textile mill/plant	*une usine textile*
a refinery	*une raffinerie*	the clothing industry	*l'industrie de l'habillement*
a gasworks	*une usine à gaz*	civil engineering	*les travaux publics*
light/heavy / engineering	*la mécanique - petite lourde*	roadworks	*travaux (d'entretien des routes)*
an assembly plant	*une usine de montage*	the building industry	*l'industrie du bâtiment*
aeronautics	*l'aéronautique*	a site	*un chantier*
the car industry	*l'industrie automobile*	a cottage industry	*une industrie à domicile*
a car factory	*une usine automobile*		
the chemical industry	*l'industrie chimique*		
a chemical plant	*une usine chimique*		

2. Raw Materials

metals	*les métaux*	aluminium	*l'aluminium*
iron [aiən]	*le fer*	gold	*l'or*
iron ore [ɔ:]	*le minerai de fer*	chemicals	*les produits chimiques*
steel	*l'acier*	acid	*l'acide*
lead [led]	*le plomb*	cyanide	*le cyanure*
copper	*le cuivre*	sodium	*le sodium*
brass	*le laiton*	soda ['səudə]	*la soude*
zinc	*le zinc*	tar	*le goudron*

chlorine ['klɔ:ri:n]	*le chlore*
dioxin [dai'ɔksin]	*la dioxine*
phosphates	*les phosphates*
textiles	*les textiles*
wool	*la laine*
cotton	*le coton*
a man-made fibre, a synthetic fibre	*une fibre synthétique*
silk	*la soie*
a material, a fabric	*un tissu, une étoffe*
cloth [klɔθ]	*du tissu*

3. Tools and Equipment

a machine tool	*une machine-outil*
a hammer	*un marteau*
a spanner	*une clef (à écrous)*
a screwdriver	*un tournevis*
a nut [nʌt]	*un écrou*
a bolt	*un boulon*
a screw	*une vis*
a nail	*un clou*
oil	*l'huile*
grease	*le cambouis*
overalls	*une salopette, un bleu de travail*
goggles	*des lunettes de protection*
a smokestack	*une cheminée d'usine*
a wind tunnel	*une soufflerie*
a drawing board	*une planche à dessin*

4. Industrial relations

a trade union (UK), a labour union (US)	*un syndicat*
a union member	*un syndiqué*
the working class	*la classe ouvrière*
class awareness	*la conscience de classe*
a delegate, a shop steward	*un délégué d'atelier*
wages ['weidʒiz]	*une paye (ouvrier)*
pay, a salary	*un salaire, traitement*
labour unrest	*l'agitation sociale*
an industrial / a labour dispute	*un conflit social*
a claim, a demand [di'ma:nd]	*une revendication*
a pay claim	*une revendication salariale*
job cuts	*les suppressions d'emploi*
a lay-off	*un licenciement*
a redundancy	*un licenciement, une mise au chômage*
a closure ['kləuʒə]	*une fermeture*
a demonstration	*une manifestation*
a strike	*une grève*
a picket	*un piquet de grève*
negotiations	*les négociations*
a settlement	*un accord*
the two sides of industry	*les partenaires sociaux*
a pay rise (UK), a pay hike (US)	*une augmentation de salaire*
severance pay	*une indemnité de licenciement*
absenteeism	*l'absentéisme*
the employment agency	*l'agence pour l'emploi (cf. ANPE)*
unemployment benefit, the dole	*l'allocation chômage*

Expressions

hi-tech industries	*les industries de pointe*
peak technologies	*les technologies de pointe*
a sunrise industry	*une industrie montante*
an ailing industry	*une industrie mal en point*
a smokestack industry	*une industrie traditionnelle*
a lame duck	*un canard boiteux*
labour-intensive industries	*les industries qui nécessitent beaucoup de main-d'œuvre*
the working conditions	*les conditions de travail*
computer-assisted production	*la production assistée par ordinateur*

a computer-controlled assembly line	*une chaîne de montage informatisée*
stringent safety standards	*des normes de sécurité sévères*
stringent safety rules/regulations	*des règles de sécurité sévères*
good-quality products	*des produits de bonne qualité*
shoddy goods	*des articles de mauvaise qualité*
vocational training	*la formation professionnelle*
the minimum wage	*le salaire minimum*
a mobile workforce	*une main d'œuvre mobile*
a plant closure	*une fermeture d'usine*
at shopfloor level	*à la base (usine)*
the closed shop system	*système où on n'embauche que des ouvriers syndiqués*
the right to hire and fire	*le droit d'embaucher et de débaucher*
to do a job	*faire un travail*
to look for (to hunt for) work/ a job	*chercher du travail*
to do odd jobs	*faire de menus travaux*
to work on the line	*travailler à la chaîne*
to step up the pace of the line	*accélérer le rythme de la chaîne*
to get down to work	*se mettre au travail*
to operate a machine	*faire fonctionner une machine*
to learn new skills	*apprendre de nouvelles compétences*
to work to capacity	*produire à plein rendement*
to churn out cheap consumer goods	*débiter des biens de consommation bon marché*
to flood the market	*inonder le marché*
to work in shifts/the 3 shifts	*travailler par roulement*
to fail to start	*ne pas (réussir à) démarrer*
to improve on a design	*apporter des améliorations à une conception*
to spearhead a technological revolution	*être le fer de lance d'une révolution technologique*
to meet the safety standards	*être conforme aux normes de sécurité*
to make a step forward	*faire un pas en avant*
to make a giant leap forward	*faire un bond en avant*
to cut jobs	*supprimer des emplois*
to be made redundant	*être mis au chômage*
to be on the dole/out of work	*être au chômage*
to go on strike	*se mettre en grève*
to work to rule	*faire la grève du zèle*
to stage a demonstration	*manifester, organiser une manifestation*
to put in a claim for a pay rise	*poser une demande d'augmentation*
to put in a claim for better working conditions	*poser une demande pour de meilleures conditions de travail*
to resume work, to go back to work	*reprendre le travail*

Phrases

A bad workman always blames his tools.
Un mauvais ouvrier se plaint toujours de ses outils.

In the 1970s Asian factories started to churn out cheap goods that flooded Western markets.
Dans les années 70 les usines asiatiques commencèrent à produire des marchandises peu chères qui envahirent les marchés occidentaux.

He was made redundant 5 years ago and he has been on the dole ever since.
Il fut licencié il y a 5 ans et depuis il est au chômage.

Can robots create as many jobs as they cause redundancies?
Les robots peuvent-ils créer autant d'emplois qu'ils en suppriment ?

Many Western firms close down their plants, relocating them in developing countries where wages are much lower.
Beaucoup d'entreprises occidentales ferment leurs usines pour les rouvrir dans des pays en voie de développement, dans lesquels les salaires sont beaucoup moins élevés..

Some machine tools have become so sophisticated that only experts can operate them.
Certaines machines-outils sont devenues si perfectionnées que seuls des experts peuvent les faire fonctionner.

The two sides of industry met to discuss wages and working conditions.
Les partenaires sociaux se sont rencontrés pour discuter des salaires et des conditions de travail.

Only stringent safety standards can prevent such accidents in the future.
Seules des normes de sécurité sévères pourront empêcher de tels accidents à l'avenir.

British industrialists then claimed the right to hire and fire.
Les industriels britanniques revendiquèrent alors le droit d'embaucher et de licencier.

Skilled workers found it hard to adapt to dull and repetitive work on the assembly line.
Les ouvriers qualifiés eurent du mal à s'adapter à la monotonie du travail à la chaîne.

Exercices

I. Compléter les phrases suivantes au moyen de mots du chapitre :

Many Western firms (1)... down their European plants, re-opening them in the Third World where a cheap labour force was ready to (2)... down to work.

Japanese industrialists have often been blamed for saving on (3)... by copying the discoveries of their Western competitors.

The revival of (4) c... industries can be considered a reaction against the mass production of standardized products.

Some experts argue that (5) s... are an inevitable ill without which our clothing industry would not survive.

Professional painters and builders cannot really compete with (6)... who do small jobs much more cheaply.

Absenteeism has often been blamed on the dull and (7) u... routine tasks that modern industry imposes.

As they did (8) p..., it was in the workers' interest to (9) t... out the items as quickly as possible.

Unskilled workers have often been replaced on the (10) a...l... by robots that are quicker and more accurate for simple jobs.

II. Compléter les phrases suivantes en apportant les modifications nécessaires mais sans changer l'ordre des mots :

1. 10 years ago - our factory - work - capacity.

2. But in 1990 - Taiwan - start - flood - market - cheap items.
3. Although - the latter - not - meet - safety standards - they - distribute - all over - Europe - USA.
4. So - company - start - cut - jobs - trim - staff.
5. Many workers - make - redundant - when - line - become - computer-assisted.
6. We - try - improve - streamline - production.
7. However - we - fail - recover - share - market.
8. Eventually - management - decide - close - plant - in 93 - lay off - 1,200 workers.
9. Today - many - my colleagues - still - out - work - and - odd jobs.
10. After - get - retrained - I - now - hunt - job.

III. Remettre les mots dans l'ordre correct :

1. Japanese / industry / shipbuilding / failed / Korean / and / to / competition / European / face / The
2. get / Fast-evolving / to / training / workers / technologies / it / for / their / further / made / have / necessary
3. compete / difficult / European / The / Asia / costs / of / it / textile / because / labour / with / industry / finds / higher / to
4. field / spearheaded / pioneer / a / in / of / the / who / He / revolution / aeronautics / a / was
5. improved / model / wind / streamlined / This / in / and / the / new / was / tunnel
6. design / machine / drawing / faulty / board / the / The / was / of / now / the / is / and / on / it / back
7. competition / shoulders / Germans / head / naturally / is / that / and / claim / product / above / their / The / the
8. working / disappear / in / tradition / class / England / today's / to / The / tending / is
9. British / strikes / decided / the / to / an / to / The / paralized / government / end / that / industry / put
10. trim / giants / engineers / their / it / Electronics / necessary / found / making / staff / to / by / redundant / even

17. Energy and natural resources
L'énergie et les ressources naturelles

Vocabulaire général

heat *la chaleur*
heating *le chauffage*
light *la lumière*
lighting *l'éclairage*
power *l'énergie*
current *le courant*
steam *la vapeur*
pressure ['preʃə] *la pression*
petrol *l'essence*
oil *le pétrole ; l'huile*

fuel	*le combustible*
a beam, a ray	*un rayon*
a kilowatt-hour	*un kilowattheure*
a megawatt	*un mégawatt*
a volt	*un volt*
voltage	*la tension*
a barrel	*un baril*
a gas cylinder	*une bouteille de gaz*
a meter ['mi:tə]	*un compteur*
fuel consumption	*la consommation d'énergie*
scarcity ['skeirsiti]	*le manque*
a shortage	*une pénurie*
waste	*le gaspillage*
the supply	*l'offre*
the demand [di'ma:nd]	*la demande*
a glut	*une surabondance*
a surplus	*un excédent*
depletion [di'pli:ʃən]	*la diminution, l'épuisement*
efficiency	*l'efficacité*
the yield	*le rendement*
safety	*la sécurité*
electric(al)	*électrique*
hybrid ['haibrid]	*hybride*
global	*planétaire*
dramatic	*spectaculaire*
infrared	*infra rouge*
ultraviolet	*ultra violet*
effective	*efficace (qui a de l'effet)*
ineffective	*sans effet*
efficient	*efficace (d'un bon rendement)*
inefficient	*inefficace*
negligible	*négligeable*
well-lit	*bien éclairé*
ill-lit	*mal éclairé*
safe	*sûr*
unsafe	*peu sûr, dangereux*
plentiful, abundant	*abondant*
finite ['fainait]	*limité*
inexhaustible	*inépuisable*
exhausted [ig'zɔ:stid]	*épuisé*
(non-) renewable	*(non) renouvelable*
scarce	*rare*
sustainable	*soutenable*
coal-fired	*chauffé au charbon*
gas-fired	*chauffé au gaz*
battery-powered	*qui fonctionne sur piles / sur batterie*
nuclear	*nucléaire*
radioactive	*radioactif*
wasteful	*gaspilleur, peu économique*

polluting [pə'lu:tiŋ]	*polluant*
irresponsible	*irresponsable*
self-sufficient	*autosuffisant*
fuel-efficient	*économique en carburant*
primary	*primaire*
secondary	*secondaire*
gigantic	*gigantesque*
huge [hju:dʒ]	*énorme*
minute [mai'nju:t]	*minuscule*
electrically	*par l'électricité*
globally	*mondialement, globalement*
dramatically	*d'une manière spectaculaire*
(in)efficiently	*(in)efficacement*
significantly	*d'une manière significative*
considerably	*considérablement*
abundantly	*abondamment*
scarcely	*à peine*
infinitely	*infiniment*
irresponsibly	*d'une manière irresponsable*
to supply	*fournir, approvisionner*
to provide	*fournir*
to consume	*consommer*
to rely on	*compter sur*
to deplete [di'pli:t]	*diminuer, réduire*
to exhaust	*épuiser*
to store	*stocker*
to yield	*produire, rapporter*
to trigger	*déclencher*
to extract, to mine	*extraire*
to dam	*faire un barrage sur*
to tap	*exploiter, utiliser*
to harness	*exploiter*
to collect	*recueillir*
to fuel	*alimenter*
to refuel	*ravitailler*
to fill up	*remplir, faire le plein*
to run* out of	*(venir à) manquer de*
to heat	*chauffer*
to boil	*bouillir*
to generate	*produire*
to radiate ['reidieit]	*rayonner, irradier*
to power	*propulser*
to ignite [i'gnait]	*(s') enflammer*
to burn*	*brûler*
to convert	*transformer*
to switch to	*changer pour, passer à*
to turn to	*se tourner vers*
to leak	*fuir*
to refine	*raffiner*

to reprocess	*retraiter*	to squander ['skwɔndə]	*dilapider*
to recycle	*recycler*	to increase	*augmenter*
to locate	*situer*	to reduce	*réduire*
to cut* (down on)	*réduire*	to fall*	*tomber, baisser*
to save	*économiser*	to soar [sɔ:]	*monter en flèche*
to conserve	*préserver*		
to waste	*gaspiller*		

Vocabulaire spécialisé

Fuels	***Les combustibles***		
charcoal ['tʃa:kəul]	*le charbon de bois*	premium /4-star petrol	*le super*
peat [pi:t]	*la tourbe*	fuel oil	*le gasoil*
firewood	*le bois de chauffage*	natural gas	*le gaz naturel*
a log	*une bûche*	ethanol ['eθənɔl]	*l'éthanol*
logging	*l'exploitation des forêts*	methane	*le méthane*
crude oil, petroleum (US)	*le pétrole brut*	propane	*le propane*
petrol, gas(oline) (US)	*l'essence*	sunlight	*la lumière solaire*
unleaded ['ʌn'ledid] petrol	*l'essence sans plomb*	hydrogen	*l'hydrogène*
		hydrocarbon fuels	*les hydrocarbures*
		fossil fuels	*les combustibles fossiles*

Different forms of energy	***Les différentes formes d'énergie***		
solar power	*l'énergie solaire*	geothermal energy	*la géothermie*
wind power	*l'énergie éolienne*	nuclear power	*l'énergie nucléaire*
hydroelectricity	*l'hydroélectricité*		

Energy-producing facilities	***Les équipements énergétiques***		
a power station / plant	*une centrale électrique*	a nuclear power station /plant (a "nuke")	*une centrale nucléaire*
a thermal power plant	*une centrale thermique*	a hydroelectric plant	*une centrale hydroélectrique*
a tidal power station	*une usine marémotrice*	a windmill	*une éolienne*
		a dam	*un barrage*

Energy-related equipment	***Le matériel énergétique***		
a stove [stəuv]	*un poêle*	a photovoltaic cell (PV cell)	*une cellule photovoltaïque*
a boiler	*une chaudière*	a solar panel	*un panneau solaire*
a radiator ['reidieitə]	*un radiateur*	a light bulb	*une ampoule électrique*
a heatpump	*une pompe à chaleur*	a wire [waiə]	*un fil, un câble*
a turbine	*une turbine*	a line	*une ligne*
a generator	*un générateur*	a pylon ['pailən]	*un pylône*
a battery	*une pile, une batterie*	a cooling tower	*une tour de refroidissement*
a circuit	*un circuit*		
a transformer	*un transformateur*		
the power network / grid	*le réseau électrique*		

Nuclear power — *L'énergie nucléaire*

a nuclear reactor	*un réacteur nucléaire*
a fast-breeder reactor (FBR)	*un surrégénérateur*
a reactor core	*le cœur d'un réacteur*
uranium rods [ju'reinjum]	*les barres d'uranium*
a chain reaction	*une réaction en chaîne*
a cooling system	*un système de refroidissement*
a meltdown	*une fusion du cœur du réacteur*
enriched uranium	*l'uranium enrichi*
plutonium	*le plutonium*
a reprocessing plant	*une usine de retraitement*
radioactive / nuclear waste	*les déchets radioactifs / nucléaires*
nuclear fallout	*les retombées radioactives*
to split*	*fissionner*
to disintegrate	*se désintégrer*
to enrich	*enrichir*
gamma rays	*les rayons gamma*

Mining — *L'exploitation minière*

a mine	*une mine*
a quarry ['kwɔri]	*une carrière*
an open-cast mine	*une mine à ciel ouvert*
coal mining	*l'extraction du charbon*
a pit	*un puits, une mine*
the pithead	*le carreau de la mine*
a gallery	*une galerie*
a seam [si:m]	*une veine*
a coal face	*un front de taille*
a mine blast	*un coup de grisou*
a pickaxe	*une pioche*
a deposit [di'pɔzit]	*un gisement*
a slag heap	*un terril*
a pit closure ['kləuʒə]	*une fermeture de mine*
iron [aiən]	*le fer*
iron ore [ɔ:]	*le minerai de fer*
a gold nugget	*une pépite d'or*
an ingot, a bar	*un lingot*
to work a mine	*exploiter une mine*
to drill	*forer*
to dig*	*creuser*

The oil industry — *L'industrie pétrolière*

oil production	*la production pétrolière*
an oil field	*un gisement pétrolifère*
an oil well	*un puits de pétrole*
an oil rig / platform	*une plate-forme de forage en mer*
an oil terminal	*un terminal pétrolier*
a refinery [ri'fainəri]	*une raffinerie*
offshore production	*la production en mer*
a tanker	*un pétrolier, un tanker*
a pipeline	*un pipeline, un oléoduc*
a filling / petrol station	*une station services*
a tank	*un réservoir*
OPEC (Organization of Petroleum -Exporting Countries)	*l'OPEP*
to strike* (oil, gold, etc.)	*découvrir*

Expressions

electric current	*le courant électrique*
electrical appliances	*les appareils électriques*
an electric meter	*un compteur électrique*
a gas meter	*un compteur à gaz*
an electricity bill	*une facture d'électricité*
central heating	*le chauffage central*
a centrally-heated house	*une maison équipée du chauffage central*
an incandescent light bulb	*une ampoule à incandescence*

a fluorescent light bulb	*une ampoule fluorescente*
energy-saving appliances	*des appareils économes en énergie*
a fuel-efficient vehicle	*un véhicule économe en carburant*
an internal combustion engine	*un moteur à explosion*
a battery-powered car	*une voiture électrique*
an array of solar cells	*un ensemble de cellules solaires*
a power cut	*une coupure de courant*
a power failure	*une panne de courant*
renewable sources of energy	*les sources d'énergie renouvelables*
non-polluting	*non polluant*
proven resources of oil / gas	*des réserves connues de pétrole / gaz*
a glut of oil / an oil glut	*une surproduction de pétrole*
the oil crisis	*la crise pétrolière*
the first oil shock	*le premier choc pétrolier*
an oil-producing country	*un pays producteur de pétrole*
a common energy policy	*une politique énergétique commune*
sustainable development	*le développement soutenable*
an EPR (European pressurized reactor)	*un EPR (réacteur pressurisé européen)*
a nuclear test	*un essai nucléaire*
a radioactive cloud	*un nuage radioactif*
the Chernobyl meltdown	*l'accident de Tchernobyl*
to cut (down on) one's energy consumption	*réduire sa consommation d'énergie*
to cut the energy bill	*réduire la facture énergétique*
to fill up the tank	*faire le plein du réservoir*
to waste / squander finite resources	*gaspiller des ressources limitées*
to be dependent on oil	*être dépendant du pétrole*
to supply energy (to a country)	*fournir de l'énergie (à un pays)*
to supply a country with energy	*fournir un pays en énergie*
to turn to (to switch to) another source of energy	*se tourner vers une autre source d'approvisionnement*
to depend on a supplier	*être tributaire d'un fournisseur*
to release energy	*libérer de l'énergie*
to trigger a chain reaction	*déclencher une réaction en chaîne*
to dig for coal	*(creuser pour) extraire du charbon*
to drill for oil	*(forer pour) extraire du pétrole*
to strike oil	*découvrir du pétrole*
to strike it rich	*trouver un filon, faire fortune*

Phrases

Since the Chernobyl meltdown, nuclear power has been questioned in many countries.
Depuis l'accident de Tchernobyl, le nucléaire est remis en question dans beaucoup de pays.

Some specialists say that the emphasis should be laid on energy conservation.
Certains spécialistes disent qu'on devrait accorder la priorité à la conservation de l'énergie.

At the turn of the century, one quarter of the world's population consumed three quarters of the world's energy.
Au tournant du siècle, un quart de la population mondiale consommait les trois quarts de l'énergie mondiale.

The building of the gigantic dam was controversial to say the least.
Le moins qu'on puisse dire est que la construction de ce barrage gigantesque fit l'objet de controverses.

Environmentalists claimed that the location was ill-chosen.
Les écologistes prétendaient que le lieu était mal choisi.

For all its attraction, wind power produces only a minute percentage of global energy.
En dépit de son attrait l'énergie éolienne ne compte que pour un infime pourcentage de l'énergie mondiale.

Gigantic arrays of solar cells could be located in desert areas.
Des ensembles gigantesques de cellules solaires pourraient être situés dans des zones désertiques.

Even though developed countries still rely heavily on fossil fuels, most governments are now aware of the need to turn to alternative sources of energy.
Bien que les pays développés dépendent encore largement des combustibles fossiles, la plupart des gouvernements sont maintenant conscients de la nécessité de passer à des sources d'énergie alternatives.

Fast breeder reactors raised fears as to the proliferation of plutonium.
Les surrégénérateurs suscitèrent des craintes quant à la prolifération du plutonium.

Nuclear fusion is unlikely to be harnessed until the middle of the 21st century.
Il est peu probable que la fusion nucléaire soit domestiquée avant le milieu du XXIe siècle.

Exercices

I. Compléter :

In Africa as in much of the Third World some 80% of the population rely on (1)... to cook their meals.

The propagation of nuclear power generates fear about terrorism and the diversion of highly (2)... material into the wrong hands.

Suddenly in the 1980s research into (3)... - ... vehicles gathered new momentum.

The major (4)... companies have often been accused of maximizing their profits to the detriment of safety and research into new energy sources.

The liquid fuel stored in the tanks may eventually (5)... into the ground and cause explosions.

As oil producing countries could not reach an agreement on the reduction of production, the (6)... of oil far exceeded the (7)... and prices fell.

(8)... from incandescent to fluorescent light bulbs would help us save a considerable amount of energy.

Fuel (9)... per head went down significantly after the first oil shock and then started rising again in the 80s.

In another 20 years our oil reserves will be (10)... and we shall have to turn to other forms of energy.

II. Apparier un élément de la colonne de droite avec un élément de la colonne de gauche pour former des phrases cohérentes :

For years researchers have tried to develop a new way of producing energy	that reduces energy waste in developed countries.
In the 1950s France launched an ambitious hydroelectric programme	that never really came true.
The notion that the wind could supply inexhaustible and cheap energy was a dream	that followed the sinking of the 'Amoco Cadiz'.
Conservationists claim that the best policy is the one	which is frightening when you come to think of it.
Scientists have yet to prove that more energy can be generated by nuclear fusion	that would be less polluting than power stations fuelled by coal or oil.
The tremendous hazards of oil tankers were demonstrated by the catastrophe	that the proven reserves of fossil fuels are far from inexhaustible.
We have to bear in mind	that would imply the building of a power station every two days somewhere in the world.
Energy consumption is expected to grow by 100% in the next 20 years,	that aims at replacing less safe plants with alternative sources of energy.
In order to guarantee long-term safety, specialists have designed a programme	than what is needed to start the reaction.
We cannot sustain a rise in energy consumption	which tapped the energy of its rivers by building gigantic dams across Alpine valleys.

III. Remettre en ordre le texte suivant et retrouver le projet d'énergie alternative proposé par la physicienne américaine Joan Ogden :

1. Since these panels work best in warm sunny areas,
2. Now hydrogen, which has the advantage of being an excellent fuel,
3. The electricity thus produced could be fed into electrolyzers,
4. where it could be used to power all sorts of engines and vehicles.
5. First and foremost we know that solar panels convert solar light into electric current.
6. we could set up arrays of thousands of panels in California or Texas.
7. Last but not least, hydrogen, being extracted from water, is a cheap and indefinitely renewable source of energy.
8. could be sent by pipeline to urban centers all over the country,
9. Another significant advantage of hydrogen fuel is that it is virtually non-polluting.
10. that would split water into its constituent elements : oxygen and hydrogen.

V. MAN'S ENVIRONMENT

18. Housing
Le logement

a bungalow	*une maison de plain-pied*
a flat, an apartment	*un appartement*
a bed-sit(ter)	*une chambre meublée, un studio*
a slum	*un taudis*
a skyscraper	*un gratte-ciel*
a lift, an elevator (US)	*un ascenseur*
a floor, a storey (US)	*un étage*
the stairs	*l'escalier*
the ground floor	*le rez-de-chaussée*
the first floor	*le premier étage (US : rez-de-chaussée)*
the landing	*le palier*
the front door	*la porte d'entrée*
a letter-box	*une boîte à lettres*
the back door	*la porte de derrière*
the doorbell	*la sonnette*
the doormat	*le paillasson*
a digital lock	*un digicode*
a shutter	*un volet*
a French window	*une porte-fenêtre*
the roof	*le toit*
the chimney	*la cheminée*
a satellite dish	*une parabole*
an aerial [‘ɛəriəl]	*une antenne*

the garden, the yard (US) ***le jardin***

the lawn [lɔ:n]	*la pelouse*
a hedge	*une haie*
a fence	*une clôture*
a gate	*une grille, un portillon*
a path	*une allée*
a garden shed	*une cabane à outils*
a greenhouse	*une serre*
a lawn-mower [‘məuə]	*une tondeuse*
a hose [həuz]	*un tuyau d'arrosage*
a summer house	*un abri de jardin*
a conservatory	*une véranda, un jardin d'hiver*
a (court)yard	*une cour*
a backyard	*une arrière-cour*

an owner ***un propriétaire***

a landlord	*un propriétaire (logeur)*
a mortgage [‘mɔ:gidʒ]	*un emprunt (hypothécaire)*
a tenant, a lodger	*un locataire*
the rent	*le loyer*
a removal	*un déménagement*
a resident	*un habitant, un riverain*
a housewife	*une ménagère*
the chores	*les corvées ménagères*

building materials ***matériaux de construction***

concrete [‘kɔnkri:t]	*le béton*
bricks	*la brique*
stone	*la pierre*
tiles	*des tuiles, des carreaux de carrelage*
slates	*des ardoises*

the layout ***l'agencement***

the cellar [‘selə]	*la cave*
the basement [‘beismənt]	*le sous-sol*
the hall	*le vestibule, l'entrée*
a passage, a corridor	*un couloir*
the dining-room	*la salle à manger*
the living-room	*la salle de séjour*

the sitting-room, the lounge	*le salon*
the kitchen	*la cuisine*
a bedroom	*une chambre*
a spare room, a guest room	*une chambre d'ami*
a nursery	*une chambre d'enfant*
the bathroom	*la salle de bain*
the toilet, the lavatory	*les toilettes*
the study	*le bureau, le cabinet de travail*

furniture and household articles — *le mobilier et les articles ménagers*

a curtain [‘kə:tn]	*un rideau*
wallpaper	*le papier peint*
a piece of furniture	*un meuble*
the carpet, (fitted-carpet)	*la moquette*
a rug, a carpet	*un tapis*
a chair	*une chaise*
a stool	*un tabouret*
a dining table	*une table de salle à manger*
a tablecloth [‘teiblklɔθ]	*une nappe*
a sideboard	*un buffet*
a cupboard [‘kʌbəd]	*un placard*
an armchair	*un fauteuil*
a settee, a sofa, a couch	*un canapé, un divan*
a three-piece suite	*un salon (mobilier)*
a coffee table, an occasional table	*une table basse*
an ashtray	*un cendrier*
a hi-fi [‘hai'fai] system	*une chaîne hi-fi*
a TV set	*un téléviseur*
a display cabinet	*une vitrine*
the fireplace	*la cheminée (l'âtre)*
the mantelpiece	*la tablette de cheminée*
a wall cupboard	*un placard mural, suspendu*
a kitchen unit	*un élément de cuisine*
a worktop	*un plan de travail*
a kitchen sink	*un évier*
a tap	*un robinet*
crockery	*la vaisselle*
kitchen utensils	*la batterie de cuisine*
a saucepan [‘sɔ:spən]	*une casserole*
a frying pan [‘fraiŋ'pæn]	*une poêle*
a pressure cooker	*une cocotte minute*
a tin opener	*un ouvre-boîtes*
a potato-peeler	*un épluche-légumes*
a dustbin	*une poubelle*
a single bed	*un lit d'une personne*
a double bed	*un lit de deux personnes*
a cot	*un lit d'enfant, un petit lit*
a sheet [ʃi:t]	*un drap*
a blanket	*une couverture*
a pillow	*un oreiller*
an eiderdown	*un édredon*
a duvet	*une couette*
a bedside table	*une table de chevet*
an alarm-clock	*un réveil*
a bedside rug	*une descente de lit*
a wardrobe	*une penderie*
a drawer [drɔ:]	*un tiroir*
a chest of drawers	*une commode*
a bath	*une baignoire*
a shower	*une douche*
a washbasin	*un lavabo*
a towel [‘tauəl]	*une serviette*
a cake of soap	*une savonnette*
a toothbrush	*une brosse à dents*
toothpaste	*du dentifrice*
a desk	*un bureau*
a waste-paper basket	*une corbeille à papier*

electrical appliances — *les appareils électriques*

a dishwasher	*un lave-vaisselle*
a gas cooker	*une gazinière*
a hot plate	*une plaque de cuisson*
a food processor	*un robot ménager*
a food mixer	*un batteur*
a liquidizer	*un mixeur*
a microwave oven	*un four à micro-ondes*
a refrigerator, a fridge	*un réfrigérateur, un frigo*
a freezer	*un congélateur*
a toaster	*un grille-pain*
an electric kettle	*une bouilloire électrique*
an automatic coffee percolator	*une cafetière électrique programmable*
a vacuum cleaner [‘vækjuəm], a hoover	*un aspirateur*

an iron [aiən]	*un fer à repasser*
a sewing-machine ['səuiŋmə,ʃi:n]	*une machine à coudre*
a knitting machine	*une machine à tricoter*
a washing machine	*un lave-linge*
a spin dryer / drier	*une essoreuse*
a tumble dryer /	*un sèche-linge*drier
a hair dryer / drier	*un sèche-cheveux*
tiny ['taini]	*minuscule*
cramped	*exigu*
roomy	*spacieux*
furnished	*meublé*
neat and tidy	*bien rangé*
clean	*propre*
shiny	*brillant, reluisant*
spotless	*impeccable*
polished	*ciré*
spick and span	*reluisant de propreté*
snug, cosy	*bien arrangé, douillet*
quiet	*calme, tranquille*
light	*clair*
comfortable	*confortable*
convenient	*commode*
well-built	*bien bâti*
inhabited	*habité*
vacant, uninhabited	*libre, inoccupé*
overcrowded	*surpeuplé*
damp	*humide*
dusty	*poussiéreux*
messy	*sale, en désordre*
dirty	*sale*
filthy ['filθi], grubby	*crasseux, dégoûtant*
noisy	*bruyant*
derelict ['derilikt]	*à l'abandon*
decrepit [di'krepit]	*délabré*
squalid ['skwɔlid]	*misérable, sordide*
shabby	*minable*

ramshackle, rickety	*branlant, en piteux état*
dilapidated	*délabré*
homeless	*sans-abri*
downstairs	*en bas, au rez-de-chaussée*
upstairs	*en haut, à l'étage*
to own	*être propriétaire*
to rent	*louer*
to let*	*louer (mettre en location)*
to turn out, to evict	*mettre à la porte*
to move in	*emménager*
to move out	*déménager*
to settle (in)	*s'installer*
to furnish	*meubler*
to install	*installer*
to build*	*construire*
to demolish, to knock down, to pull down	*démolir*
to renovate	*rénover*
to insulate	*isoler*
to revamp, to refurbish	*retaper, remettre en état*
to redecorate [ri:'dekəreit]	*« refaire » une pièce (tapisserie et peinture)*
to lock	*fermer à clé*
to sweep*	*balayer*
to polish	*cirer*
to dust	*faire les poussières*
to wipe	*essuyer*
to vacuum, to hoover	*passer l'aspirateur*
to wake* up	*se réveiller*
to get* up	*se lever*
to shave	*se raser*

Expressions

"To let"	*« À louer »*
"For sale"	*« À vendre »*
to have a house built	*se faire construire une maison*
to move into a house	*emménager*
to have a house-warming party	*pendre la crémaillère*
to keep up with the Joneses	*ne pas être en reste avec les voisins*
to break into a house	*pénétrer par effraction*
to be cramped for space	*être à l'étroit*
to be in good repair	*être en bon état*
to ring the bell	*sonner*
to knock at the door	*frapper à la porte*

to dig the garden	*bêcher le jardin*
to trim the hedge	*tailler la haie*
to mow the lawn	*tondre la pelouse*
to do the housework	*faire le ménage*
to do the washing-up	*faire la vaisselle*
to do the cooking	*faire la cuisine*
to lay the table	*mettre la table*
to make the bed	*faire le lit*
to go to sleep	*s'endormir*
to take (to have) a shower	*prendre une douche*
to take (to have) a bath	*prendre un bain*
to wash one's hair	*se laver les cheveux*
to brush / to clean one's teeth	*se laver les dents*
to dry one's hair	*se sécher les cheveux*
home cooking	*la cuisine familiale*
household expenses	*les dépenses du ménage*
modern conveniences	*confort moderne*
a detached house	*un particulier*
a semi-detached house	*une maison jumelée*
a well-groomed garden	*un jardin bien entretenu*
a second home, a country home, a house in the country, a holiday home	*une résidence secondaire*
terraced houses (GB)	*maisons attenantes et toutes identiques*
council houses, council flats	*logements sociaux*
a block of flats	*un immeuble d'habitation*
a tower block, a highrise block	*une tour*
a two-storey(ed) house	*une maison à un étage*
the building trade	*le secteur du bâtiment*
a building contractor	*un entrepreneur en bâtiment*
a real-estate agent, an estate agent	*un agent immobilier*

Phrases

The Joneses have just had the whole house painted green.
Les Jones viennent de faire peindre toute la maison en vert.

I think I'll have double glazing fitted.
Je crois que je vais faire installer un double vitrage.

Her husband spends most of his time lying on the sofa watching TV.
Son mari passe le plus clair de son temps étendu sur le canapé à regarder la télévision.

Some landlords prefer to keep their flats vacant rather than have to evict undesirable tenants.
Certains propriétaires préfèrent conserver leurs appartements inoccupés plutôt que d'avoir à expulser des locataires indésirables.

A burglar broke into their house and stole all their jewellery.
Un cambrioleur a pénétré par effraction dans leur maison et a dérobé tous leurs bijoux.

Rents have kept increasing for the last ten years or so.
Les loyers ne cessent d'augmenter depuis une dizaine d'années.

Please wipe your feet on the doormat! I've just done the housework.
S'il vous plaît, essuyez vos pieds sur le paillasson ! Je viens de faire le ménage.

I'd like to see your bedroom neat and tidy for once!
J'aimerais voir ta chambre bien rangée, pour une fois !

How is it all the towels in the bathroom are wet?
Comment se fait-il que toutes les serviettes de la salle de bain sont mouillées ?

They lived in a tiny apartment and were terribly cramped for space.
Ils habitaient un appartement minuscule et étaient terriblement à l'étroit.

Exercices

I. Trouver les réponses aux définitions suivantes :

1. it wakes you up in the morning.
2. you spread some of it on your toothbrush.
3. you hang your clothes in it.
4. the postman rings it when he has a parcel for you.
5. an appliance in which food can be warmed up very quickly.
6. most people mow it once a week in the summer.
7. it needs trimming from time to time.
8. the person to whom the rent is due.
9. in which frozen foods are kept.
10. smoke comes out of it in the winter.

II. Retrouver les mots en remettant les lettres dans le bon ordre :

1. tsdwsnoari 2. orenw 3. hysatar 4. bdsniut 5. rhoews 6. sreaott 7. ssstlpeo 8. pradocbu 9. teesmanb 10. ctoreenc

III. Traduire :

1. Dans beaucoup de maisons britanniques, les toilettes sont dans la salle de bain.
2. Pourquoi est-ce que tu laisses toujours les plats sales dans l'évier ?
3. Beaucoup de gens rêvent de posséder une maison à la campagne.
4. Il y a un beau tapis au milieu de leur salon.
5. Une famille vient d'emménager dans la maison voisine.
6. Pourrais-tu vider le lave-vaisselle pendant que je fais la cuisine ?
7. Ils habitent une maison à un étage au coin de la rue.
8. Elle se lave toujours les cheveux dans le lavabo.
9. N'oublie pas de te laver les dents !
10. Il s'endort toujours en regardant la télévision.

19. City life
La vie urbaine

a town	*une ville*
a city	*une (grande) ville*
a city dweller	*un citadin*
townspeople	*les gens des villes*
an inhabitant	*un habitant*
a resident ['rezidənt]	*un habitant (immeuble)*
a commuter	*un migrant pendulaire (journalier)*
a town planner	*un urbaniste*
real estate	*l'immobilier*
a street	*une rue*
a one-way street	*une rue à sens unique*
the main street (the high street)	*la rue principale*
an avenue ['ævinju:]	*une avenue*
a cul-de-sac [kuldə'sæk]	*une impasse*
a crossroads	*un carrefour*
traffic lights	*les feux de circulation*
a roundabout	*un sens giratoire*
a square	*une place*
a circus ['sə:kəs]	*une place*
*(circulaire)*a lamppost	*un réverbère*
a pillar box, a mail box (US)	*une boîte aux lettres (publique)*
a bus stop	*un arrêt de bus*
a road sign [sain]	*un panneau indicateur*
the pavement (sidewalk US)	*le trottoir*
a phone box	*une cabine téléphonique*
a pedestrian	*un piéton*
a pedestrian crossing	*un passage pour piétons*
a passer-by (pl. passers-by)	*un passant*
the kerb	*la bordure du trottoir*
the gutter ['gʌtə]	*le caniveau*
a block (US)	*un pâté d'immeubles*
a neighbourhood, a district	*un quartier*
the surroundings	*le cadre, l'environnement*
the town centre	*le centre ville*
the inner city	*les vieux quartiers du centre*
a slum [slʌm]	*un taudis, un quartier pauvre*

a vagrant	*un vagabond*
a tramp, a bum	*un clochard*
a beggar	*un mendiant*
a busker ['bʌskə]	*qqn qui fait la manche*
a ghetto	*un ghetto*
the suburbs	*la banlieue*
the outskirts	*la périphérie*
a ring road, an orbital road	*un périphérique*
a shop	*une boutique*
a store	*un magasin*
a café ['kæfei]	*un café*
a pub (a public house)	*un pub*
the local	*le pub du quartier*
a restaurant ['restərɔ̃:ŋ]	*un restaurant*
a fast-food place	*un fast food*
a hotel [həu'tel]	*un hôtel*
a guest house	*un hôtel modeste, une pension de famille*
a bed-and-breakfast (B&B)	*une chambre d'hôtes*
facilities	*équipements, installations*
utilities	*les services publics*
monuments	*les monuments*
sights	*les curiosités*
the tourist office	*le syndicat d'initiative*
public conveniences	*les toilettes publiques*
a bus [bʌs]	*un autobus*
a tramcar, a streetcar (US)	*un tramway*
a conductor	*un contrôleur*
a coach	*un autocar, un car de tourisme*
a taxi (a cab US)	*un taxi*
the fare	*le prix (de la course)*
the underground, the subway (US)	*le métro*
a vigilante [ˌvidʒi'lænti]	*un vigile (police privée)*
a railway station	*une gare*
a coach station	*une gare routière*
an airport	*un aéroport*
a petrol station (gas station US)	*une station essence*
a post office	*un bureau de poste*
a police station	*un commissariat*

a fire station	*une caserne de pompiers*
a barracks	*une caserne*
the town hall (city hall US)	*la mairie*
the Registry Office	*le bureau d'État Civil*
a library ['laibrəri]	*une bibliothèque*
a librarian [lai'brɛəriən]	*un bibliothécaire*
a university	*une université*
a museum	*un musée*
an art gallery	*un musée, une galerie d'art*
an exhibition	*une exposition*
a concert hall	*une salle de concert*
an opera house ['ɔpərə]	*un opéra*
a cinema (a movie theater US)	*une salle de cinéma*
a park	*un parc*
a public garden	*un square, un jardin public*
open, green spaces	*les espaces verts*
a playground	*un terrain de jeu*
a swimming pool	*une piscine*
a skating rink	*une patinoire*
a sports ground	*un terrain de sports*
a market	*un marché*
a church	*une église*
a cathedral [kə'θi:drəl]	*une cathédrale*
a cemetery ['semitri]	*un cimetière*
a grave	*une tombe*
ugly ['ʌgli]	*laid*
bleak, grim, dismal	*sinistre, lugubre*
sordid	*sordide*
grimy ['graimi]	*sale, encrassé, noirci*
smelly	*malodorant*
derelict ['derilikt]	*à l'abandon*
ramshackle	*délabré*
gutted	*vandalisé, dévasté*
populous	*populeux*
noisy	*bruyant*
congested	*embouteillé*
relentless	*incessant, sans répit*
deafening ['defniŋ]	*assourdissant*
unmanageable	*ingérable*
suffocating	*suffocant, étouffant*
unbreathable	*irrespirable*
unsafe	*dangereux*
safe	*sûr, sans danger*
quiet	*calme*
busy ['bizi], lively	*animé*
bustling	*grouillant d'activité*
open	*ouvert*
closed	*fermé*

crowded	*bondé (transports en commun)*
overcrowded, overpopulated	*surpeuplé*
empty	*vide*
pleasant	*agréable*
attractive	*attrayant, attirant*
vibrant ['vaibrənt]	*plein de vie*
idle [aidl]	*oisif*
ragged ['rægid]	*en haillons*
to lack (in)	*manquer de*
to plan, to lay* out	*planifier*
to run*	*gérer*
to erect	*ériger*
to complete [kəm'pli:t]	*terminer (une construction)*
to pull down	*démolir*
to reclaim	*réhabiliter*
to sweep*	*balayer*
to collect	*ramasser (les ordures)*
to commute	*faire la navette journalière*
to get* on	*monter (transports en commun)*
to get* off	*descendre (transports en commun)*
to rush	*se précipiter*
to hurry, to hasten ['heisn]	*se dépêcher*
to queue (up) [kju:]	*faire la queue*
to cross	*traverser*
to run* over	*écraser*
to knock down	*renverser*
to hit*	*frapper, percuter*
to collide with	*entrer en collision avec*
to walk about (around)	*se promener*
to stroll	*flâner*
to flock, to gather	*se rassembler*
to hang* about, to loiter ['lɔitə]	*rôder, errer, traîner*
to threaten	*menacer*
to mug	*agresser (pour de l'argent)*
to assault	*agresser (voies de fait)*
to rape	*violer*
to vandalize	*saccager*
to smash up	*tout casser, tout démolir*
to tag	*« tagger »*
to beg	*mendier*
to busk	*faire la manche*
to sleep* out	*dormir à la belle étoile*
to follow	*suivre*
to scare	*effrayer*
to strain	*surmener, mettre à rude épreuve*

Expressions

a block of flats	*un immeuble d'habitation*
an office block	*un immeuble de bureaux*
a building site	*un chantier de construction*
a mushroom town	*une ville champignon*
a dormitory town	*une ville dortoir*
a gated community	*un lotissement sécurisé*
a CCTV camera	*une caméra de surveillance*
a shanty town	*un bidonville*
to live on the street	*vivre dans la rue*
to stand in a line (US)	*faire la queue*
a parking meter	*un parcmètre*
a no-parking area	*une zone de stationnement interdit*
a parking area	*une aire de stationnement*
a car park, a parking lot (US)	*un parking*
a multi-storey car park	*un parking à étages*
to go through a red light	*brûler un feu rouge*
a pedestrian area, a paved zone	*une zone piétonne*
an adventure playground	*une aire de jeu aménagée*
recreational activities	*les activités de loisir*
recreational facilities	*les équipements de loisir*
an indoor swimming pool	*une piscine couverte*
to go into town, to go downtown	*aller en ville*
downtown Chicago	*le centre de Chicago*
a department store	*un grand magasin*
a shopping mall, a shopping precinct	*un centre commercial*
the corner shop	*la boutique / l'épicerie du coin*
commuter trains	*les trains de banlieue*
a double-decker	*un bus à deux étages*
rush-hour traffic	*la circulation aux heures de pointe*
to be in a hurry	*être pressé*
the hustle and bustle of city life	*l'intense activité de la vie citadine*
the rumble of heavy lorries	*le bruit sourd des poids lourds*
the squeal of brakes	*le crissement des freins*
the screech of tyres	*le grincement des pneus*
the urban landscape	*le paysage urbain*
a residential area	*une zone résidentielle*
an industrial estate	*une zone industrielle*
public lighting	*l'éclairage public*
the outer suburbs	*la grande banlieue*
a housing shortage	*une pénurie de logements*
the property market	*le marché immobilier*
a property developer	*un promoteur*
a housing scheme	*un programme de construction de logements*
a housing benefit	*une allocation logement*
a housing policy	*une politique du logement*
a housing estate	*un lotissement, un ensemble*
the quality of life, life quality	*la qualité de la vie*

Phrases

There are shops on either side of the street.
Il y a des boutiques des deux côtés de la rue.

Real estate prices in London have reached staggering heights.
Le prix de l'immobilier à Londres a atteint des sommets ahurissants.

—Could you tell me the way to the tourist office, please?
— Pourriez-vous m'indiquer le chemin de l'office de tourisme, s'il vous plaît ?

—Turn left at the next crossroads; it is by the railway station.
— Prenez à gauche au prochain carrefour ; il se trouve près de la gare.

More and more homeless people live on the streets of our cities.
De plus en plus de sans logis vivent dans les rues de nos villes.

Many young couples buy houses in the country to escape the hustle and bustle of city life.
Beaucoup de jeunes couples achètent des maisons à la campagne pour échapper au tourbillon de la vie dans les grandes villes.

Some affluent executives had rather live in gated communities.
Certains cadres aisés préfèrent vivre dans des lotissements sécurisés.

While living in the suburbs is the dream of many an American, it is a nightmare for most Europeans.
Alors que la vie en banlieue est le rêve de maints Américains, c'est un cauchemar pour la plupart des Européens.

Property developers should stop building blocks of flats in the outer suburbs.
Les promoteurs devraient mettre un terme à la construction d'immeubles d'habitation dans la grande banlieue.

Many US inner cities are gradually turning into ghettos.
De nombreux centres villes américains se transforment peu à peu en ghettos.

To my mind, all town centres ought to be banned to traffic and made into pedestrian areas.
D'après moi, on devrait interdire les centres villes à la circulation automobile et en faire des zones piétonnières.

Sprawling urban centres are rife with problems.
Les problèmes abondent dans les grands centres urbains tentaculaires.

By the turn of the century, there will be 21 megacities with populations of 10 million or more.
D'ici à la fin du siècle, il y aura 21 mégalopoles avec des populations dépassant les 10 millions.

Exercices

I. Compléter les phrases suivantes :

1. A dead-end street is called a ... .
2. On the bus, you may have to show your ticket to the ... .
3. The arrow on this ... indicates that this is a one-way street.
4. There are some very old graves in that ... .
5. Piccadilly ... is not very far from Trafalgar ... .
6. You can fill up at the ... station.
7. He was fined for going ... a red light.
8. I go to the ... swimming-pool in the winter.
9. Harrods is the most famous ... store in Britain.

II. Retrouver les adjectifs correspondant aux définitions suivantes :

1. hideous
2. having a bad smell
3. making so much noise that hearing is almost impossible
4. doing no work
5. free from danger
6. that never stops
7. with little or no movement or sound
8. extremely dirty
9. badly torn or in rags
10. that has been vandalized

III. Traduire :

1. *Elle a été agressée alors qu'elle allait pénétrer dans l'ascenseur.*
2. *Il devrait y avoir davantage d'espaces verts dans nos villes.*
3. *À Tokyo, on est presque obligé de porter un masque car l'air est irrespirable.*
4. *Je crois que la bibliothèque est à côté de l'hôtel de ville.*
5. *N'oublie pas de mettre une pièce dans le parcmètre !*
6. *J'aime flâner dans les jardins publics le dimanche.*
7. *Es-tu allé voir la dernière exposition au musée ?*
8. *Il y a de plus en plus de vagabonds qui mendient dans les rues.*
9. *Le samedi après-midi, les rues sont embouteillées et les bus sont bondés.*
10. *Il regardait une fille attirante qui marchait sur le trottoir et il a percuté un réverbère.*

20. Nature
La nature

1. The natural habitat
Le milieu naturel

The wild	*La nature sauvage*	a hill	*une colline*
a wilderness	*une étendue déserte, une région sauvage,*	a plateau ['plætəu]	*un plateau*
		a mountain range	*une chaîne de montagnes*
the savannah	*la savane*		
the bush	*la brousse*	a valley	*une vallée*
a desert ['dezət]	*un désert*	a peak	*un pic, une cime*
the jungle	*la jungle*	a summit	*un sommet*
the rainforest	*la forêt tropicale*	a stream	*un ruisseau*
a heath [hi:θ], a moor	*une lande*	a river	*une rivière, un fleuve*
a swamp	*un marécage*	a lake	*un lac*
a marsh	*un marais*	a bank	*une rive, un bord/un banc (de sable)*
a plain	*une plaine*		

Natural catastrophes ***Les catastrophes naturelles***

a hurricane	*un ouragan*	an eruption	*une éruption*
a typhoon [tai'fu:n]	*un typhon*	the Richter Scale	*l'échelle de Richter*
a flood [flʌd]	*une inondation*	lava ['la:və]	*la lave*
a tidal wave ['taidl]	*un raz-de-marée*	ashes	*des cendres*
a drought	*une sécheresse*	a landslide	*un glissement de terrain*
an earthquake	*un tremblement de terre*	a mudslide	*une coulée de boue*
a fault	*une faille*	extinct	*éteint*
a tremor	*une secousse*	active	*en activité*
a volcano	*un volcan*	dormant	*en sommeil*

Plants ***Les végétaux***

greenery	*la verdure*	a creeper	*une plante grimpante*
a tree	*un arbre*	ivy	*le lierre*
a sapling	*un jeune arbre*	a walnut	*une noix*
a leaf (leaves)	*une feuille*	a hazel nut ['heizl'nʌt]	*une noisette*
foliage	*le feuillage*	a chestnut [tʃesnʌt]	*une châtaigne*
a trunk	*un tronc*	a horse chestnut	*un marron(nier)*
a branch	*une branche*	a mushroom	*un champignon*
a twig	*un rameau*	a berry	*une baie*
a root	*une racine*	heather ['heðə]	*la bruyère*
bark	*l'écorce*	a forest	*une forêt*
sap	*la sève*	the rainforest	*la forêt tropicale*
a bush	*un buisson, un arbuste*	a wood	*un bois*
a hedge	*une haie*	an evergreen	*un arbre à feuilles persistantes*

a conifer	*un conifère*	a chestnut tree	*un châtaignier*
a fir (tree)	*un sapin*	a hazel	*un noisetier*
a pine cone	*une pomme de pin*	a willow	*un saule*
an oak	*un chêne*	a lime tree	*un tilleul*
an elm	*un orme*	a cypress	*un cyprès*
a maple	*un érable*	exotic trees	*les arbres exotiques*
a beech	*un hêtre*	a cedar	*un cèdre*
a birch	*un bouleau*	a palm tree	*un palmier*
a poplar	*un peuplier*	a coconut palm	*un cocotier*
a plane tree	*un platane*		

Human activities ***Les activités humaines***

a lumberjack	*un bûcheron*	rocky	*rocheux, rocailleux*
an axe	*une hache*	sandy	*sablonneux*
a saw [sɔ:]	*une scie*	marshy	*marécageux*
a chainsaw	*une tronçonneuse*	wooded	*boisé*
deforestation	*le déboisement*	deciduous	*à feuilles caduques*
a clearing	*une clairière*	overgrown	*envahi (végétation)*
logging	*l'abattage*	tall	*grand, haut*
pine(wood)	*le pin*	lofty	*haut, élevé*
mahogany	*l'acajou* [mə'hɔgəni]	wooden	*de/en bois*
teak	*le teck*	edible	*comestible*
ebony ['ebəni]	*l'ébène*	poisonous	*vénéneux*
a board	*une planche*	prickly, thorny	*épineux*
a log	*un rondin, une bûche*	to decay	*pourrir*
firewood	*le bois de chauffage*	to grow*	*pousser/ faire pousser, cultiver*
timber	*le bois d'œuvre*		
cork	*le liège*	to dry up	*se dessécher, tarir*
charcoal	*le charbon de bois*	to flow	*couler*
dense	*dense, épais*	to flood	*inonder*
sparse [spa:s]	*clairsemé*	to erupt	*entrer en éruption*
remote	*isolé*	to shake*	*secouer*
quiet	*tranquille*	to quake	*trembler*
silent	*silencieux*	to swell*	*grossir (eaux)*
wild	*sauvage*	to overflow*	*déborder*
desolate	*désolé, désert*	to carry along	*emporter*
unspoilt	*qui n'est pas défiguré*	to fell	*abattre*
inhospitable	*inhospitalier*	to saw*	*scier*
flat	*plat*	to chop	*couper (à la hache)*
mountainous	*montagneux*	to split*	*fendre*
hilly	*accidenté*	to shrink*	*rétrécir*
jagged	*irrégulier, déchiqueté*		

2. Wildlife La faune

Mammals ***Les mammifères***

an animal	*un animal*	a bear [bɛə]	*un ours*
a beast	*une bête*	a fox	*un renard*
a species ['spi:ʃi:s]	*une espèce*	a wolf [wulf]	*un loup*
a shelter	*un abri*	a mole [məul]	*une taupe*
a sanctuary	*une réserve*	a squirrel	*un écureuil*

a weasel ['wi:zl]	*une belette*
a badger	*un blaireau*
a rabbit	*un lapin*
a hare [hɛə]	*un lièvre*
deer	*les cervidés*
a roe deer	*un chevreuil*
a stag	*un cerf*
a doe	*une biche*
a fawn [fɔ:n]	*un faon*
a wild boar	*un sanglier*
a monkey	*un singe (petit)*
an ape	*un singe anthropoïde*
an elephant	*un éléphant*
a giraffe	*une girafe*
a tiger/tigress ['taigə]	*un(e) tigre(sse)*
a lion(ess)	*un(e) lion(ne)*
a jackal ['dʒækɔ:l]	*un chacal*
a cub	*un petit (lion, etc.)*
a camel	*un chameau*
a buffalo	*un buffle*
a bat	*une chauve-souris*
a marsupial	*un marsupial*
a kangaroo	*un kangourou*
a paw [pɔ:]	*une patte*
a claw [klɔ:]	*une griffe*
a fang	*un croc*
a footprint	*une empreinte*
fur	*la fourrure*

Birds	***Les oiseaux***
birds of prey	*les oiseaux de proie*
a hawk, a falcon	*un faucon*
a vulture	*un vautour*
an eagle	*un aigle*
an owl [aul]	*un hibou*
a raven	*un corbeau*
a crow [krəu]	*une corneille*
a magpie ['mægpai]	*une pie*
a migratory bird	*un oiseau migratoire*
a swallow	*une hirondelle*
a stork	*une cigogne*
a crane	*une grue*
a partridge	*une perdrix*
a pheasant	*un faisan*
a nightingale	*un rossignol*
a robin	*un rouge-gorge*
a starling	*un étourneau*
a blackbird	*un merle*
a lark	*une alouette*
a sparrow	*un moineau*
a thrush [θrʌʃ]	*une grive*
a swan	*un cygne*
an ostrich	*une autruche*
a budgerigar ['bʌdʒəriga:]	*une perruche*
a parrot	*un perroquet*
a wing	*une aile*
a feather ['feðə]	*une plume*
a beak	*un bec*
down [daun]	*le duvet*

Insects	***Les insectes***
a mosquito	*un moustique*
a wasp	*une guêpe*
a fly [flai]	*une mouche*
a beetle	*un scarabée*
a ladybird	*une coccinelle*
a dragonfly	*une libellule*
a bug	*une punaise*
a cockroach	*un cafard*
a flea [fli:]	*une puce*
a louse [laus] (pl.lice)	*un pou*
a worm [wə:m]	*un ver*
a caterpillar	*une chenille*
a butterfly	*un papillon*
an ant	*une fourmi*
an ant hill	*une fourmilière*
a spider [spaidə]	*une araignée*
a cobweb	*une toile d'araignée*

Other creatures	***Autres bêtes***
a tortoise ['tɔ:təs]	*une tortue*
a snake	*un serpent*
an adder	*une vipère*
a grass snake	*une couleuvre*
a rattlesnake	*un serpent à sonnette*
a boa constrictor	*un boa constricteur*
a lizard	*un lézard*
a frog	*une grenouille*
a tadpole	*un têtard*
a toad	*un crapaud*
an eel	*une anguille*
fresh water fish	*poissons d'eau douce*
a trout [traut]	*une truite*
a perch	*une perche*
a pike	*un brochet*
a goldfish	*un poisson rouge*

Human activities	***Activités humaines***		
shooting	*la chasse*	to devour [di'vauə]	*dévorer*
hunting	*la chasse à courre*	to suck	*téter, sucer*
fox-hunting	*la chasse au renard*	to tear* [tɛə]	*déchirer*
poaching ['pəutʃiɲ]	*le braconnage*	to crouch [krautʃ]	*se tapir*
game	*le gibier*	to lurk	*se tapir, se cacher*
a gamekeeper	*un garde-chasse*	to scurry	*se précipiter (petits animaux)*
a hunter	*un chasseur*		
a poacher	*un braconnier*	to flutter	*voleter*
a pack	*une meute*	to soar [sɔ:]	*prendre son essor, planer*
a hound [haund]	*un chien de chasse*		
the kill	*la mise à mort*	to hover	*voltiger, planer*
a snare [snɛə]	*un piège*	to swoop	*fondre, piquer*
a trap	*un piège, un collet*	to alight	*se poser*
a game reserve	*une réserve de chasse*	to hop	*sautiller*
shy	*timide*	to nest	*nicher*
fierce, ferocious	*féroce*	to peck	*picorer*
venomous	*venimeux*	to whistle [wisl]	*siffler*
wary	*méfiant*	to twitter	*gazouiller*
cunning	*malin*	to sting*	*piquer*
striped ['straipt]	*rayé*	to buzz	*bourdonner*
furry	*à poil (gibier)*	to hiss	*siffler (serpent)*
noxious	*nocif*	to swallow [swɔləu]	*avaler*
harmless	*inoffensif*	to smother	*étouffer*
rare	*rare*	to creep*, to crawl	*ramper*
extinct	*disparu*	to croak	*croasser*
endangered	*en voie de disparition*	to dive	*plonger*
to roar	*rugir*	to trap	*piéger*
to howl [haul]	*hurler*	to shoot*	*abattre, tirer*
to grunt	*grogner*	to poison ['pɔizn]	*empoisonner*
to bite* [bait]	*mordre*		

3.The sea   La mer

a coast	*une côte*	a bay	*une baie*
a shore	*une rive*	a cliff	*une falaise*
a beach [bi:tʃ]	*une plage*	a ledge	*une corniche, un rebord*
a wave	*une vague*		
a tide	*une marée*	a promontory	*un promontoire*
ebb and flow	*le flux et le reflux*	a cape	*un cap*
the ebb tide	*la marée descendante*	a strait	*un détroit*
low tide	*la marée basse*	a gulf	*un golfe*
an island	*une île*	a breeding ground	*un lieu de reproduction*
an archipelago [,a:ki'peligəu]	*un archipel*	a (coral) reef	*un récif (de corail)*
a peninsula	*une péninsule*		
Sea birds	***Les oiseaux marins***		
a (sea) gull	*une mouette*	a cormorant	*un cormoran*
an albatross	*un albatros*	a penguin	*un pingouin / un manchot*

Fish	*Les poissons*		
salmon ['sæmən]	*le saumon*	a shark	*un requin*
herring	*le hareng*	the scales	*les écailles*
cod	*le cabillaud*	a fin	*une nageoire*
mackerel	*le maquereau*	the bones	*les arêtes*
tuna ['tju:nə]	*le thon*	a jaw [dʒɔ:]	*une mâchoire*
a sardine [sa:'di:n]	*une sardine*		

Shellfish	*Les crustacés*		
an oyster ['ɔistə]	*une huître*	a scallop	*une coquille St Jacques*
a cockle	*une coque*		
a mussel	*une moule*	a lobster	*un homard*
		a prawn [prɔ:n]	*une crevette*

Sea mammals	*Les mammifères marins*		
a whale	*une baleine*	a seal	*un phoque*
a walrus	*un morse*	a dolphin	*un dauphin*

Others	*Autres*		
a turtle	*une tortue*	a squid	*un calmar*
an octopus ['ɔktəpəs]	*une pieuvre*	a jelly fish	*une méduse*
a tentacle	*un tentacule*		

Human activities	*Les activités humaines*		
fishing	*la pêche*	rough [rʌf]	*agité*
a fisherman	*un pêcheur*	fresh(ly)	*frais (fraîchement)*
a net	*un filet*	fishy	*de poisson, louche*
a trawl [trɔ:l]	*un chalut*	smelly	*qui sent mauvais*
a trawler	*un chalutier*	to fish	*pêcher*
the catch	*la prise*	to dive	*plonger*
a fishing ground	*un lieu de pêche*	to float	*flotter*
overfishing	*la surpêche*	to swim*	*nager*
powerful(ly)	*puissant, (puissamment)*	to sail	*naviguer*
		to bait [beit]	*appâter*
smooth(ly)	*lisse, calme(ment)*	to catch*	*attraper, prendre*
deep	*profond*	to sink*	*sombrer*
shallow	*peu profond*	to drown	*se noyer*
choppy	*un peu agité*		

Expressions

a desert area	*une région désertique*
a desert island	*une île déserte*
sparse vegetation	*une végétation éparse*
a densely-wooded area	*une région couverte de forêts*
to become extinct	*disparaître*
the shrinking rainforest	*la forêt tropicale en régression*
pine/mahogany furniture	*des meubles en pin/acajou*
to climb a tree	*grimper à un arbre*
to be afraid of one's shadow	*avoir peur de son ombre*
a bird sanctuary	*une réserve ornithologique*

a nature reserve	*une réserve naturelle*
wildlife protection	*la protection de la faune*
an endangered species	*une espèce menacée de disparition*
an extinct species	*une espèce disparue*
to be on the lookout	*être à l'affût*
to lurk in the darkness	*se tapir dans l'ombre*
the struggle for life	*la lutte pour la survie*
the survival of the fittest	*la survie des plus forts*
to tear to pieces	*mettre en pièces*
a smell of fish	*une odeur de poisson*
a shoal of herring	*un banc de harengs*
a mosquito bite	*une piqûre de moustique*

Métaphores

shark-infested waters	*des eaux infestées de requins*
a fishy business	*une histoire louche*
there's a fly in the ointment	*il y a un hic*
a white elephant	*objet/construction démesuré et inutile*
that's a red herring	*c'est pour brouiller les pistes*
to have butterflies	*avoir le trac*
to be as happy as a lark	*être gai comme un pinson*
to kill two birds with one stone	*faire d'une pierre deux coups*
to make a mountain out of a molehill	*(se) faire une montagne d'un rien*
to take the lion's share	*prendre la part du lion*
as the crow flies	*à vol d'oiseau*
a storm in a teacup	*une tempête dans un verre d'eau*

Phrases

A bird in the hand is worth two in the bush.
Un tiens vaut mieux que deux tu l'auras.

It's the last straw that breaks the camel's back.
C'est la goutte d'eau qui fait déborder le vase.

Birds of a feather flock together.
Qui se ressemble s'assemble.

The early bird catches the worm.
L'avenir appartient à qui se lève matin.

He can't see the wood for the trees.
Les arbres lui cachent la forêt.

She sells sea shells on the sea shore. (a tongue twister)
Elle vend des coquillages sur le rivage. (phrase difficile à prononcer)

«Tiger, tiger, burning bright/In the forests of the night,/What immortal hand or eye/Could frame thy fearful symmetry?» (William Blake)
« Tigre, tigre, brillant comme le feu/Dans les forêts de la nuit/Quelle main ou quel œil immortel/A pu forger ta terrible harmonie ? »

Poaching should be stopped to save endangered species.
Il faudrait mettre fin au braconnage pour sauver les espèces menacées de disparition.

Due to overfishing there is less and less cod in the North Sea.
Du fait de la pêche trop intensive il y a de moins en moins de morues en mer du Nord.

He was as ferocious as a shark, preying on his fellow creatures.
Il avait la férocité du requin, considérant ses semblables comme des proies.

Exercices

I. Trouver les mots et expressions correspondant aux définitions suivantes :

1. a large monkey
2. illegal hunting
3. a group of fish
4. with a lot of inhabitants
5. the largest sea mammal
6. a group of islands
7. an exceptionally strong tide
8. the ability of the strongest to survive
9. a fishing vessel
10. the most common sea-bird

II. Compléter les phrases suivantes :

1. Being on the San Andreas Fault, California is subject to major ... .
2. He rarely came to town, where he was like a ... out of water.
3. In that crowded bus we felt like ... in a tin.
4. In spite of protests the government decided to build a motorway through a wildlife ... .
5. The world of politics is often compared to ... - ... waters.
6. We were terrified and thought that there were fierce animals ... everywhere in the dark.
7. The World Wide Fund for Nature's aim is to save the elephant and other ... .
8. Indiscriminate ... threatens the rainforest.
9. Like other species, the leopard has been hunted to the verge of extinction because of its ... .
10. As ... ... Paris is less than 200 miles from London.

III. Retrouver les expressions et maximes en complétant les phrases à l'aide de la liste suivante : (fish, lark, hares, poacher, swallow, oyster, lion, fox, owl, wolves)

1. If you run after two ... you will catch neither.
2. A ... is not taken twice in the same snare.
3. One ... does not make a summer.
4. as strong as a ...
5. a wise old ...
6. to shut up like an ...
7. I have other ... to fry.
8. Who keeps company with the ... will learn to howl.
9. Go to bed with the lamb and rise with the ... .
10. An old ... makes the best gamekeeper.

21. Farming
L'agriculture

Vocabulaire général

the countryside	*la campagne*
a farmer	*un agriculteur*
a farmer's wife	*une agricultrice*
a farm hand, a farm worker	*un ouvrier agricole*
a peasant ['pezənt]	*un paysan*
a farm	*une ferme*
land	*les terres*
the land	*la terre*
a field	*un champ*
a fence	*une barrière*
agriculture	*l'agriculture*
cultivation	*la culture*
farm produce (sing)	*les produits agricoles*
the harvest	*la moisson*
a crop	*une récolte, une culture*
the yield [ji:ld]	*le rendement*
irrigation	*l'irrigation*
watering	*l'arrosage*
manure [mə'njuə]	*le fumier*
a fertilizer	*un engrais*
a pesticide ['pestisaid]	*un pesticide*
a weed-killer	*un désherbant*
phosphates ['fɔsfeits]	*les phosphates*
nitrates ['naitreits]	*les nitrates*
hormones	*des hormones*
antibiotics ['æntibai'ɔtiks]	*des antibiotiques*
a nutrient ['nju:triənt]	*un élément nutritif*
farm buildings	*des bâtiments agricoles*
a farmhouse	*une ferme*
outhouses	*les dépendances*
a farmyard	*une cour de ferme*
a barn	*une grange*
a stable	*une écurie*
a shed	*une remise*
a cowshed	*une étable*
a pigsty ['pigstai]	*une porcherie*
a greenhouse	*une serre*
a well	*un puits*
farming implements	*le matériel agricole*
a tractor	*un tracteur*
a plough [plau]	*une charrue*
a trailer	*une remorque*
a combine harvester	*une moissonneuse-batteuse*
a fork	*une fourche*
a rake	*un râteau*

a spade [speid]	*une bêche*
a shovel ['ʃʌvl]	*une pelle*
a blade	*une lame*
a basket	*un panier*
a scarecrow	*un épouvantail*
a pound	*une livre (454 g)*
a ton	*une tonne*
an acre ['eikə]	*une acre (0,4 hect.)*
industrial farming	*l'agriculture industrielle/ intensive*
foodstuffs	*les denrées alimentaires*
a commodity	*une denrée*
the agribusiness	*l'agro-alimentaire*
a glut	*une surabondance*
a surplus ['sə:pləs]	*un surplus*
overproduction	*la surproduction*
a quota ['kwəutə]	*un quota*
a shortage	*un manque, une pénurie*
rural	*rural*
agricultural	*agricole*
arable	*arable*
fertile ['fə:tail]	*fertile*
tropical	*tropical*
dry	*sec*
wet	*humide*
barren	*improductif*
archaic [a:'keiik]	*archaïque*
self-sufficient	*autarcique*
modern	*moderne*
brand new	*flambant neuf*
early	*hâtif*
late	*tardif*
vegetable	*végétal*
ripe	*mûr*
unripe	*vert*
juicy ['dʒu:si]	*juteux*

mature [mə'tjuə]	*mûr, à maturité*
healthy, wholesome	*sain*
plentiful	*abondant*
natural(ly)	*naturel(lement)*
industrial(ly)	*industriel(lement)*
organic(ally)	*biologique(ment)*
transgenic	*transgénique*
genetic(ally)	*génétique(ment)*
intensive(ly)	*intensif (-vement)*
extensive(ly)	*extensif (de manière extensive)*
to farm	*cultiver*
to till	*labourer, cultiver*
to grow*	*cultiver (tr.) ; pousser (intr.)*
to fence (in)	*clôturer*
to plough [plau]	*labourer*
to sow* [səu]	*semer*
to harvest	*récolter*
to mow* [məu]	*tondre, faucher*
to pick	*cueillir*
to yield	*rendre, produire*
to irrigate	*irriguer*
to water	*arroser*
to sprinkle	*arroser, asperger*
to fertilize ['fətilaiz]	*fertiliser, amender*
to spread* [spred]	*épandre*
to spray	*pulvériser*
to feed*	*nourrir ; se nourrir*
to stockpile	*stocker*
to subsidize ['sʌbsidaiz]	*subventionner*
to pour [pɔ:]	*verser*
to spill*	*renverser*
to contaminate	*contaminer*
to regulate	*réglementer*
to set* aside	*mettre en jachère*
to dump	*jeter, vendre à bas prix*

Vocabulaire spécialisé

topsoil	*l'humus*
seeds	*des semences*
hydroponics [ˌhaidrəu'pɔniks]	*la culture hors-sol*
grain(s), cereals	*les céréales*
a cereal ['siəriəl]	*une céréale*
corn	*le blé (GB), le maïs (US)*
maize [meiz]	*le maïs (GB)*
wheat	*le blé, le froment*
straw	*la paille*

flour ['flauə]	*la farine*
a mill	*un moulin*
sugar beet	*la betterave sucrière*
hops	*le houblon*
pulses	*les légumineuses*
oil seeds	*les oléagineux*
sunflower	*le tournesol*
rice	*le riz*
soya	*le soja*
cotton	*le coton*
fruit farming	*l'arboriculture*

a vineyard ['vinjəd]	*un vignoble*
a vine	*un pied de vigne*
grapes	*le raisin*
a wine grower	*un viticulteur*
a barrel	*une barrique*
an orchard ['ɔ:tʃəd]	*un verger*
an apple (tree)	*une pomme (un pommier)*
a pear [pɛə] (tree)	*une poire (un poirier)*
a cherry (tree)	*une cerise (un cerisier)*
an apricot ['eiprikɔt]	*un abricot(ier)*
a peach (tree)	*une pêche (un pêcher)*
a walnut (tree)	*une noix (un noyer)*
an almond ['a:mənd]	*une amande* (tree) *(un amandier)*
a blossom	*une fleur (d'arbre)*
a strawberry ['strɔ:bəri]	*une fraise*
a raspberry (bush)	*une framboise (un framboisier)*
a blackberry	*une mûre*
a tomato	*une tomate*
an avocado (pear)	*un avocat*
a pineapple	*un ananas*
a mango	*une mangue*
a banana [bə'na:nə]	*une banane*
citrus ['saitrəs] fruit	*les agrumes*
an orange	*une orange*
a tangerine	*une mandarine*
a lemon	*un citron*
a grapefruit	*un pamplemousse*
vegetable growing	*l'horticulture*
early produce	*les primeurs*
a potato	*une pomme de terre*
a leek	*un poireau*
a carrot	*une carotte*
a bean	*un haricot*
French beans	*les haricots verts*
a pea	*un petit pois*
a cabbage ['kæbidʒ]	*un chou*
a cauliflower	*un chou-fleur*
a pumpkin	*une citrouille*
an onion	*un oignon*
Brussels sprouts	*des choux de Bruxelles*
lettuce ['letis]	*de la laitue, de la salade*
spinach ['spinidʒ]	*des épinards*
a radish	*un radis*
parsley	*du persil*
garlic	*de l'ail*
gardening	*le jardinage*
a gardener	*un jardinier*
a landscape gardener	*un paysagiste*
a lawn [lɔ:n]	*une pelouse*
a lawn-mower	*une tondeuse*
turf	*le gazon*
a blade of grass	*un brin d'herbe*
a flower bed	*un parterre*
a rose-bush	*un rosier*
a carnation	*un œillet*
a tulip ['tjulip]	*une tulipe*
a lily	*un lis*
lily-of-the-valley	*du muguet*
a daisy	*une pâquerette*
a daffodil	*une jonquille*
lilac	*du lilas*
a poppy	*un coquelicot ; un pavot*
a chrysanthemum	*un chrysanthème*
a petal	*un pétale*
a stem	*une tige*
a thorn	*une épine*
a bud	*un bouton ; un bourgeon*
a leaf	*une feuille*
hay	*le foin*
hay-making	*la fenaison*
stockbreeding	*l'élevage*
a herd [hə:d]	*un troupeau (bovins)*
a cattle breeder	*un éleveur de bovins*
a cattle dealer	*un marchand de bestiaux*
a slaughter-house	*un abattoir*
a cow	*une vache*
a calf (calves)	*un veau*
dairy farming	*l'élevage laitier*
dairy produce	*les produits laitiers*
milk	*le lait*
a bull [bul]	*un taureau*
an ox (oxen)	*un bœuf*
fodder	*le fourrage*
a sheep (inv.)	*un mouton*
sheep farming	*l'élevage de moutons*
a shepherd ['ʃepəd]	*un berger*
a sheepdog	*un chien de berger*
a flock	*un troupeau*
a lamb [læm]	*un agneau*
wool	*la laine*
a goat	*une chèvre*
a kid	*un chevreau*
a horse	*un cheval*
a mare	*une jument*
a foal	*un poulain*
a pony ['pəuni]	*un poney*
a donkey, an ass	*un âne*
a pig	*un cochon, un porc*
a sow [sau]	*une truie*
a piglet	*un porcelet*
a horn	*une corne*

a hoof	*un sabot*	sweet	*doux*
a mane	*une crinière*	sour ['sauə]	*aigre*
a cat	*un chat*	bitter	*amer*
a kitten	*un chaton*	rotten	*pourri*
a dog	*un chien*	fragrant ['freigrənt]	*parfumé*
a bitch	*une chienne*	lean	*maigre*
a watchdog	*un chien de garde*	fat	*gras*
a puppy	*un chiot*	aggressive	*agressif*
rabies	*la rage*	aggressively	*avec agressivité*
a mouse (mice) [mais]	*une souris*	shy(ly)	*timide(ment)*
a rat	*un rat*	woolly	*laineux*
a bee	*une abeille*	rabid ['ræbid]	*enragé*
bee-keeping	*l'apiculture*	to bloom, to flower	*fleurir*
a hive [haiv]	*une ruche*	to smell*	*sentir*
a swarm	*un essaim*	to wither	*se faner*
poultry farming	*l'élevage de volailles*	to fade [feid]	*passer (couleurs)*
a fowl [fəul]	*une volaille*	to breed*, to raise	*élever*
a chicken	*un poulet*	to keep*	*faire l'élevage de*
a chick	*un poussin*	to graze [greiz]	*paître*
a hen	*une poule*	to milk	*traire*
an egg	*un œuf*	to shear* [ʃiə]	*tondre (animaux)*
a rooster	*un coq*	to fatten	*engraisser*
a turkey ['tə:ki]	*un dindon*	to forcefeed*	*gaver*
a duck	*un canard*	to slaughter ['slɔ:tə]	*abattre*
a duckling	*un caneton*	to moo	*meugler*
a goose (geese)	*une oie*	to bleat	*bêler*
a guinea fowl	*une pintade*	to neigh [nei]	*hennir*
a (turtle) dove	*une tourterelle*	to squeal	*crier, pousser des cris perçants*
a pigeon ['pidʒin]	*un pigeon*		
a peacock	*un paon*	to bite* [bait]	*mordre*
a rabbit	*un lapin*	to lick	*lécher*
mellow	*fondant*	to cackle	*caqueter*
tasty ['teisti]	*goûteux*	to sting*	*piquer*
tasteless	*insipide*		

Expressions

to live on a farm	*vivre à la ferme*
to work on a farm	*travailler à la ferme*
high standards of cultivation	*un haut niveau de technique agricole*
crop rotation	*l'assolement*
genetically-modified crops	*des organismes génétiquement modifiés*
systemic weed-killers	*des désherbants systémiques*
a bumper crop	*une récolte exceptionnelle*
a good cash crop	*une bonne culture de rente*
a high-yield crop	*une culture à haut rendement*
to reap the benefits of	*récolter les bénéfices de*
a vegetable garden	*un (jardin) potager*
organic farming	*l'agriculture biologique*
organically-grown vegetables	*des légumes biologiques*
10 tons per hectare/per acre	*10 tonnes à l'hectare/à l'acre*

the food processing industry	*l'industrie agro-alimentaire*
EEC farm subsidies	*les subventions agricoles de la CEE*
a farming policy	*une politique agricole*
milk quotas	*les quotas laitiers*
the Common Agricultural Policy (CAP)	*la Politique Agricole Commune (PAC)*
a grain mountain	*une montagne de céréales*
milk surpluses	*les surplus laitiers*
the farmers' lobby	*le lobby des agriculteurs*
set-aside land	*les terres en jachère*
the Corn Belt (US)	*la région de culture du maïs*
the Wheat Belt (US)	*la région de culture du blé*
hormone-fed beef (US)	*du bœuf aux hormones*
to make hay	*faire les foins*
to chew the cud	*ruminer*
500 head of cattle	*500 têtes de bétail*
extensive sheep farming	*l'élevage intensif de moutons*
to milk a cow	*traire une vache*
machine milking	*la traite mécanisée*
to lay eggs	*pondre des œufs*
2 dozen eggs	*2 douzaines d'œufs*
free-range chickens	*des poulets élevés en plein air*
battery chickens	*des poulets élevés en batterie*
«Fresh-laid eggs for sale»	*«Œufs du jour à vendre»*
«Pick your own strawberries, 50p a pound»	*«Cueillez vous-même vos fraises, 50 pence la livre»*

Métaphores

to nip in the bud	*tuer dans l'œuf*
a black sheep	*une brebis galeuse*
to spill the beans	*vendre la mèche*
to have gooseflesh	*avoir la chair de poule*

Phrases

He farms 1,000 acres of good, fertile land.
Il cultive 400 hectares de bonne terre fertile.

Traditionally, Lincolnshire farmers mainly grow cereals and potatoes.
Traditionnellement, les agriculteurs du Lincolnshire cultivent surtout les céréales et la pomme de terre.

Many farmers went bankrupt after borrowing heavily to buy expensive implements.
Beaucoup d'agriculteurs firent faillite après s'être lourdement endettés pour acheter du matériel couteûx.

Angry farmers demonstrated in Brussels against the Common Agricultural Policy.
Les paysans en colère ont manifesté à Bruxelles contre la P.A.C.

Periodically, they would dump manure in front of the administrative headquarters.
À intervalles réguliers ils déversaient du fumier devant les locaux administratifs.

Milk quotas have failed to solve the problem of surpluses.
Les quotas laitiers n'ont pas résolu le problème des surplus.

How could small European farmers compete with US industrial farming?
Comment les petits paysans européens pourraient-ils concurrencer l'agriculture industrielle américaine ?

Thanks to hydroponics, Spanish farmers produce tasteless strawberries even in winter.
Grâce à la culture hors-sol les fermiers espagnols produisent des fraises insipides même en hiver.

Shouldn't the government give incentives to organic farming?
Le gouvernement ne devrait-il pas accorder des incitations à l'agriculture biologique ?

Farmers used to keep chickens and rabbits and were self-sufficient.
Autrefois les fermiers élevaient poulets et lapins et vivaient en autarcie.

Exercices

I. Classer les 20 mots ci-dessous en 5 groupes égaux par affinité de sens. Donner un titre à chaque groupe (par exemple, «breeding», «implements», etc.)

barley, blade, cabbage, corn, fatten, flour, garlic, grapes, juicy, lettuce, pineapple, plough, raise, raspberry, trailer, sow, spinach, sprinkler, stable, wheat.

II. Compléter les phrases en utilisant des mots dérivés des termes suivants : aggressively, wholesome, fertilizer, subsidise, tasteless, pesticides, extensively, combine-harvester, organically, surpluses.

We can no longer afford to (1)... the grain mountain.

Farmers still spread massive amounts of (2)... to improve the yield.

(3)... -grown products have two advantages : they are better quality and more (4)... .

Such crops would significantly reduce (5)... in Western Europe.

These beautiful apples have probably been sprayed with (6)... .

He ran into debt to buy a brand new (7)... - ... .

I hate the unripe, (8)... fruit that they sell in supermarkets these days.

Sheep are raised (9)... on the moors of Northern England.

The US administration reacted (10)... to what is called a protectionist European agricultural policy.

III. Former des phrases cohérentes en remettant dans le bon ordre les éléments de la colonne de droite :

1. The extensive use of fertilizers has improved the crops,	a. who work with computers and sophisticated machinery.
2. The Common Agricultural Policy was widely criticized	b. that fertile land should be set aside.
3. The food-processing industry dictates its standards and prices	c. but you also pay much lower prices for fresher produce.
4. Better yields may mean lower prices for the consumer	d. on the other hand it has seriously damaged the land.
5. There is a tremendous difference between Third World peasants and American farmers,	e. for suppressing some subsidies.
6. Old-time farmers grew everything they needed	f. which is no longer true as many people have given up smoking.
7. Some farmers are shocked at the EC decision	g. to compete with large agribusiness companies.
8. EC regulations make it difficult for small family businesses	h. to feed themselves and their families.
9. Not only is it fun to pick your own fruit,	i. they may also bring about the death of less efficient farms.
10. Tobacco used to be a good cash crop,	j. to be able to supply supermarkets with competitive products.

22. The environment and pollution
L'environnement et la pollution

Vocabulaire général

The Earth	*la Terre*
the Planet	*la planète*
the ecosystem	*l'écosystème*
Nature [‘neitʃə]	*la nature*
the air	*l'air*
a current	*un courant*
the scenery	*le paysage*
the countryside	*la campagne*
the atmosphere	*l'atmosphère*
an aquifer	*une nappe phréatique*
the ozone layer	*la couche d'ozone*
the fauna	*la faune*
the flora	*la flore*
wildlife	*la faune, la vie sauvage*
a species [‘spiːʃiːz]	*une espèce*
damage [dæmidʒ]	*les dégâts*
a threat [θret]	*une menace*
a hazard, [‘hæzəd] a risk	*un risque*
a plague, a scourge	*un fléau*
death	*la mort*
survival	*la survie*
a balance	*un équilibre*
a lack	*un manque*
a surplus	*un surplus*
a glut [glʌt]	*une surabondance*
a shortage	*une pénurie*
the Greens	*les Verts*
the Green Party	*le Parti des Verts*
an environmentalist	*un écologiste*
a conservationist	*un protecteur de l'environnement*

environmental(ly)	*écologique(ment)*
ecological(ly)	*écologique(ment)*
(non-) polluting	*(non) polluant*
spoilt	*abîmé, défiguré*
unspoilt	*intact*
harmful	*nocif, nuisible*
hazardous [‘hæzədəs]	*dangereux*
devastating	*dévastateur, catastrophique*
lethal#, deadly	*mortel (destructeur)*
radioactive	*radioactif*
unbreathable	*irrespirable*
poisonous, toxic	*toxique*
noxious [‘nɔkʃəs]	*nocif*
barren	*stérile, aride*
extinct	*disparu (espèce), éteint (volcan)*
rampant	*incontrôlé*
appalling	*épouvantable*
dire	*affreux, extrême*
energy-guzzling	*gourmand en énergie*
profligate	*prodigue, gaspilleur*
congested	*embouteillé*
scarce	*rare, peu abondant*
widespread	*répandu*
indiscriminate(ly)	*sans discernement*
pollution-related	*lié à la pollution*
annoying	*agaçant, ennuyeux*
ugly [‘ʌgli]	*laid*
polluted	*pollué*
befouled	*souillé*
dramatic(ally)	*spectaculaire(ment)*
tragic(ally)	*tragique(ment)*
dead	*mort*
irreparable [i’repərəbl]	*irréparable*
grimy [‘graimi]	*encrassé*
dusty	*poussiéreux*
short-term	*à court terme*
long-term	*à long terme*
medium-term	*à moyen terme*
organic	*biologique*
natural	*naturel*
biodegradable [‘baiəudi’greidəbl]	*biodégradable*
disposable	*jetable*
drastic(ally)	*énergique, sévère(ment)*
viable [‘vaiəbl]	*viable*
sustainable	*viable, soutenable*
(non-)renewable	*(non) renouvelable*
alternative	*alternatif, de rechange*
undrinkable	*non potable*
(in)edible	*(non) comestible*
unleaded [‘ʌn’ledid]	*sans plomb*
lead-free	
ozone-friendly	*respectueux de la couche d’ozone*

economical [ˌi:kə’nɔmikəl]	*économique (peu cher)*
cost-effective	*rentable*
fuel-efficient	*économe en carburant*
well insulated	*bien isolé*
organically grown	*de culture biologique*
drastically	*radicalement, sévèrement*
irretrievably, irremediably	*irrémédiablement*
currently	*actuellement*
scarcely, hardly	*à peine*
for ever	*à jamais*
evermore	*à tout jamais*
to pollute [pə’lu:t]	*polluer*
to damage	*abîmer, endommager*
to wreck	*détruire, démolir*
to spoil*, to mar	*abîmer, défigurer*
to disfigure	*défigurer*
to foul [faul]	*souiller*
to destroy	*détruire*
to wipe out	*anéantir, effacer*
to vanish	*disparaître*
to endanger	*mettre en danger*
to threaten	*menacer*
to deplete	*réduire, épuiser*
to reject	*rejeter*
to pour [pɔ:]	*verser, se déverser*
to spill*	*renverser, se déverser*
to get* rid of	*se débarrasser de*
to throw* away	*jeter*
to dump	*jeter, déverser*
to dispose of	*se défaire de, se débarrasser de*
to discard	*jeter, se débarrasser de*
to belch (out)	*vomir, cracher (fumée, etc.)*
to leak	*fuire*
to stink*	*puer, empester*
to asphyxiate	*asphyxier*
to guzzle	*consommer en grandes quantités*
to waste	*gaspiller*
to fell	*abattre (arbres)*
to recycle	*recycler*
to sort	*trier*
to collect	*ramasser, recueillir*
to save	*économiser*
to clean up	*nettoyer*
to sustain	*soutenir*
to insulate	*isoler*
to conserve	*préserver*
to survive	*survivre*
to ban	*interdire*
to cut* out	*supprimer*
to cut* down on	*réduire*

Vocabulaire spécialisé

1. Causes of pollution

urban sprawl	*l'extension tentaculaire de la ville*
population growth	*la croissance démographique*
a mobile phone mast	*une antenne-relais*
a smokestack	*une cheminée (d'usine)*
a car exhaust pipe	*un tuyau d'échappement*
an emission	*une émanation*
a chemical ['kemikəl]	*un produit chimique*
a fossil fuel	*un combustible fossile*
hydrocarbon fuels ['haidrəu'ka:bən]	*les hydrocarbures*
an aerosol, a spray	*un aérosol*
a spray can	*un atomiseur*
a pollutant	*un polluant*
a polluter	*un pollueur*
sewage ['sju(:)idʒ]	*eaux usées, eaux d'égout*
a sewer ['sjuə]	*un égout*
industrial waste	*les déchets industriels*
domestic/household waste	*les déchets ménagers*
waste disposal	*l'élimination des déchets*
refuse ['refjus], garbage, rubbish	*les ordures*
a dustman	*un éboueur*
a tip, a rubbish dump	*une décharge*
plastic	*les matières plastiques*
packaging	*les emballages*
a fertilizer	*un engrais*
a pesticide	*un pesticide*
nitrogen ['naitrədʒən]	*l'azote*
asbestos	*l'amiante*
dioxin	*la dioxine*
lead [led]	*le plomb*
mercury	*le mercure*
nitrates ['naitreits]	*les nitrates*
a detergent	*un détergent*
soot [sut]	*la suie*

2. Manifestations

an effluent	*un écoulement polluant*
a leak	*une fuite*
noise	*le bruit*
a din	*un vacarme*
smoke	*la fumée*
smog	*brouillard mêlé de fumée*
a cloud	*un nuage*
fumes [fju:mz]	*des vapeurs, des émanations*
grime [graim]	*la crasse*
litter	*détritus (sur le sol)*
a stench	*une puanteur*
a drought [draut]	*une sécheresse*
acid rain	*les pluies acides*
extinction	*l'extinction*
destruction	*la destruction*
carbon monoxide	*l'oxyde de carbone*
carbon dioxide	*le dioxyde de carbone*
nitrogen oxide	*l'oxyde d'azote*
sulphur dioxide	*l'anhydride sulfureux*
an oil slick	*une nappe de pétrole*
a black tide an oil slick,	*une marée noire*
the greenhouse effect	*l'effet de serre*
global warming	*le réchauffement de la Terre*
climate change	*le changement climatique*
a disease	*une maladie*
an epidemic	*une épidémie*
skin cancer	*le cancer de la peau*
lung cancer	*le cancer du poumon*
lead poisoning	*le saturnisme*
an eyesore ['ai-sɔ:]	*une horreur (dans le paysage)*

3. Cures

a catalytic converter	*un pot catalytique*
unleaded petrol	*l'essence sans plomb*
car-pooling	*l'utilisation collective d'un véhicule*
a cleanup	*un nettoyage*
a substitute	*un produit de remplacement*
a filter	*un filtre*
a scrubber	*un épurateur*
conservation	*la préservation*
a sewage treatment plant	*une station d'épuration*
a solar panel	*un panneau solaire*
a windmill	*une éolienne*

insulation	*l'isolation*	a framework	*une structure, un cadre*
a bottle bank	*un conteneur à verre*	a measure ['meʒə]	*une mesure*
returnable packaging	*les emballages consignés*	an incentive	*une incitation*
savings	*les économies*	a commitment	*un engagement*
a regulation	*un réglement*	a pledge	*une promesse*
a ban	*une interdiction*	awareness	*la conscience*
a moratorium	*un moratoire*		

Expressions

the natural balance	*l'équilibre naturel*
an ecological disaster	*une catastrophe écologique*
an environmental crisis	*une crise écologique*
irreparable damage	*des dégâts irréparables*
dire consequences	*des conséquences désastreuses*
a devastating environmental impact	*un impact écologique accablant*
the greening of business	*l'orientation des entreprises vers l'écologie*
an environment-friendly product	*un produit sans danger pour l'environnement*
greenwashing	*l'écoblanchiment (donner l'image écologiste d'une firme qui ne l'est pas)*
the throwaway society	*la société de gaspillage*
an endangered species	*une espèce en voie de disparition*
drinking water	*l'eau potable*
an unspoilt landscape	*un paysage qui n'est pas défiguré*
energy-saving appliances	*des appareils économes en énergie*
energy-guzzling appliances	*des appareils gaspilleurs d'énergie*
a well insulated loft	*un grenier bien isolé*
a garbage disposal unit	*un broyeur de déchets*
renewable sources of energy	*des sources d'énergie renouvelables*
photovoltaic cells	*des cellules photovoltaïques*
selective waste collection	*la collecte sélective des déchets*
congested roads	*les routes encombrées*
exhaust fumes	*les gaz d'échappement*
a radioactive cloud	*un nuage radioactif*
lethal gases	*des gaz mortels*
rising sea levels	*la montée du niveau des mers*
coastal flooding	*les inondations côtières*
nuclear fallout	*les retombées radioactives*
a threat on our environment	*une menace pour notre environnement*
zero growth	*la croissance zéro*
sustainable growth	*la croissance soutenable, raisonnable*
the supply-side approach	*la théorie de l'offre qui devance la demande*
the survival of the fittest	*la persistance du plus apte (la loi du plus fort)*
to gather pace / momentum	*prendre de la vitesse*
to be at risk	*être en danger*
to break a cycle	*rompre un cycle*
to be littered with	*être jonché de*
to dump waste into the sea	*déverser des déchets dans la mer*
to deplete the ozone layer	*épuiser / diminuer la couche d'ozone*
CFCs (chlorofluorocarbons)	*les chlorofluorocarbones*
to wreak havoc (on)	*faire des ravages, dévaster*
to jeopardize life on earth	*compromettre la vie sur terre*
to pledge to take measures	*promettre de prendre des mesures*
to be committed to taking measures	*être engagé à prendre des mesures*
to take drastic steps	*prendre des mesures radicales*

to clean up one's act	*«balayer devant sa porte»*
to call for urgent action	*demander des mesures d'urgence*
to ban urban traffic	*interdire la circulation urbaine*
to put human life in jeopardy	*mettre la vie humaine en péril*

Phrases

Waste not, want not.
L'économie protège du besoin.

The European bear, like many species, is on the verge of extinction.
L'ours européen, comme beaucoup d'espèces, est en voie de disparition.

The survival of future generations is at stake.
C'est la survie des générations futures qui est en jeu.

The advance of the desert is already beyond control.
L'avancée du désert échappe déjà à tout contrôle.

Deforestation in Amazonia is going on at an alarming pace.
La déforestation en Amazonie se poursuit à un rythme inquiétant.

Can Third World economies grow without wrecking the global environment?
L'économie des pays du Tiers Monde peut-elle se développer sans détruire l'écologie de la planète ?

Conservation measures ought to be emphasized.
On devrait privilégier les mesures visant à économiser les ressources.

We have indiscriminately dumped waste into the sea, fouling it for ever.
Nous avons, sans discernement, jeté nos déchets à la mer, la souillant à jamais.

Rampant population growth leaves few regions unspoilt.
La croissance démographique galopante épargne peu de régions.

Car fumes and industrial smoke put historical buildings in jeopardy.
Les émanations des automobiles et les fumées des industries mettent les bâtiments historiques en danger.

When landscapes are not spoilt by electricity pylons, they are marred by mobile phone masts or gigantic windmills.
Quand les paysages ne sont pas gâchés par des pylônes électriques, ils sont abîmés par des antennes-relais ou des éoliennes gigantesques.

Exercices

I. Reformuler les phrases suivantes en utilisant, à la forme donnée, les mots entre parenthèses :

The Californian Administration has promised to ban fossil fuel vehicles by 2020. (committed)
In the past twenty years deforestation increased dramatically in Brazil's Amazonian forest. (pace)

The commercial stripping of forests is already having devastating effects on the global balance. (wreaking)

Detritus gradually covers Mediterranean beaches during the tourist season. (littered)

If we are to sustain our way of life we must take drastic steps to reduce waste. (down)

Western governments call for urgent action but what the planet needs is a commitment by them to stop fouling their own environment. (their act)

The indiscriminate use of fertilizers and pesticides threatens our drinking water. (jeopardy)

Millions of dead fish floated in the Rhine after the dumping of lethal chemicals into the river by a Swiss pharmaceutical company. (poured)

Sustainable growth can only be achieved through the use of products that do not damage the environment. (friendly)

Thanks to high-tech energy-saving devices we can achieve greater efficiency. (enable)

II. À l'aide des indices donnés, compléter les phrases suivantes au moyen d'adjectifs ou d'adverbes figurant dans le chapitre :

(1) D... legislation will have to be taken to protect city centres that are (2) c... overwhelmed by motor vehicles.

More (3) e... stoves would reduce Africa's dependence on (4) s... firewood.

It is hard to believe that the (5) r... cloud from Chernobyl power station stopped at the French border.

(6) S... waste collecting could be a first step towards a cleaner world.

Taller smokestacks belch out their (7) n... fumes higher into the atmosphere, thus polluting larger areas.

Incentives and grants may encourage industrialists to (8) d... reduce industrial effluents.

(9) E... - ... motor cars help deplete our oil resources.

Well-insulated buildings are (10) s... more expensive to build than bad quality ones and they are much cheaper to maintain.

III. Traduire :

en français :

1. the rampant destruction of the rain forest
2. a green lobby
3. a lack of political commitment
4. to cut down on packaging
5. the indiscriminate use of spray cans

en anglais :

6. *des vapeurs mortelles*
7. *une quantité croissante d'ordures ménagères*
8. *un paysage irrémédiablement défiguré*
9. *une plage souillée par la marée noire*
10. *des conséquences dramatiques à long terme*

VI. LIVING IN SOCIETY

23. Social life
La vie sociale

mankind	*l'humanité*
society	*la société*
a community	*une communauté*
an association	*une association*
a club	*un club*
a neighbourhood	*un quartier*
a citizen	*un citoyen*
a city-dweller	*un citadins*
townspeople	*les citadins*
a crowd [kraud]	*une foule*
a mob	*une populace*
charity	*la charité*
welfare	*l'aide sociale*
an allowance	*une allocation*
a status ['steitəs]	*un statut*
success, achievement	*le succès*
failure ['feiljə]	*l'échec*
mediocrity [ˌmi:di'ɔkriti]	*la médiocrité*
ambition	*l'ambition*
drive	*le dynamisme*
an upstart	*un arriviste*
a career [kə'riə]	*une carrière*
optimism	*l'optimisme*
confidence	*la confiance*
an incentive	*une incitation*
a goal [gəul]	*un but*
an ideal [ai'diəl]	*un idéal*
a dream	*un rêve*
a fashion	*une mode*
a trend	*une tendance*
a fad	*une vogue*
hopelessness	*le désespoir*
a burden ['bə:dn]	*un fardeau*
drudgery	*le travail pénible et ingrat*
poverty	*la pauvreté*
wretchedness	*la misère*
wealth	*la richesse*
affluence	*l'aisance*
the rich	*les riches*
the poor	*les pauvres*
the homeless	*les sans-abri*
an outcast	*un paria*

inactivity	*l'inactivité*
idleness ['aidlnis]	*l'oisiveté*
isolation	*l'isolement*
weakness	*la faiblesse*
discontent	*le mécontentement*
bitterness	*l'amertume*
activism	*le militantisme*
unrest	*l'agitation*
a demonstration	*une manifestation*
a riot ['rai-ət]	*une émeute*
hostility	*l'hostilité*
a quarrel	*une querelle*
repression	*la répression*
rivalry ['raivəlri]	*la rivalité*
expectations	*les attentes, l'espoir*
promotion	*la promotion*
(in)equality	*l'(in)égalité*
tolerance	*la tolérance*
intolerance	*l'intolérance*
rejection	*le rejet*
oppression	*l'oppression*
persecution	*la persécution*
equity	*l'équité*
solidarity	*la solidarité*
selfishness	*l'égoïsme*
a prejudice, a bias ['baiəs]	*un préjugé*
gossip	*les ragots, les commérages*
a scapegoat	*un bouc émissaire*
a stereotype	*un stéréotype*
racism	*le racisme*
segregation	*la ségrégation*
rejection	*le rejet*
apartheid [ə'pa:theid]	*l'apartheid*
propaganda	*la propagande*
hostility	*l'hostilité*
persecution	*la persécution*
a minority	*une minorité*
the mainstream	*le courant dominant*
xenophobia [ˌzenə'fəubjə]	*la xénophobie*
alienation [ˌeiljə'neiʃən]	*l'aliénation*

a gap	*un fossé*
a discrepancy	*un écart, une antinomie*
homosexuality	*l'homosexualité*
sex	*le sexe*
a taboo [tə'bu:]	*un tabou*
discrimination	*la discrimination*
depravation	*l'avilissement*
prostitution	*la prostitution*
a prostitute	*une prostituée*
a pimp	*un souteneur*
a sexist	*un sexiste*
harassment	*le harcèlement*
a feminist	*une féministe*
emancipation	*l'émancipation*
contraception	*la contraception*
abortion [ə'bɔ:ʃən]	*l'avortement*
tension	*la tension*
the aged, ['eidʒid] the elderly	*les personnes âgées*
the young	*les jeunes*
a teenager	*un adolescent*
a lifestyle	*un style de vie*
a habit	*une habitude*
a custom ['kʌstəm]	*une coutume*
manners	*les manières*
lucrative	*lucratif*
luxurious	*luxueux, de luxe*
ambitious	*ambitieux*
determined	*décidé, résolu*
bold	*hardi, osé*
optimistic	*optimiste*
social	*social*
societal [sə'saiətəl]	*sociétal*
polite	*poli*
rude	*grossier*
brutal	*brutal*
violent	*violent*
friendly	*amical, sympathique*
charitable	*charitable*
generous	*généreux*
selfish	*égoïste*
reliable, [ri'laiəbl] dependable	*sur qui on peut compter*
sly [slai]	*sournois*
right	*bon, juste*
wrong [rɔŋ]	*mauvais, injuste*
irresponsible	*irresponsable*
inferior	*inférieur*
broke [brəuk]	*fauché*
destitute	*démuni*
uprooted	*déraciné*
degrading	*dégradant*
desperate	*désespéré*
underprivileged	*défavorisé*
rejected	*rejeté*

battered	*battu*
idle [aidl]	*oisif*
illegal	*illégal, clandestin*
undocumented	*sans papiers*
undesirable	*indésirable*
prejudiced, biased	*partial*
intolerant	*intolérant*
xenophobic	*xénophobe*
anti-Semitic	*antisémite*
jealous]'dʒeləs]	*jaloux*
frustrated	*frustré*
adverse	*hostile, défavorable*
suicidal [sjui'saidl]	*suicidaire*
homosexual, gay	*homosexuel*
to succeed	*réussir*
to fail	*échouer*
to trust	*faire confiance à*
to depend on / upon	*dépendre de*
to stick* together	*se serrer les coudes*
to improve	*améliorer*
to tolerate	*tolérer*
to promote	*promouvoir*
to emancipate	*émanciper*
to adapt (to)	*s'adapter (à)*
to integrate into	*s'intégrer (à)*
to settle	*s'installer*
to complain	*se plaindre*
to claim	*revendiquer*
to demand [di'ma:nd]	*exiger*
to shelter	*abriter, donner asile à*
to fund [fʌnd]	*financer*
to spend*	*dépenser*
to relieve	*venir en aide, soulager*
to support	*soutenir*
to benefit from	*bénéficier de*
to struggle	*s'efforcer, se débattre*
to evolve [i'vɔlv]	*évoluer*
to compete (with)	*concurrencer*
to envy ['envi]	*envier*
to dream*	*rêver*
to misbehave	*se conduire mal*
to take* to (+ing)	*s'adonner à*
to disadvantage	*désavantager*
to neglect [ni'glekt]	*négliger*
to humiliate	*humilier*
to repress [ri'pres]	*réprimer*
to persecute	*persécuter*
to harass ['hærəs]	*harceler*
to deprive	*priver*
to manipulate	*manipuler*
to influence	*influencer*
to exploit, to sweat [swet]	*exploiter*
to evict	*expulser*
to abort [[ə'bɔ:t]	*avorter*

Expressions

a social issue	*un problème de société*
a two-tier society	*une société à deux vitesses*
to bridge the gap	*combler le fossé*
one's station in life	*son rang social*
social status	*le prestige, le standing*
a status symbol	*une marque de standing*
the social fabric	*la trame sociale*
to climb the social ladder	*gravir l'échelle sociale*
living conditions	*les conditions de vie*
one's living standard	*son niveau de vie*
the man in the street	*l'homme de la rue*
to be at the top of the ladder	*être au sommet de l'échelle*
social mobility	*la mobilité sociale*
to drive someone to do something	*inciter quelqu'un à réagir*
to be full of drive	*être très entreprenant*
the rat race	*la course au succès, la foire d'empoigne*
to go from rags to riches	*faire fortune en partant de rien*
to fight one's way to the top	*se battre pour arriver au sommet*
to keep up with the Joneses	*ne pas être en reste avec les voisins*
to be well-off	*vivre dans l'aisance*
to live in luxury	*vivre dans le luxe*
the affluent society	*la société d'abondance*
class struggle	*la lutte des classes*
the privileged classes	*les classes privilégiées*
the ruling class	*la classe dirigeante*
the upper classes	*les classes supérieures*
the middle class	*la classe moyenne*
the working class	*la classe ouvrière*
the lower ranks	*les bas échelons*
equal rights	*l'égalité des droits*
social conflicts	*les conflits sociaux*
to make both ends meet	*joindre les deux bouts*
poverty-stricken	*pauvre*
to be below the poverty line	*être au-dessous du seuil de pauvreté*
to live in poverty	*vivre dans la pauvreté*
the bare necessities	*le strict minimum*
to be in dire straits	*être dans une situation désespérée*
double-digit inflation	*une inflation supérieure à 10%*
a welfare worker	*un travailleur social*
welfare benefits, social aids	*les aides sociales*
the dregs / scum of society	*la lie de la société*
human rights	*les droits de l'homme*
the women's liberation movement	*le mouvement de libération de la femme*
sex discrimination	*la discrimination sexuelle*
a single-parent family	*une famille monoparentale*
the Sex Discrimination Act	*la loi pour l'abolition de la discrimination sexuelle*
equal opportunity	*l'égalité des chances*
sexual harassment	*le harcèlement sexuel*

battered wives	*les femmes battues*
child abuse	*mauvais traitement à enfant*
battered children	*les enfants battus*
a broken family	*une famille désunie*
to commit suicide	*se suicider*
a teenage mother	*une mère adolescente*
senior citizens	*les personnes âgées, le troisième âge*
meals on wheels	*repas à domicile (pour le 3e âge)*
the generation gap	*le fossé des générations*

Phrases

They will never manage to make both ends meet on such a low income.
Ils ne parviendront jamais à joindre les deux bouts avec des revenus si faibles.

How come that so many people live below the poverty line in wealthy nations?
Comment se fait-il que tant de gens vivent en-dessous du seuil de pauvreté dans les pays riches ?

The man in the street feels that the gap between the poor and the rich keeps widening.
L'homme de la rue a le sentiment que le fossé entre les riches et les pauvres ne cesse de s'élargir.

However ambitious you may be, climbing the social ladder is not that easy when you start from the bottom.
Quelle que soit votre ambition, il n'est pas facile de vous hisser dans l'échelle sociale quand vous partez du bas.

72% of German women complain they have been sexually harassed.
72 % des femmes en Allemagne se plaignent d'avoir été victimes d'harcèlement sexuel.

In Japan, the average woman's income amounts to only half that of a man's.
Au Japon, le revenu moyen des femmes ne représente que la moitié de celui des hommes.

Even after segregation was officially abolished in South Africa, pockets of white resistance kept fighting integration.
Même après que la ségrégation fut officiellement abolie en Afrique du Sud, des poches de résistance blanche ont continué à lutter contre l'intégration.

Educational success is often the only chance for the children of immigrants to escape from ghettos.
La réussite scolaire est souvent la seule chance qu'ont les enfants d'immigrés d'échapper au ghetto.

The local authorities have decided to grant poor families financial benefits to enable them to pay their rent.
Les autorités locales ont décidé d'accorder des aides financières aux familles démunies pour leur permettre de payer leur loyer.

In the US, the poverty rate for blacks is 31% as against 11% for whites.
Aux États Unis, le taux de pauvreté est de 31 % pour les noirs, comparé à 11 % pour les blancs.

Exercices

I. Retrouver les adjectifs correspondant aux définitions suivantes :

1. chiefly thinking of one's own needs and welfare
2. expecting the best
3. without a proper sense of responsibility
4. on whom you can depend
5. filled with despair
6. penniless
7. bringing in money
8. beaten
9. lower in rank
10. ready to give

II. Quel est le contraire des mots suivants :

1. achievement 2. equality 3. contentment 4. desirable 5. to worsen

III. Reformuler les phrases suivantes en utilisant les mots entre parenthèses :

1. Without welfare benefits, they could not survive. (to depend on)
2. His ambition is to climb the social ladder. (to dream)
3. There are very few Italians in that town. (a minority)
4. When he was born, his father had already left his mother. (a broken family)
5. The number of children who are ill-treated by their parents unfortunately seems to be increasing. (battered)

IV. Traduire :

en français :

1. The essential American promise is that individuals will rise or fall on their own merits.
2. Most US blacks find themselves cut off from the mainstream.
3. Young men who have been the victims of broken families are often the perpetrators of new ones.
4. In China, only-children are entitled to monthly health-care allowances.
5. Idle people have too much time on their hands, they get depressed and sometimes take to drinking.

en anglais :

6. *Ce sont les classes privilégiées qui bénéficient le plus de la société d'abondance.*
7. *Il était très entreprenant et s'efforçait de réussir.*
8. *Il était déterminé à atteindre le sommet de l'échelle.*
9. *Les immigrés clandestins sont souvent sans papiers d'identité.*
10. *Ils étaient fauchés et on les a expulsés de leur logement.*

24. The media
Les médias

the news (toujours singulier)	*les nouvelles, les informations*
a newspaper	*un journal*
an issue ['iʃu:]	*un numéro*
a copy	*un exemplaire*
a reader	*un lecteur*
the readership	*le nombre de lecteurs*
a subscription	*un abonnement*
a subscriber	*un abonné*
a newsagent	*un dépositaire*
a news vendor	*un vendeur de journaux*
a publisher	*un éditeur*
an editor ['editə]	*un rédacteur*
the newsroom	*la salle de rédaction*
the circulation	*le tirage*
typesetting	*la composition*
the layout	*la mise en page*
a misprint	*une coquille*
the content(s)	*le contenu*
the contents page	*le sommaire*
a tabloid	*un quotidien populaire (demi-format)*
a rag	*une feuille de chou, un torchon*
a rumour ['ru:mə]	*une rumeur*
journalese	*le jargon journalistique*
a magazine	*un magazine*
a daily	*un quotidien*
a weekly	*un hebdomadaire*
a monthly	*un mensuel*
a piece of news	*une nouvelle*
a news item ['aitəm]	*une information, un fait divers*
a topic	*un sujet*
an event [i'vent]	*un événement*
an issue	*un problème, une question*
an article, a feature ['fi:tʃə]	*un article*
a column ['kɔləm]	*une colonne, une rubrique, une chronique*
a columnist	*un chroniqueur*
a report [ri'pɔ:t]	*un reportage*
a headline	*un titre*
a scoop	*une exclusivité*

a review	*une critique*
a cartoon	*un dessin humoristique*
a caption	*une légende*
an insert	*un encart*
a crossword	*des mots croisés*
games	*les jeux*
an editorial	*un éditorial*
a disclosure	*une révélation*
libel ['laibəl]	*la diffamation*
a survey ['sə:vei]	*une étude*
a poll [pəul]	*un sondage*
a journalist, a newsman	*un journaliste*
a reporter	*un reporter*
a correspondent	*un correspondant*
a photograph ['fəutəgra:f]	*une photographie*
a photographer [fə'tɔgrəfə]	*un photographe*
a critic	*un critique*
a TV set	*un téléviseur*
the box, the telly	*la télé*
a VCR	*un magnétoscope*
a TV viewer	*un téléspectateur*
interference	*les parasites*
a channel	*une chaîne*
a network	*un réseau*
ratings	*l'indice de popularité (l'Audimat)*
a programme	*une émission*
an announcer	*un présentateur*
a newsreader	*un présentateur du journal*
an anchorman ['æɲkəmæn]	*un présentateur-réalisateur*
a host [həust]	*un présentateur (jeux)*
a commentator	*un commentateur*
the weatherman	*M. Météo*
a newsflash	*un flash*
a dispatch	*une dépêche*
the highlights	*les grands titres de l'actualité*
a crew [kru:]	*une équipe*
a teleplay	*une dramatique*
a film	*un film*
a subtitle	*un sous-titre*
a videoclip	*un clip*

ads, commercials	*les pubs*
a serial, ['siəriəl]	*un feuilleton*
a series ['siəri:z]	
a documentary	*un documentaire*
a talkshow	*un débat*
a quiz	*un jeu-concours*
the quiz master	*l'animateur*
a prize	*un prix*
a sponsor	*un sponsor*
the audience	*le public*
a repeat [ri'pi:t]	*une rediffusion*
the radio	*la radio*
a station	*une station*
a radio set	*un poste de radio*
a transistor	*un transistor*
a hifi ['hai'fai]	*une chaîne hi-fi*
a tuner ['tju:nə]	*un tuner*
an amplifier	*un ampli*
a turntable	*une platine*
a loudspeaker	*un haut-parleur*
a headphone	*un écouteur*
a listener ['lisnə]	*un auditeur*
a broadcast	*une émission*
the newsreel	*les actualités filmées (au cinéma)*
state-owned	*public*
private	*privé*
journalistic	*journalistique*
political	*politique*
arbitrary	*arbitraire*
biased ['baiəst]	*partial*
unbiased	*impartial*
objective	*objectif*
accurate ['ækjurit]	*précis, exact*
dependable, reliable	*sûr, fiable*
truthful	*véridique*
circumstantial	*détaillé*
live [[aiv]	*en direct*
newsworthy	*qui vaut la peine d'être publié*
harmful	*nuisible*
dull [[dʌl]	*morne*
boring [bɔ:riŋ]	*ennuyeux*
exciting	*passionnant*

thrilling	*qui vous tient en haleine*
mesmerized	*hypnotisé*
addicted [ə'diktid]	*drogué, « accro »*
to cover	*couvrir, faire un reportage sur*
to broadcast*	*diffuser*
to show*	*montrer, passer*
to print	*imprimer*
to report	*rapporter, relater, faire un reportage*
to review	*faire la critique*
to write*	*écrire*
to rewrite*	*remanier*
to quote	*citer*
to sensitize	*sensibiliser*
to expose [iks'pəuz]	*révéler*
to antagonize	*contrarier, soulever l'hostilité*
to run* down	*dénigrer*
to libel ['laibəl]	*diffamer*
to infringe (on)	*empiéter (sur)*
to apologize	*s'excuser*
to censor	*censurer*
to boycott	*boycotter*
to edit	*mettre en forme*
to set*	*composer*
to publish	*publier*
to translate	*traduire*
to subtitle	*sous-titrer*
to dub [dʌb]	*doubler*
to subscribe (to)	*s'abonner*
to receive	*recevoir*
to record, to tape	*enregistrer*
to videotape	*enregistrer sur bande vidéo*
to shoot* [ʃu:t]	*filmer*
to switch on	*allumer*
to switch off	*éteindre*
to turn down	*baisser le volume*
to turn up	*augmenter le volume*
to tune in (to)	*se mettre à l'écoute (de)*
to implode [im'pləud]	*imploser*

Expressions

current events	*l'actualité*
a topical issue	*une question d'actualité*
the national press	*la presse nationale*
the popular press	*la presse populaire*

the consumer press	*la presse grand public*
the gutter press	*la presse à sensation*
a press cutting / clipping	*une coupure de presse*
a press tycoon	*un magnat de la presse*
a press conference	*une conférence de presse*
a freelance photographer	*un photographe indépendant*
a press conference	*une conférence de presse*
a news agency	*une agence de presse*
news-in-brief	*les nouvelles brèves, les faits divers*
to cover an event	*couvrir un événement*
the Sunday papers	*les journaux du dimanche*
a comic strip	*une bande dessinée*
the sports page/column	*la rubrique sportive*
classified advertisements	*les petites annonces*
to hit the front page	*faire la une*
the front page	*la première page*
the correspondence column, letters to the editor	*le courrier des lecteurs*
to pull to pieces	*éreinter*
to be shown on TV	*passer à la télé (programme, etc.)*
to appear on TV	*passer à la télé (personne)*
independent TV	*les chaînes privées*
a privately-owned channel	*une chaîne privée*
a pay channel	*une chaîne payante*
cable TV	*la télévision par câble*
a satellite dish	*une antenne parabolique*
a TV addict	*un mordu de la télé*
a couch potato	*personne qui passe tout son temps devant la télé*
to have a high rating	*avoir un indice d'écoute élevé*
prime time	*les heures de grande écoute*
a live broadcast	*une émission en direct*
to be on the air	*être à l'antenne*
a recorded broadcast	*une émission en différé*
an educational programme	*une émission éducative*
a sit-com (situation-comedy)	*une comédie (en situation)*
a soap opera	*un feuilleton à l'eau de rose*
the feature film	*le grand film, le film de la soirée*
a variety show	*un spectacle de variétés*
a news bulletin	*un bulletin d'information*
from knowledgeable sources	*de sources bien informées*
a running commentary	*un commentaire suivi*

Phrases

Scandal has sold newspapers for more than a century.
Cela fait plus d'un siècle que les journaux se vendent grâce aux scandales.

I do not approve of the press prying into famous people's lives.
Je suis opposé à ce que la presse s'immisce dans la vie privée des gens célèbres.

It is time that the press in general and the scandal press in particular established a set of rules on defending people's image.
Il est temps que la presse en général et la presse à scandale en particulier établissent un ensemble de règles pour protéger l'image des gens.

The average American watches thirty hours of TV each week.
L'Américain moyen regarde trente heures de télévision chaque semaine.

It has been calculated that by the time they leave school, young Americans have watched some 17,000 hours of TV.
On a calculé que lorsqu'ils arrivent à la fin de leurs études secondaires, les jeunes Américains ont regardé quelque 17 000 heures de télévision.

It is the third time this week that this tabloid has been sued for libel.
C'est la troisième fois cette semaine que ce quotidien populaire est poursuivi pour diffamation.

She would not miss a single episode of her favourite serial for anything on earth.
Elle ne manquerait un seul épisode de son feuilleton préféré pour rien au monde.

That journalist was given the sack after writing an inaccurate account of the events.
Ce journaliste a été renvoyé après avoir écrit un compte-rendu inexact des événements.

I find commercials often more exciting than the boring debates that are shown on TV.
Je trouve souvent les spots publicitaires plus passionnants que les débats ennuyeux qui passent à la télévision.

I cannot stand watching films that have been dubbed.
Je ne peux pas supporter de regarder des films qui ont été doublés.

Exercices

I. What do you call someone who... :

1. reads the news on TV.
2. takes pictures.
3. listens to the radio.
4. forecasts the weather conditions.
5. watches TV.
6. sells newspapers in the street.
7. regularly contributes an article of special interest to a paper or magazine.
8. directs the publication of a newspaper.
9. issues books to the public through booksellers.
10. reports from abroad.

II. Compléter les phrases suivantes :

1. Turn the telly ... ; it's much too loud!
2. A ... can rerun yesterday's shows and preserve today's for tomorrow.
3. The debate was so ... that I went to sleep.

4. It is not always easy to read the ... when you watch foreign films.
5. This programme had already been ... on Radio Four the year before.
6. That show is very popular and has a high ... .
7. The freedom of the press means that papers cannot be ... .
8. How many ... can you get on your TV?
9. It was a huge scandal and it ... the front page.
10. The latest ... shows an increase in the Prime Minister's popularity.

III. Trouver les réponses aux définitions suivantes :

1. a magazine that is published once a month
2. the period when the number of viewers is at its peak
3. a film or programme that has already been shown
4. an excerpt cut out from a newspaper
5. run by the state
6. a press magnate
7. fully detailed
8. prejudiced
9. shown in instalments at regular intervals
10. to disclose, to make public

25. Transport
Le transport

General Vocabulary

public transport	*les transports en commun*
a means of transport	*un moyen de transport*
a passenger	*un passager*
a ticket	*un billet*
the fare [fɛə]	*le tarif*
a counter	*un comptoir*
a seat [si:]	*un siège, une place*
luggage [‘lʌgidʒ]	*les bagages*
a shuttle	*une navette*
city transport	*les transports urbains*
a vehicle]'vi:ikl]	*un véhicule*
traffic	*la circulation*
speed	*la vitesse*
speeding	*l'excès de vitesse*
an accident, a crash	*un accident*
a casualty [‘kæʒjuəlti]	*une victime*
the mileage [‘mailidʒ]	*le kilométrage*
the consumption	*la consommation*
congestion	*les embouteillages*
a traffic jam	*un embouteillage*
a bus	*un bus*
a bus driver	*un chauffeur de bus*
a bus station	*une gare routière*
a bus conductor	*un contrôleur*
a school bus	*un car scolaire*
a coach [kəutʃ]	*un car*
a tram	*un tram(way)*
the underground (GB)	*le métro*

the subway (US)	*le métro*	crowded, packed	*bondé*
the metro (F)	*le métro*	jammed, congested [kənˈdʒestid]	*embouteillé*
a station	*une station*	punctual	*ponctuel*
a line	*une ligne*	late	*en retard*
a commuter [kəˈmju:tə]	*un navetteur*	regular [ˈregjulə]	*régulier*
commuting	*les migrations journalières*	frequent [ˈfri:kwənt]	*fréquent*
a journey [ˈdʒə:ni]	*un trajet, un voyage*	economical	*économique*
a trip	*un voyage*	free	*gratuit*
departure	*le départ*	unleaded, leadfree	*sans plomb*
arrival	*l'arrivée*	air conditioned	*climatisé*
a delay [diˈlei]	*un retard*	streamlined	*aérodynamique*
a cancellation	*une annulation*	watertight	*étanche*
a map	*une carte*	to take* off	*décoller*
a route [ru:t]	*un itinéraire*	to land	*atterrir (avion), débarquer (bateau)*
a road	*une route*	to load [ləud]	*charger*
a stop	*un arrêt*	to unload	*décharger*
a tunnel	*un tunnel*	to park	*se garer, stationner*
a path	*un sentier*	to back, to reverse	*faire marche arrière*
a track	*une voie, une piste*	to double-park	*se garer en double file*
a waterway	*une voie navigable*	to pull out	*déboîter*
a network	*un réseau*	to overtake*	*doubler*
a link	*une liaison*	to skid	*déraper*
a canal [kəˈnæl]	*un canal*	to overturn	*se retourner*
a river	*un fleuve*	to collide [kəˈlaid]	*entrer en collision*
a bridge	*un pont*	to brake [breik]	*freiner*
a lock	*une écluse*	to slow down	*ralentir*
a barge [ba:dʒ]	*une péniche*	to accelerate	*accélérer*
airborne	*transporté par avion*	to break* down	*tomber en panne*
seaborne	*transporté par bateau*	to maintain	*entretenir*
careful	*prudent*	to service	*réviser*
reliable, [riˈlaiəbl] dependable	*fiable*	to lubricate	*lubrifier*
careless, reckless	*imprudent*	to whistle	*siffler*
hazardous [ˈhæzədəs]	*dangereux*	to pull up	*s'arrêter*
fast	*rapide*	to derail	*dérailler*
slow	*lent*	to climb [klaim]	*grimper*
slippery	*glissant*	to hijack	*détourner*
icy [ˈaisi]	*verglacé*	to crash	*avoir un accident, s'écraser*
comfortable	*confortable*	to steer [stiə]	*gouverner*
restful	*reposant*	to pitch	*tanguer*
tiring [ˈtaiəriŋ]	*fatigant*	to roll	*rouler (navire)*
(to be) seasick	*avoir le mal de mer*	to moor [muə]	*amarrer*
(to be) airsick	*être malade en avion*	to drift	*dériver*
empty	*vide*	to capsize	*chavirer*
vacant [ˈveikənt]	*libre (place)*	to sink*	*couler*
roomy	*spacieux*	to rescue	*sauver*
full	*plein*		

Specialized Vocabulary

Road transport	***Le transport routier***
a car, an automobile	*une voiture*
a sportscar	*une voiture de sport*
a motorist, a car driver	*un automobiliste*
a caravan, a trailer (US)	*une caravane*
a van	*une camionnette*
a lorry, a truck	*un camion*
a removal van	*un camion de déménagement*
a tanker	*un camion-citerne*
a lorry driver, a truckdriver	*un camionneur*
a trucker, a teamster (US)	*un routier*
a trailer	*une remorque*
a juggernaut	*un mastodonte*
haulage [‘hɔ:lidʒ]	*le transport routier*
a make	*une marque*
the engine	*le moteur*
the gearbox	*la boîte de vitesses*
the brakes	*les freins*
the body	*la carrosserie*
a headlight	*un phare avant*
the bonnet, the hood (US)	*le capot*
the windscreen	*le pare-brise*
the steering wheel	*le volant*
the dashboard	*le tableau de bord*
a headrest	*un appui-tête*
the speedometer	*le compteur*
a rear mirror	*un rétroviseur*
a wheel	*une roue*
a tyre / tire (US)	*un pneu*
the spare wheel	*la roue de secours*
the tank	*le réservoir*
petrol, gas (US)	*de l'essence*
the boot, the trunk (US)	*le coffre*
a diversion [dai’və:ʃən]	*une déviation*
roadworks	*un chantier routier*
a bend	*un virage*
a roundabout	*un sens giratoire*
a crossroads	*un croisement, un carrefour*
a junction	*une bifurcation, un carrefour*
a ringroad	*un boulevard périphérique*
a bypass [‘baipa:s]	*une rocade*

a motorway	*une autoroute*
a toll [təul]	*un péage (somme à payer)*
a tollgate	*une barrière de péage*
a highway	*une route à grande circulation*
a lay-by	*une aire de stationnement*
an exit	*une sortie*
a car park	*un parking*
a garage [‘gæra:dʒ]	*un garage*
a mechanic	*un mécanicien*
a service station, a filling station	*une station-service*
Rail transport	*Le transport ferroviaire*
the railways / railroad (US)	*les chemins de fer*
a train station	*une gare*
a railwayman	*un cheminot*
a railway line	*une ligne de chemin de fer*
a track	*une voie*
a rail [reil]	*un rail*
a platform	*un quai*
a subway	*un passage souterrain*
a bookstall, a news stand	*un kiosque*
refreshments	*rafraîchissements, sandwichs, boissons*
a timetable, a schedule	*un horaire*
a connection	*une correspondance*
a train	*un train*
an express train	*un express*
a fast train	*un rapide*
a high speed train	*un TGV*
the engine [‘endʒin]	*la locomotive*
the guard	*le chef de train*
a ticket inspector, a ticket collector	*un contrôleur*
a carriage, a coach	*une voiture*
a dining car, a diner (US)	*un wagon restaurant*
a compartment	*un compartiment*
a corridor	*un couloir*
a window	*une vitre*
a door	*une portière*
the alarm	*le signal d'alarme*
derailment [di’reilmənt]	*le déraillement*

Air transport — *Le transport aérien*

an aeroplane, a plane	*un avion*	takeoff	*le décollage*
an airline	*une compagnie aérienne*	landing	*l'atterrissage*
		a stopover	*une escale*
an aircraft (pl. aircraft)	*un avion, un appareil*	an air ticket	*un billet d'avion*
a helicopter	*un hélicoptère*	the schedule [ʃedju:l], the timetable	*les horaires de vol*
a balloon [bə'lu:n]	*un ballon*		
a jet	*un avion à réaction*	a flight	*un vol*
a jumbo jet	*un gros porteur*	the flight number	*le numéro de vol*
a carrier,	*un avion-cargo,*	a time zone	*un fuseau horaire*
a freighter	*un transporteur*	a crash	*un accident*
the hold	*la soute*	a parachute [pærəʃu:t]	*un parachute*
a propeller	*une hélice*		
a jet engine	*un réacteur*	speed	*la vitesse*
the cockpit	*le poste de pilotage*	an airport	*un aéroport*
the joystick	*le manche à balai*	an air terminal	*un aérogare*
a pilot ['pilət]	*un pilote*	a gate	*une porte*
the crew [kru:]	*l'équipage*	an airfield	*un terrain d'aviation*
a steward [stju:ət]	*un steward*	a runway	*une piste*
an air hostess, a stewardess	*une hôtesse*	the tarmac ['ta:mæk]	*l'aire d'envol*

Sea transport — *Le transport maritime*

a ship	*un navire*	the gangway	*la passerelle d'embarquement*
a shipyard	*un chantier naval*		
a shipbuilder	*un constructeur*	the deck	*le pont*
a shipowner	*un armateur*	a deck-chair	*un transat*
a vessel	*un vaisseau*	a cabin	*une cabine*
a tanker	*un pétrolier*	a porthole	*un hublot*
a supertanker	*un pétrolier géant*	a bunk, a berth	*une couchette*
the cargo	*la cargaison*	a stowaway	*un passager clandestin*
a tug [tʌg]	*un remorqueur*		
a ferry	*un ferry*	a shipwreck	*un naufrage*
a hovercraft	*un aéroglisseur*	a wreck [rek]	*une épave*
a catamaran [ˌkætəmə'ræn]	*un catamaran*	a knot [nɔt]	*un nœud (vitesse)*
		a port	*un port (ville)*
the captain	*le capitaine*	a harbour ['ha:bə]	*un port (installations portuaires)*
a sailor	*un marin*		
the crew	*l'équipage*	a dock	*un bassin*
a crewman	*un membre de l'équipage*	a pier [piə]	*une jetée*
		a quay,	*un quai,*
a flag	*un pavillon*	a wharf [wɔ:f]	*un appontement*
the hull	*la coque*	a lighthouse	*un phare*
the wake	*le sillage*	a container	*un conteneur*
a lifeboat	*une chaloupe de sauvetage*	a warehouse	*un entrepôt*

Expressions

the driving test	*l'examen du permis de conduire*
a driving licence	*un permis de conduire*
a luxury car	*une voiture de luxe*

a car maker	*un constructeur automobile*
a traffic offence	*une infraction*
the road tax (GB)	*la vignette*
a number plate	*une plaque d'immatriculation*
a petrol station, a gas station, a filling station	*une station service*
a seat belt	*une ceinture de sécurité*
the right of way	*la priorité*
a speed limit	*une limitation de vitesse*
heavy traffic	*une circulation dense*
road casualties	*les victimes des accidents de la route*
the death toll	*le nombre des morts*
the road network	*le réseau routier*
a trunk road	*une route principale («nationale»)*
a dual carriageway	*une route à quatre voies*
a service area	*une aire de services*
mileage per gallon (mpg) (GB), gas mileage (US)	*la consommation*
public transport	*les transports en commun*
a double-decker	*un autobus à deux étages*
road haulage	*le transport routier*
handle with care	*fragile / manipuler avec précaution*
a road haulage contractor	*un entrepreneur de transports routiers*
an articulated lorry	*un semi-remorque*
a heavy goods vehicle (HGV)	*un poids lourd*
maintenance costs	*les coûts d'entretien*
a transport café	*un routier (restaurant)*
British Rail (BR)	*la Compagnie des chemins de fer britanniques*
a waiting room	*une salle d'attente*
the entrance hall	*la salle des pas perdus*
the left-luggage office	*la consigne*
a passenger train	*un train de voyageurs*
a reduced-fare ticket	*un billet à tarif réduit*
a full-fare ticket	*un billet plein tarif*
a monthly ticket	*une carte (d'abonnement) mensuelle*
a one-way ticket, a single (ticket)	*un aller simple*
a return (ticket)	*un aller-retour*
a non-smoking compartment	*un compartiment non-fumeurs*
a steam train	*un train à vapeur*
the engine driver	*le mécanicien*
a level crossing	*un passage à niveau*
airport facilities	*les infrastructures de l'aéroport*
the control tower	*la tour de contrôle*
the departure lounge	*la salle d'attente*
the information desk	*le guichet des renseignements*
the registration desk	*le guichet d'enregistrement*
the sound barrier	*le mur du son*
an air pocket	*un trou d'air*
an emergency landing	*un atterrissage forcé*
port facilities	*les installations portuaires*
the port authority	*les autorités portuaires*
a cargo boat	*un cargo*

the merchant navy	*la marine marchande*
to crisscross the seas	*sillonner les mers*
the open sea	*le large*
a round-the-world cruise	*une croisière autour du monde*
to be at the helm	*être au gouvernail*
a convenience flag	*un pavillon de complaisance*

Phrases

In some big cities, road users are locked in perpetual traffic jams.

Dans certaines grandes villes, les usagers de la route restent bloqués dans des embouteillages perpétuels.

In London, some of the Underground stations have to be closed in the rush hour.

À Londres, certaines stations de métro doivent être fermées aux heures de pointe.

One solution to urban traffic congestion is to incite more people to use public transport.

Une des solutions aux encombrements de la circulation urbaine est d'inciter plus de gens à utiliser les transports en commun.

Passengers in the high-speed trains using the Chunnel will travel from London to Paris in three hours.

Les passagers des trains à grande vitesse empruntant le tunnel sous la Manche voyageront de Paris à Londres en trois heures.

In Britain, speed is limited to 70 miles per hour on motorways.

En Grande Bretagne, la vitesse est limitée à 112 km/h sur les autoroutes.

Tragedies are being caused, and lives lost, because seatbelts are not being used.

Le fait de ne pas utiliser la ceinture de sécurité est la cause de tragédies et de pertes de vies humaines.

French lorry drivers brought the traffic to a standstill by blocking the roads into and out of main cities.

Les chauffeurs routiers français ont paralysé la circulation en bloquant les routes d'accès aux grandes villes.

The traffic was diverted because of major road works.

La circulation a été déviée à cause d'importants travaux routiers.

Whenever he sails to Britain, he is seasick.

Chaque fois qu'il va en Grande Bretagne en bateau, il a le mal de mer.

"The crossing will be rather rough and we advise passengers not to go out on deck."

« La traversée va être plutôt agitée et nous conseillons aux passagers de ne pas sortir sur le pont. »

Exercices

I. Compléter les phrases suivantes :

1. As the train was packed, he had to stand in the ... .
2. He lifted the ... to have a look at the engine of his car.
3. The ... indicates the speed at which you are driving.
4. The duty-free shop will open once we have reached the ... sea.
5. Look in your ... mirror before overtaking!
6. Once he is sitting at the ... wheel, he becomes a different man altogether.
7. I think you'd better show your driving ... to that policeman.
8. Double-parking is a traffic ... .
9. You can put your suitcases on the ... rack.
10. The death ... on French roads has dramatically increased lately.

II. What vehicle is it?

1. a public motor vehicle for long runs.
2. a ship which transports oil.
3. it moves along on a cushion of compressed air.
4. a sailing vessel with two hulls.
5. it flies thanks to rotating rotors.
6. a small boat used for towing.
7. a freighter used on canals.
8. a vehicle designed to be towed by another.
9. an aircraft supported by a large envelope of gas.
10. a locomotive.

III. Former dix paires :

a wheel, icy, a quay, jammed, a crossroads, a trucker, a tyre, a carriage, an accident, a teamster, slippery, a carrier, a truck, a coach, a crash, a roundabout, a lorry, congested, a wharf, a freighter.

VII. SOCIAL INSTITUTIONS

26. Education
L'éducation

Pre-school education (age 3-5) ***L'enseignement préscolaire***

a day nursery, a day-care centre	*une crèche*	a playschool, a playgroup	*une garderie*
a nursery rhyme	*une comptine*	a nursery school	*une école maternelle*

Secondary education (age 5-18) ***L'enseignement secondaire***

-in the US:

compulsory education	*l'enseignement obligatoire (sa durée varie selon les états; elle commence entre 5 et 8 ans et se termine entre 16 et 18 ans)*
kindergarten (age 5-6)	≈ *maternelle*
elementary school (age 6-11) (grade 1 to grade 5)	≈ *école élémentaire (primaire)*
junior high school (ou Middle School) (age 11-14) (grade 6 to grade 8)	≈ *collège d'enseignement secondaire*
high school (age 14-18) (grade 9 to grade 12)	≈ *lycée*
high school graduation	≈ *baccalauréat (diplôme de fin d'études secondaires)*

-in the UK:

compulsory education	*l'enseignement obligatoire (de 5 à 16 ans)*
infant school (age 5-7)	≈ *école primaire*
junior school (age 7-11)	≈ *école primaire*
secondary school (11-16) (form 1 to 5)	≈ *collège d'enseignement secondaire*
GCSE (General Certificate of Secondary Education) = a set of single-subject examinations	≈ *certificat d'enseignement secondaire (il s'agit d'un ensemble d'épreuves distinctes par discipline ; les élèves en passent généralement entre 5 et 10)*
secondary school (lower sixth and upper sixth) or sixth-form college (16-18)	≈ *lycée (première et terminale)*
"AS" levels (advanced subsidiary) / "A" levels (advanced) (also officially called CGE-AS and CGE-A) (CGE=General Certificate of Education)	≈ *baccaulauréat (diplôme de fin d'études secondaires) (comme les GCSEs, ce sont des épreuves monodisplinaires ; les élèves en passent généralement 3 ; les « AS » se passent en fin de première année (ou sous forme modulaire), et sont une étape pour l'obtention des « A » levels)*

Note : l'appellation des établissements d'enseignement secondaire (« secondary schools ») *est variable, (quelques exemples :* « Cardiff High School », « Wilmington Hall School », « Bexley Grammar School » – : *les* « grammar schools » *pratiquent généralement une sélection plus ou moins sévère et ne sont pas nécessairement mixtes*: « Sutton Coldfield Grammar School for Girls », « Queen Elizabeth's Grammar School for Boys »). « Scarborough Sixth Form College » *fait partie des quelque cent établissements de ce type en Angleterre et au Pays de Galles actuellement.*

Higher education — *L'enseignement supérieur*

a university [ˌju:'vɜ:siti]	*une université*
a faculty ['fækəlti]	*une faculté*
a department	*un département*
a medical school	*une faculté de médecine*
a faculty of Arts	*une faculté de lettres*
an engineering college ['kɔlidʒ]	*une école d'ingénieurs*
a business school	*une école de commerce*
a law [lɔ:] school	*une faculté de droit*
a diploma [di'pləumə]	*un diplôme*
a degree in science, a science degree	*une licence de sciences*
an Arts degree [di'gri:]	*une licence ès lettres*
a Master's degree	*une maîtrise*
a doctor's degree, a doctorate	*un doctorat*
a Bachelor of Arts ['bætʃələ]	*un licencié ès* (B.A.) *lettres*
a Bachelor of Science (B.Sc.)	*un licencié ès sciences*
a Master of Arts Science (M.Sc.)	*un titulaire* (M.A.)/ *d'une maîtrise ès lettres / sciences*
a Doctor of Law / Science / etc.	*un docteur en droit / sciences / etc.*
a Doctor of Philosophy (PhD)	*un titulaire d'un doctorat d'état*

Schooling — *La scolarité*

a schoolboy, a schoolgirl	*un écolier, une écolière*
a schoolmate	*un (une) camarade d'école*
a pal	*un copain, une copine*
a student	*un étudiant*
a pupil ['pju:pl]	*un élève*
a timetable	*un emploi du temps*
a lesson	*une leçon*
a class	*un cours*
a period ['piəriəd]	*une heure (de cours)*
a break	*une récréation*
lunch break	*la pause de midi*
a form (division)	*une classe*
a level	*un niveau*
tuition [tju:'iʃən] fees	*les frais de scolarité*
a state grant	*une bourse d'état*
a scholarship	*une bourse universitaire (sur concours)*
a mark	*une note*
the average ['ævəridʒ]	*la moyenne*
a school report	*un bulletin scolaire*
a grade sheet (US)	*un relevé de notes*
a school record	*un dossier scolaire*
an exercise ['eksəsaiz]	*un exercice*
a school paper	*un devoir*
an essay ['esei]	*une composition, une dissertation*
a test	*une épreuve*
a proficiency test	*un test de niveau*
an examination, an exam	*un examen*
an exam paper	*une copie*
a bully ['buli]	*une petite brute, une « terreur »*
a school outing	*une sortie scolaire*
a schoolbus	*un car de ramassage scolaire*
school attendance	*scolarisation*
absenteeism, truancy	*l'absentéisme*

Types of schools — *Différents types d'écoles*

a private school	*une école privée*
a state school	*une école publique*
a public school (US)	*une école publique*
a Public School (GB)	*un grand collège (privé)*
a day school	*un externat*
a boarding school	*un internat*
a boarder ['bɔ:də]	*un interne*
a day pupil	*un externe*

School subjects — *Les matières scolaires*

the curriculum, [kə'rikjuləm] the syllabus	*le programme*
foreign languages ['fɔrin]	*les langues étrangères*
modern languages	*les langues vivantes*
classical languages	*les langues mortes*
Greek	*le grec*
Latin	*le latin*
literature ['litəritʃə]	*la littérature*
grammar	*la grammaire*
spelling	*l'orthographe*
religious instruction	*l'instruction religieuse*
history ['histəri]	*l'histoire*
geography [dʒi'ɔgrəfi]	*la géographie*
economics	*l'économie*

science	*les sciences*
biology	*la biologie*
geology	*la géologie*
zoology	*la zoologie*
botany	*la botanique*
physics	*la physique*
chemistry ['kemistri]	*la chimie*
mathematics (maths)	*les mathématiques (les maths)*
algebra ['ældʒibrə]	*l'algèbre*
geometry [dʒi'ɔmetri]	*la géométrie*
technology	*la technologie*
drawing ['drɔ:iŋ]	*le dessin*
engineering drawing	*le dessin industriel*
painting	*la peinture*
philosophy	*la philosophie*
metaphysics	*la métaphysique*
music	*la musique*
singing	*le chant*
physical training (P.T.)	*l'éducation* (P.T.) *physique*
handicrafts	*les travaux manuels*
domestic science	*l'économie ménagère*
citizenship	*l'éducation civique*

The school year — *L'année scolaire*

a semester	*un semestre*
a term [tə:m]	*un trimestre*
half-term	*congé de mi-trimestre*
holidays, a vacation (US)	*des vacances*
the Christmas holidays	*les vacances de Noël*
the Easter Holidays	*les vacances de Pâques*
the summer holidays	*les grandes vacances*

The staff — *Le personnel*

the headmaster / headmistress	*le directeur, la directrice (le principal, le proviseur)*
a deputy headmaster / headmistress	*le sous-directeur / la directrice (l'adjoint(e), le censeur)*
the board of governors	≈ *le conseil d'établissement*
a teacher	*un enseignant*
the teaching profession	*le corps enseignant*
a primary-school teacher	*un instituteur, une institutrice*
a secondary-school teacher	*un professeur de l'enseignement secondaire*
an English teacher	*un professeur d'anglais*
a form master	≈ *un professeur principal*
a school librarian	*un documentaliste*
an inspector	*un inspecteur*
a lecturer ['lekʃərə]	*un maître-assistant*
a tutor ['tju:tə]	*un directeur d'études*
a senior lecturer, a reader	*un maître de conférence*
a professor	*un professeur (d'université)*
a head of department	*un directeur de département*
a dean	*un doyen*
a president	*un président*

The premises — *Les locaux*

the school buildings	*les bâtiments scolaires*
the staffroom	*la salle des professeurs*
the head's office	*le bureau du principal, du proviseur*
a classroom	*une salle de classe*
a desk	*un bureau, un pupitre*
the board	*le tableau*
chalk [tʃɔ:k]	*de la craie*
a piece of chalk	*un morceau de craie*
a duster ['dʌstə]	*un tampon effaceur*
a playing-field, a sportsground	*un terrain de sports*
a playground	*une cour de récréation*
a gymnasium	*un gymnase*
a cloakroom	*un vestiaire*
a laboratory, a lab	*un laboratoire*
a language laboratory	*un laboratoire de langues*
a booth [bu:ð]	*une cabine*
a tape-recorder	*un magnétophone*
a dining-hall	*un réfectoire*
a dormitory	*un dortoir*
a library ['laibrəri]	*une bibliothèque, un C.D.I.*
a bookcase	*une bibliothèque (meuble)*
shelves (a shelf)	*des étagères*
a workshop	*un atelier*

School materials	***Le matériel scolaire***
a satchel, a schoolbag	*un cartable*
a copybook, an exercise-book	*un cahier*
a textbook	*un manuel*
a jotter	*un cahier de brouillon*
a jotting-pad	*un bloc-notes*
a notebook	*un carnet*
a diary ['daiəri]	*un agenda*
a sheet	*une feuille*
drawing-paper	*du papier à dessin*
a pencil-case	*une trousse*
a pencil ['pensl]	*un crayon*
a pencil-sharpener	*un taille-crayon*
a fountain-pen	*un stylo*
a ball-point pen	*un stylo-bille*
a biro ['baiərəu]	*un bic*
a felt-tip pen	*un feutre*
a ruler ['ru:lə]	*une règle*
an eraser, a rubber	*une gomme*
compasses, a pair of compasses	*un compa*
a square	*une équerre*
a protractor	*un rapporteur*
a stapler	*une agrafeuse*
a paper clip	*un trombone*
glue [glu:]	*de la colle*
a box of paints	*une boîte de peinture*
a brush	*un pinceau*
clever, intelligent, bright	*intelligent*
gifted ['giftid], brainy	*doué*
outstanding	*brillant*
sharp	*à l'esprit vif*
hard-working	*bûcheur*
painstaking	*sérieux, appliqué*
obedient [ə'bi:djənt]	*obéissant*
pliable ['plaiəbl]	*docile*
quiet, still	*tranquille, sage*
illiterate [i'litərit]	*analphabète*
backward	*arriéré*
dumb [dʌm]	*bête, nigaud*
stupid, foolish, silly	*stupide, bête*
dull [dʌl]	*peu doué*
absent-minded	*distrait*
passive	*passif*
careless	*négligent*
untidy	*sans soin*
talkative	*bavard*
disruptive	*perturbateur*
restless	*agité*
bad	*mauvais*
poor [puə]	*insuffisant*
tolerable	*passable*
fair	*assez bien*
good	*satisfaisant*

very good	*très bien*
excellent	*excellent*
lenient ['li:njənt]	*indulgent*
strict	*sévère*
to teach*	*enseigner*
to lecture	*faire une conférence, un cours (univ.)*
to learn*	*apprendre*
to memorize	*mémoriser, apprendre par cœur*
to study	*étudier*
to enrol	*s'inscrire*
to graduate	*obtenir un diplôme*
to pass [pa:s]	*être reçu à un examen*
to fail [feil]	*échouer*
to train	*former*
to head	*diriger*
to research	*faire de la recherche*
to understand*	*comprendre*
to puzzle	*laisser perplexe*
to mean*	*signifier, vouloir dire*
to listen	*écouter*
to ask	*demander*
to check	*vérifier*
to answer	*répondre*
to repeat [ri'pi:t]	*répéter*
to remark [ri'ma:k]	*faire remarquer*
to observe [əb'zə:v]	*faire observer*
to obey [ə'bei]	*obéir*
to behave oneself	*bien se conduire*
to dream*	*rêver*
to talk [tɔ:k]	*parler*
to chat	*bavarder*
to fidget	*s'agiter*
to disrupt	*perturber*
to giggle ['gigl]	*pouffer de rire*
to cheat [tʃi:t]	*tricher*
to shut* up	*se taire*
to scold, to tell* off	*réprimander*
to punish	*punir*
to expel [iks'pel]	*mettre à la porte*
to suspend	*exclure*
to reward [ri'wɔ:d]	*récompenser*
to deserve [di'zə:v]	*mériter*
to improve	*s'améliorer*
to write* down	*noter, mettre par écrit*
to scribble	*griffonner, gribouiller*
to spell*	*épeler, orthographier*
to read*	*lire*
to recite	*réciter*
to sum up	*résumer*
to sing*	*chanter*
to paint	*peindre*

to draw*	*dessiner*	to add up	*additionner*
to wipe	*effacer (le tableau)*	to multiply	*multiplier*
to erase, [i'reiz] to rub out	*effacer, gommer*	to subtract	*soustraire*
		to divide	*diviser*
to count	*compter*	to solve	*résoudre*

Expressions

compulsory school attendance	*scolarité obligatoire*
school leaving age	*âge de fin de scolarité*
academic standards	*le niveau des études*
to meet pupils' needs	*répondre aux besoins des élèves*
to achieve high academic standards	*avoir un niveau d'études élevé*
to raise the school leaving age	*prolonger la scolarité*
to enrol in a university	*s'inscrire dans une faculté*
to enrol for a course	*s'inscrire à un cours*
to win a scholarship	*obtenir une bourse universitaire (par concours)*
to go on to higher education	*poursuivre ses études*
to go to university, to go to college	*faire des études supérieures*
school leavers	*jeunes gens qui ont terminé leurs études secondaires*
to be fresh from school	*être frais émoulu de l'école*
to drop out of school	*abandonner ses études*
to drop a subject	*abandonner une matière*
to be a low achiever	*être en situation d'échec scolaire*
to play truant	*faire l'école buissonnière, «sécher» les cours*
to be late	*être en retard*
to take one's seat	*prendre place, s'asseoir*
to be a chatterbox	*être bavard, être une pipelette*
to disrupt the class	*perturber le cours*
to be punished for chattering	*être puni pour bavardage*
to be reported to the head	*être signalé au directeur*
to be well-educated	*avoir une bonne instruction*
to be self-educated	*être autodidacte*
to sit an exam, to take an exam	*se présenter à un examen*
to pass an exam	*réussir à un examen*
to fail an exam	*échouer à un examen*
an examination board	*un comité chargé de l'organisation des examens nationaux*
to do one's homework	*faire ses devoirs*
to learn by heart	*apprendre par cœur*
to revise for an exam	*réviser un examen*
to read over one's lessons	*revoir ses leçons*
to look up a word in a dictionary	*chercher un mot dans le dictionnaire*
to get an average mark	*obtenir une note moyenne*
to get fifteen out of twenty	*avoir quinze sur vingt*
to make progress	*progresser*
to have an English class	*avoir cours d'anglais*

to have a free period	*avoir une heure d'étude*
to drill students in maths	*faire faire des exercices de maths aux élèves*
to read law at Oxford	*étudier le droit à Oxford*
to lecture in law	*être professeur de droit*
to graduate from high school (US)	*terminer ses études au lycée*
to graduate from Oxford	*être diplômé d'Oxford*

Phrases

Far too many young blacks drop out of high school in the States.
Beaucoup trop de jeunes noirs quittent le lycée avant la fin de leurs études aux États Unis.

If you don't know what that word means, look it up in the dictionary.
Si tu ne sais pas ce que veut dire ce mot, cherche-le dans le dictionnaire.

He's got a degree in Arts and hopes to get his Master's next year.
Il a une licence de lettres et espère obtenir sa maîtrise l'année prochaine.

After winning a scholarship, he went to Cambridge to read law.
Après avoir obtenu une bourse, il est allé étudier le droit à Cambridge.

Tuition fees are very high in French business colleges.
Les frais de scolarité sont très élevés dans les écoles de commerce françaises.

The teacher called the roll and realized John was skipping classes once more.
Le professeur fit l'appel et se rendit compte que John séchait les cours une fois de plus.

He was not given the job because his academic qualifications were too low.
On ne lui donna pas le poste parce qu'il n'avait pas suffisamment de diplômes universitaires.

He is an entirely self-educated man and is very knowledgeable on many topics.
C'est un autodictate complet et il sait beaucoup de choses sur de nombreux sujets.

Mathematics is far from being my favourite subject!
Les maths sont loin d'être ma matière préférée !

The latest cut in grants will mean fewer students going into higher education.
La dernière réduction des bourses va entraîner une diminution du nombre d'étudiants dans le supérieur.

Exercices

I. Retrouver les phrases en remettant les mots dans le bon ordre :

1. never / don't / your / will / if / of / improve / make / results / an / effort / more / you
2. went / Oxford / teaching / after / he / graduating / into / from / the / profession

3. lower / teachers / getting / many / standards / lower / that / claim / are / and
4. 'O' levels / their / British / end / take / students / the / of / at / form 5
5. eighteen / outstanding / rule / pupil / as / twenty / this / a / out of / gets
6. teaching / complain / often / students / too / far / some / theoretical / is / that
7. having / he / heart / dislikes / things / learn / by /to
8. extra / expelled / was / from / John / classroom / some / given / and / the / work
9. with / a lot/ he / catch / has / homework /up / to / of
10. streets / unemployed / must / the / kept / off / teenagers / be

II. Trouver un synonyme :

1. to tell off 2. to go to university 3. to rub out 4. a grade sheet 5. foolish 6. a reader 7. to sit an exam 8. a satchel 9. a playing-field 10. a day-care center

III. Traduire :

1. *Il fut mis à la porte pour avoir perturbé le cours.*
2. *Quel est l'âge de fin de scolarité en France ?*
3. *Il apprend toujours ses leçons par cœur.*
4. *Il avait revu sa leçon, mais il n'a obtenu qu'une note moyenne.*
5. *C'est un bûcheur, mais il n'est pas très bon.*
6. *Il est bon en sciences, mais ses résultats en maths sont insuffisants.*
7. *Conduisez-vous correctement ou je vais vous signaler au directeur !*
8. *Il est très distrait et n'arrête pas de rêver.*
9. *Il a échoué à son examen et n'a pu s'inscrire dans une faculté.*
10. *Nous avons une heure d'étude après le cours d'anglais.*

27. Law
La loi

1. Law and order — ***L'ordre public***

a police station	*un commissariat*
a policeman	*un agent de police*
a policewoman	*une femme-agent*
a traffic warden	*un(e) contractuel(le)*
a cop, a bobby	*un « flic »*
a constable (GB)	*un agent, un gardien de la paix*
a police officer	*un policier*
a police inspector	*un inspecteur de police*
a detective	*un policier en civil*
a private detective, a private eye	*un détective privé*
a superintendent	*un commissaire*
a squad [skwɔd]	*une brigade*
the drugs squad	*la brigade des stupéfiants*
the crime squad	*la brigade criminelle*
a raid [reid]	*une descente*
a patrol car	*une voiture de police*

a Black Maria [mə'riə]	*un fourgon cellulaire*
handcuffs	*des menottes*
a rubber bullet ['bulit]	*une balle en caoutchouc*
the riot police ['raiət]	*la police anti-émeute*
a truncheon, a baton ['bætən]	*une matraque*
a riot shield	*un bouclier*
a helmet	*un casque*
tear gas [tiə]	*du gaz lacrymogène*
a fingerprint	*une empreinte*
a breathalyser	*un alcootest*
a clue [klu:]	*un indice*
a lead	*une piste*
an arrest [ə'rest]	*une arrestation*
a fine	*une amende*
a ticket	*une contravention, un P.V.*
an investigation, an inquiry	*une enquête*
evidence	*des preuves*
a piece of evidence	*une preuve*

2. Lawbreakers — *Ceux qui ne respectent pas la loi*

the underworld	*la pègre, le milieu*
the Mafia, the mob the Syndicate	*la Mafia*
organized crime	*le grand banditisme*
the crime syndicate	*le syndicat du crime*
an offender	*un contrevenant*
a criminal	*un criminel*
an accomplice	*un complice*
an outlaw ['autlɔ:]	*un hors-la-loi*
a delinquent	*un délinquant*
a hooligan	*un voyou*
a vandal	*un vandale*
a looter ['lu:tə]	*un pillard*
a thug [θʌg]	*un casseur*
a mugger	*un agresseur*
a thief [θi:f]	*un voleur*
a robber	*un voleur (à main armée)*
a burglar ['bə:glə]	*un cambrioleur*
a pickpocket	*un voleur à la tire*
a shoplifter	*un voleur à l'étalage*
a crook, a swindler	*un escroc*
a blackmailer	*un maître-chanteur*
a forger ['fɔ:dʒə]	*un faussaire*
a tax evader [i'veidə]	*un fraudeur fiscal*
a smuggler	*un contrebandier, un trafiquant*
a drug peddler, a drug pusher	*un revendeur*
a drug addict	*un toxicomane*
a prostitute	*un(e) prostitué(e)*
a kidnapper	*un ravisseur*
a hostage ['hɔstidʒ]	*un otage*
a hijacker ['hai,dʒækə]	*un pirate de l'air*
a hacker	*un pirate informatique*
a terrorist	*un terroriste*
an arsonist	*un pyromane*
a gang	*une bande*
a gangster	*un gangster*
a mobster	*un mafioso*
a murderer, a killer	*un meurtrier, un assassin*
a serial killer	*un tueur en série*
a sex offender	*un délinquant sexuel*
a paedophile	*un pédophile*
a rapist ['reipist]	*un violeur*
a victim	*une victime*
a traitor	*un traître*
a spy	*un espion*

3. Criminal offences — *Les délits*

an offence	*un délit, une infraction*
a crime [kraim]	*un crime*
crime	*la criminalité*
petty crime	*la petite criminalité*
serious crime	*la grande criminalité*
delinquency	*la délinquance*
a theft [θeft]	*un vol*
a motive	*un mobile*
shoplifting	*le vol à l'étalage*
armed robbery	*vol (attaque) à main armée*
a hold-up	*un hold-up, un braquage*
a kidnapping, an abduction	*un enlèvement*
hostage taking	*la prise d'otages*
a ransom	*une rançon*
a mugging	*une agression*
a burglary	*un cambriolage*
forgery	*contrefaçon*
blackmail	*le chantage*
a bribe	*un pot-de-vin*
tax evasion	*la fraude fiscale*

insider trading	*le délit d'initié (bourse)*
a hijacking	*un détournement d'avion*
hacking	*le piratage informatique*
embezzlement	*détournement de fonds*
speeding	*excès de vitesse*
drinking and driving	*conduite en état d'ébriété*
drug trafficking	*le trafic de drogue*
drug abuse [ə'bju:s]	*l'usage de stupéfiants*
an overdose	*une overdose*
laundering	*le blanchiment*
infanticide	*l'infanticide*
incest	*l'inceste*
sexual harassment	*le harcèlement sexuel*
a rape	*un viol*
a murder ['mə:də]	*un meurtre*
manslaughter	*homicide involontaire*
an assassination	*un assassinat (politique)*
a shooting	*une fusillade*
a slaughter ['slɔ:tə]	*un massacre*
lynching	*le lynchage*
a weapon ['wepən]	*une arme*
a permit	*un permis*
a gun	*une arme à feu*
a handgun	*un pistolet*
a rifle	*une carabine*
a knife [naif]	*un couteau*
a flick knife	*un cran d'arrêt*

4. Justice — *La justice*

the legal profession	*les hommes de loi*
a lawyer ['lɔ:jə]	*un homme de loi*
a solicitor	*un notaire, un avocat, un juriste*
a judge, a justice	*un juge*
a magistrate	*un magistrat*
the defense counsel	*l'avocat de la* (US) *défense*
the defending counsel (GB)	*l'avocat de la défense*
the public prosecutor	*le procureur*
the prosecuting attorney (US), thecounsel for theprosecution (GB)	*l'avocat général*
a coroner	*un médecin légiste*
a forensic laboratory	*un laboratoire médico-légal*
a court [kɔ:t]	*un tribunal*
the court room	*la salle d'audience*
caselaw	*la jurisprudence*
civil law [lɔ:]	*le code civil*
the penal code	*le code pénal*
a trial, a lawsuit	*un procès*
a case [keis]	*une affaire*
a jury ['dʒuəri]	*un jury*
a juror	*un juré*
a witness	*un témoin*
a court hearing	*une audience*
a charge	*un chef d'accusation*
a testimony	*un témoignage*
an oath [əuθ]	*un serment*
the defendant, the accused	*l'accusé*
a verdict	*un verdict*
a sentence	*une condamnation*
damages ['dæmidʒiz]	*dommages-intérêts*
probation	*liberté surveillée*
clemency	*la clémence*
an acquittal	*un acquittement*
a death sentence	*une condamnation à mort*
the death penalty, capital punishment	*la peine de mort*
the electric chair ("Old Smoky")	*la chaise électrique*
the gallows	*la potence*
a lethal [li:θəl] injection	*une injection mortelle*
a firing squad	*un peloton d'exécution*
a gas chamber	*une chambre à gaz*
a deterrent	*un moyen de dissuasion*
a prison, a jail, [dʒeil] a gaol	*une prison*
a convict, an inmate	*un détenu*
a cell	*une cellule*
a prison guard (US), a prison warder (GB)	*un gardien de prison*
lawful, legal	*légal, licite*
lawless	*sans loi, anarchique*
illegal, unlawful	*illégal*
criminal	*criminel, délictueux*
prohibited, banned	*interdit*
compulsory, mandatory	*obligatoire*
innocent	*innocent*
guilty	*coupable*
respectful	*respectueux*
sane	*sain d'esprit*
insane	*dément*
honest ['ɔnist]	*honnête*
dishonest	*malhonnête*
safe	*sûr, sans danger*
unsafe	*dangereux*

strict	*sévère, rigoureux*
tough	*dur, sévère*
true	*vrai*
untrue	*faux, erroné*
fair	*juste*
unfair	*injuste*
evil, malevolent, wicked [‘wikid]	*mauvais, malfaisant*
violent	*violent*
wilful	*délibéré, prémédité*
deceitful [di’si:tful]	*trompeur, fourbe*
cunning	*rusé, malin*
shady	*louche*
crooked [‘krukid]	*malhonnête*
dubious [‘dju:biəs]	*douteux, suspect*
suspect, suspicious	*suspect*
disreputable	*de mauvaise réputation*
depraved	*dépravé, perverti*
hardened	*endurci*
abusive	*injurieux, grossier*
shameful	*honteux*
revolting	*révoltant*
shocking	*choquant*
degrading	*dégradant*
vicious	*malveillant, brutal*
atrocious	*atroce*
outrageous	*scandaleux, monstrueux*
bloody	*sanglant*
beastly	*bestial, brutal*
cruel [‘kru:əl]	*cruel*
ruthless [‘ru:θlis]	*cruel, sans pitié*
guilty	*coupable*
innocent	*innocent*
(un)fair	*(in)juste*
tough [tʌf]	*dur, sévère*
lenient [‘li:njənt]	*clément*
to pass	*voter, faire passer*
to implement	*appliquer*
to enforce	*faire respecter*
to prove	*prouver*
to deter [di’tə:]	*dissuader*
to prevent	*prévenir, empêcher*
to investigate	*enquêter*
to chase [dʃeis]	*poursuivre*
to track	*pister*
to hunt down	*traquer*
to search	*fouiller*
to fine	*frapper d’une amende*
to breathalyse	*soumettre à l’alcootest*
to book	*dresser procès-verbal à*
to surrender	*se rendre*
to arrest [ə’rest]	*arrêter*
to strip search	*fouiller au corps*
to club	*matraquer*

to beat* up	*tabasser*
to abuse [ə’bju:s]	*maltraiter*
to torture	*torturer*
to sue, to prosecute	*poursuivre en justice*
to judge, to try	*juger*
to examine, to question	*interroger*
to confess	*avouer*
to witness	*être le témoin de*
to testify	*témoigner, faire une déposition*
to defend	*défendre*
to plead	*plaider*
to appeal	*faire appel*
to rule	*décider*
to suspend	*suspendre*
to convict	*déclarer coupable*
to condemn, to sentence	*condamner*
to acquit	*acquitter*
to amnesty	*amnistier*
to pardon	*gracier*
to bail	*mettre en liberté sous caution*
to imprison, to jail	*emprisonner*
to lock up	*mettre sous les verrous*
to release, to set* free	*relâcher, libérer*
to execute	*exécuter*
to behead [bi’hed]	*décapiter*
to hang* someone	*pendre quelqu’un*
to shoot* someone	*fusiller quelqu’un*
to steal*	*voler*
to escape (from)	*s’échapper (de)*
to break* into	*pénétrer par effraction*
to burglarize	*cambrioler*
to bribe	*corrompre*
to swindle	*escroquer*
to blackmail	*faire chanter*
to spy (on)	*espionner*
to betray	*trahir*
to forge	*contrefaire*
to smuggle	*faire la contrebande de*
to vandalize	*saccager*
to mug, [mʌg] to assault	*agresser*
to rape	*violer*
to loot [lu:t]	*piller*
to blow up*	*faire sauter, faire exploser*
to stab	*poignarder*
to kill	*tuer*
to murder	*assassiner*
to assassinate [ə’sæsineit]	*assassiner (politique)*

Expressions

to abide by the law	*respecter la loi*
law-abiding citizens	*les citoyens respectueux de la loi*
the law of the jungle	*la loi de la jungle*
to take the law into one's own hands	*(se) faire justice soi-même*
to join the police force	*entrer dans la police*
police harassment	*le harcèlement policier*
a police blunder	*une bavure policière*
a strip search	*une fouille corporelle*
a plain-clothes policeman	*un policier en civil*
to launch an investigation	*ouvrir une enquête*
to be on duty	*être en service*
to be off duty	*ne pas être en service*
in the course of duty	*en service commandé*
to be on police files	*être fiche par la police*
an identity card	*une carte d'identité*
a forged passport	*un faux passeport*
to be caught red-handed	*être pris la main dans le sac, en flagrant délit*
to steal something from someone, to rob someone of something	*voler quelque chose à quelqu'un*
to give oneself up	*se rendre*
to take someone hostage	*prendre quelqu'un en otage*
to take someone prisoner	*faire prisonnier*
the Metropolitan Police	*la police londonienne*
New York Police Department (NYPD)	*la police de New York*
the Intelligence Service (GB)	*les services secrets*
the Federal Bureau of Investigation (US)	*le FBI*
the Central Intelligence Agency	*la CIA*
the DEA (Drug Enforcement Administration) (US), the drugs squad (GB)	*la brigade des stupéfiants*
the immigration authorities	*les services d'immigration*
to have a long criminal record	*avoir un casier judiciaire chargé*
not to have a criminal record	*avoir un casier judiciaire vierge*
to go to law	*recourir à la justice*
to take a case to law	*porter une affaire devant les tribunaux*
to bring someone before a court	*intenter un procès à quelqu'un*
to stand trial	*passer en jugement*
to appear before court	*comparaître*
to take the oath	*prêter serment*
to give evidence	*témoigner*
to question a witness	*interroger un témoin*
to charge someone with something, to indict someone for something	*inculper quelqu'un de quelque chose*
to accuse someone of something	*accuser quelqu'un de quelque chose*
in someone's defence	*à la décharge de quelqu'un*
extenuating circumstances	*circonstances atténuantes*
to be in the dock	*être sur le banc des accusés*
to be convicted of	*être reconnu coupable de*
to plead guilty	*plaider coupable*
to plead not guilty	*plaider non coupable*
a strong body of evidence	*une forte accumulation de preuves*
to be put on probation	*être mis en liberté surveillée*
to be on remand	*être en détention préventive*

to release on bail	*relâcher sous caution*
a 10-year prison sentence	*une condamnation à 10 ans de prison*
to send someone to jail for 5 years	*condamner quelqu'un à 5 ans de prison*
to sentence someone to death	*condamner quelqu'un à mort*
to serve a prison sentence	*purger une peine de prison*
a life sentence	*une condamnation à perpétuité*
solitary confinement	*réclusion*
death row (US)	*le quartier des condamnés à mort*
to break out of jail	*s'évader de prison*

Phrases

No person, for any reason, may be denied the protection of the law.
On ne peut refuser à quiconque, pour quelque raison que ce soit, la protection de la justice.

The prosecuting attorney presents the case against the accused.
Le procureur général présente les charges contre l'accusé.

The accused was found guilty of armed robbery and sentenced to ten years' imprisonment.
L'accusé a été jugé coupable de vol à main armée et condamné à dix ans de prison.

Although there was a strong body of evidence against him, he pleaded not guilty.
Bien qu'il y eût des preuves accablantes contre lui, il plaida non coupable.

Witnesses must take the oath before giving evidence.
Les témoins doivent prêter serment avant de témoigner.

Studies have never found anything to suggest that capital punishment deters murderers better than the prospect of long prison terms.
Les études n'ont jamais rien trouvé qui puisse laisser penser que la peine capitale soit un meilleur moyen de dissuasion que les longues peines d'emprisonnement.

Fear is behind the advocacy of the death penalty.
C'est la peur qui pousse les gens à défendre la peine de mort.

Someone once said that one street lamp was worth more than six policemen.
Quelqu'un a dit un jour qu'un lampadaire valait mieux que six agents de police.

He was caught red-handed as he was trying to leave the shop with stolen goods.
On le prit la main dans le sac alors qu'il tentait de quitter le magasin avec des marchandises volées.

He lost his driving licence after being convicted of drunken driving.
On lui a retiré son permis de conduire après avoir été reconnu coupable de conduite en état d'ébriété..

Exercices

I. Retrouver les prépositions :

1. Someone broke ... his house and stole his paintings.
2. The convicts managed to escape ... the prison.
3. This Japanese was accused of spying ... American firms.
4. After hearing the evidence, the judge charged him ... murder.
5. My parents always told me I should abide ... the law.

6. When he is ... duty, he wears a uniform.
7. He was put ... probation before standing trial.
8. No one understands how they succeeded in breaking ... of jail.
9. They should not have taken the law ... their own hands.
10. The pickpocket stole his wallet ... him.

II. Traduire en français les extraits suivants de la constitution américaine :

The fifth amendment forbids trial for a major crime except after indictment by a grand jury. It prohibits repeated trials for the same offence, forbids punishment without due process of law and provides that an accused person may not be compelled to testify against himself.

The sixth amendment of the American Constitution guarantees speedy trial for criminal offences. It requires trial by an unbiased jury, guarantees legal counsel for the accused and provides that witnesses shall be compelled to attend the trial and testify in presence of the accused.

The seventh assures trial by jury in civil cases involving anything valued at more than $20.

The eighth forbids excessive bail or fines, and cruel or unusual punishment.

III. What is the offence called?

1. stealing something
2. stealing goods that are on display in a store
3. unauthorized entry into someone else's computer system
4. killing someone
5. forcing someone to make a payment of money for not disclosing some facts
6. giving someone money in order to get him to do something
7. forcing a pilot to change routes
8. being at the wheel when you have drunk too much
9. trying to cheat the Inland Revenue
10. smuggling and selling drugs

28. Government and politics
Le gouvernement et la politique

Political institutions Les institutions politiques

a country	*un pays*	homeland	*la patrie*
a nation	*une nation*	a democracy	*une démocratie*
a state	*un État*	freedom	*la liberté*
a major power	*une grande puissance*	a republic	*une république*

a dictatorship	*une dictature*
a dictator [dik'teitə]	*un dictateur*
totalitarianism	*le totalitarisme*
nationalism	*le nationalisme*
isolatonism	*l'isolationnisme*
ideology [ˌaidi'ɔlədʒi]	*l'idéologie*
propaganda	*la propagande*
tyranny ['tirəni]	*la tyrannie*
a tyrant ['taiərənt]	*un tyran*
a police state	*un état policier*
centralization	*la centralisation*
a monopoly	*un monopole*
a monarchy ['mɔnəki]	*une monarchie*
a kingdom	*un royaume*
a monarch	*un monarque*
sovereignty	*la souveraineté*
a sovereign ['sɔvrin]	*un souverain*
a king	*un roi*
a queen	*une reine*
a prince	*un prince*
a princess	*une princesse*
a crown [kraun]	*une couronne*
a throne	*un trône*
a coronation	*un couronnement*
a reign	*un règne*
a statesman	*un homme d'état*
diplomacy	*la diplomatie*
a diplomat	*un diplomate*
an embassy	*une ambassade*
an ambassador	*un ambassadeur*
a citizen	*un citoyen*
a census ['sensəs]	*un recensement*
a parliament	*un parlement*
a president	*un président*
a vice-president	*un vice-président*
an adviser	*un conseiller*
a term (of office)	*un mandat*
a constitution	*une constitution*
a chart [tʃa:t]	*une charte*
a right	*un droit*
a duty ['dju:ti]	*un devoir*
a bill	*un projet de loi*
a motion	*une motion*
a law, an act	*une loi*
an amendment	*un amendement*
enforcement	*la mise en application*
a showdown	*une épreuve de force*
an embargo	*un embargo*
a reform [ri'fɔ:m]	*une réforme*
a reformer	*un réformateur*
a project, a plan	*un projet*

a proposal	*une proposition*
a measure ['meʒə]	*une mesure*
a priority	*une priorité*
a stake	*un enjeu*
a setback	*un revers*
a crisis (crises)	*une crise*
a plot	*un complot*
a coup [ku:]	*un coup d'état*
a collapse	*un effondrement*
an upheaval [ʌp'hi:vəl]	*un bouleversement*
a treaty	*un traité*
the cabinet	*le cabinet*
a sitting	*une séance*
a session	*une session*
a side issue ['iʃu:]	*une question secondaire*
a topic	*un thème, un sujet*
a delegate	*un délégué*
a council	*un conseil*
a committee	*une commission, un comité*
an assembly	*une assemblée*
talks	*des pourparlers*
a veto ['vi:təu]	*un veto*
a summit	*un sommet*
a seat	*un siège*
a title	*un titre*
corruption	*la corruption*
a report	*un rapport*
an inquiry [in'kwaiəri]	*une enquête*
a resignation	*une démission*
a ministry	*un ministère*
a minister	*un ministre*
a subsidy ['sʌbsidi]	*une subvention*
a budget	*un budget*
a tax	*un impôt*
a form	*un formulaire*
a taxpayer	*un contribuable*
a townhall, a city hall	*une mairie*
a mayor, a mayoress	*un maire*
a city council	*un conseil municipal*
a councillor	*un conseiller municipal*
a county ['kaunti]	*un comté*
a borough ['bʌrə]	*un district*
the civil service	*la fonction publique*
a civil servant	*un fonctionnaire*

The United States — *Les États-Unis*

the President	*le Président*
the Vice President	*le Vice président*
the White House	*la Maison Blanche*
the State Capitol	*le Capitole*
a secretary	*un ministre*
a department	*un ministère*

the State Secretary	*le Secrétaire d'État*	a congressman	*un député*
Congress	*le Congrès*	the Senate ['senit]	*le Sénat*
the House of Representatives	*la Chambre des Représentants*	a senator ['senətə]	*un sénateur*

The President's cabinet

Department of Agriculture (USDA)	Secretary of Agricultue
Department of Commerce (DOC)	Secretary of Commerce
Department of Defense (DOD)	Secretary of Defense
Department of Education (ED)	Secretary of Education
Department of Energy (DOE)	Secretary of Energy
Department of Health and Human Services (HHS)	Secretary of Health and Human Services
Department of Homeland Security (DHS)	Secretary of Homeland Security
Department of Housing and Urban Development (HUD)	Secretary of Housing and Urban Development
Department of Justice (DOJ)	Attorney General
Department of Labor (DOL)	Labor Secretary
Department of the Interior (DOI)	Secretary of the Interior
Department of State (affaires étrangères)	State Secretary, the Secretary of State
Department of Transportation (DOT)	Secretary of Transportation
Department of the Treasury	Secretary of the Treasury
Department of Veterans Affairs (VA)	Secretary of Veteran Affairs

Great Britain — *La Grande-Bretagne*

the Queen	*la Reine*	the House of Commons	*la Chambre des Communes*
the Privy council ['praivi]	*le Conseil Privé*	the Speaker	*le Président de la Chambre des Communes*
the Prime Minister	*le Premier Ministre*		
Parliament ['pa:ləmənt]	*le parlement*	a division	*un vote (au parlement)*
the House of Lords	*la Chambre des Lords*	a Member of Parliament (an MP)	*un député*

Her Majesty's government

Les ministres du gouvernement (cabinet ministers) *portent généralement le titre de secrétaire d'État* (Secretary of State). *Quelques-uns ont une appellation particulière :*

the Home Secretary	*le ministre de l'Intérieur*
the Foreign Secretary	*le ministre des Affaires étrangères*
the Attorney General	*le ministre de la Justice*
the Chancellor of the Exchequer	*le ministre des Finances*

UK Ministerial Departments (2009)

Home Office (HO)
Ministry of Defence (MoD)
Ministry of Justice (MoJ)
Her Majesty's Treasury (HMT)
Department of Health (DH)
Department for Communities and Local Government (DCLG)
Department for Business, Innovation and Skills (BIS)
Department for Children, Schools and Families (DCSF)
Department for Culture, Media and Sport (DCMS)
Department of Energy and Climate Change (DECC)
Department for Environment, Food and Rural Affairs (DEFRA)
Department for International Development (DfID)
Department for Transport (DfT)
Department for Work and Pensions (DWP)
Foreign and Commonwealth Office (FCO)
Government Equalities Office (GEO)
Northern Ireland Office (NIO)
Scotland Office (SO)
Wales Office (WO)

state-controlled	*étatisé*
state-maintained	*public*
state-subsidized	*subventionné par l'état*
official	*officiel*
nationwide	*national*
worldwide	*à l'échelle mondiale*
authoritarian	*autoritaire*
totalitarian	*totalitaire*
uncompromising	*intransigeant*
presidential	*présidentiel*
republican	*républicain*
parliamentary	*législatif*
municipal	*municipal*
self-governing	*autonome*
stable	*stable*
unsteady	*instable*
shaky	*chancelant*
lame [leim]	*boiteux*
corrupt [kə'rəpt]	*corrompu*
unfair	*injuste*
polemical	*polémique*
to head	*diriger, être à la tête de*
to run*	*gérer, diriger*
to rule, to govern ['gʌvən]	*gouverner*
to overcome	*triompher de*
to plot	*comploter*
to conceal [kən'si:l]	*dissimuler*
to interfere [ˌintə'fiə]	*intervenir, s'ingérer*
to collapse	*s'effondrer*
to overthrow*	*renverser*
to oppress	*opprimer*
to deprive (of)	*priver (de)*
to appoint	*nommer*
to approve	*agréer, ratifier, approuver*
to approve of	*approuver (un fait)*
to promote	*promouvoir*
to reform	*réformer*
to dismiss	*renvoyer*
to resign [ri'zain]	*démissionner*
to reject	*rejeter*
to dissolve	*dissoudre*
to delay	*ajourner*
to ensure [in'ʃuə]	*s'assurer de*
to subsidize	*subventionner*
to sit*	*siéger*
to deliberate	*délibérer*
to vote	*voter*

Expressions

to come into office	*entrer en fonctions*
to gain control of	*prendre le contrôle de*
to go on / make a state visit to a country	*se rendre en / faire un voyage officiel dans un pays*
an unofficial visit	*une visite privée*
a summit conference meeting	*une conférence au sommet*
state apartments	*les appartements officiels*
the legislative body	*le corps législatif*
the executive body	*le corps exécutif*
the party in opposition	*le parti de l'opposition*
an overall majority	*une majorité absolue*
the ruling party	*le parti au pouvoir*
a foreign policy	*une politique étrangère*
a domestic policy	*une politique intérieure*
to draft a bill	*rédiger un projet de loi*
a vote of confidence	*un vote de confiance*
a package of measures	*un paquet de mesures*
to address an issue	*s'attaquer à un problème*
to reach a settlement	*parvenir à un accord*
red tape	*documents officiels, paperasserie*
the state opening of Parliament	*l'ouverture solennelle du Parlement*
the storming of the Bastille	*la prise de la Bastille*
the separation of powers	*la séparation des pouvoirs*
a confederation of states	*une confédération d'états*
the Constitution of the United States	*la Constitution des États-Unis*
the Bill of Rights (US)	*les amendements à la Constitution (1791)*
the Bill of Rights (GB)	*loi de 1689 déterminant les droits du citoyen anglais*
the Inland Revenue, the Treasury	*le fisc*
income tax	*l'impôt sur le revenu*
the rates	*les impôts locaux*
the real estate tax (US)	*les impôts fonciers*
the National Health Service (NHS) (GB)	*la Sécurité sociale*
a senior civil servant	*un haut fonctionnaire*
a public official	*un responsable public*
the management of public affairs	*la gestion des affaires publiques*

II. Politics and elections La politique et les élections

a policy	*une politique*
a politician	*un homme politique*
a party	*un parti*
a leader	*un chef*
a member	*un membre*
a (trade) union	*un syndicat*
a representative	*un représentant*
a spokesperson	*un porte-parole*
a supporter [[sə'pɔ:tə]	*un partisan*
a proponent	*un adepte*
an advocate	*un défenseur*
an activist	*un militant*
a dissident	*un dissident*
an opponent	*un adversaire, un opposant*
a critic	*un censeur, un détracteur*
criticism	*les critiques*
a foe [fəu]	*un ennemi*
a system	*un système*
ideology [ˌaidi'ɔlədʒi]	*l'idéologie*
an ideologist	*un idéologue*

loyalty	*le loyalisme*
Fascism	*le fascisme*
Marxism	*le marxisme*
communism	*le communisme*
liberalism	*le libéralisme*
socialism	*le socialisme*
capitalism	*le capitalisme*
anarchy ['ænəki]	*l'anarchisme, l'anarchie*
a Fascist	*un fasciste*
a Marxist	*un marxiste*
a communist	*un communiste*
a liberal	*un libéral*
a socialist	*un socialiste*
a capitalist	*un capitaliste*
an anarchist	*un anarchiste*
a democrat	*un démocrate*
a republican	*un républicain*
an aristocrat	*un aristocrate*
a terrorist	*un terroriste*
a coalition	*une coalition*
a tie [tai]	*un lien*
a commitment	*un engagement*
an oath [əuθ]	*un serment*
a statement	*une déclaration*
a denial [di'naiəl]	*un démenti*
a side	*un camp*
a demonstration	*une manifestation*
a demonstrator	*un manifestant*
a rally	*un rassemblement*
a march	*un défilé*
a riot [raiət]	*une émeute*
a debate	*un débat*
a controversy	*une controverse*
a dispute, a conflict	*un conflit*
a negotiation	*une négociation*
an agreement	*un accord*
a deal	*un marché, un accord*
a compromise	*un compromis*
a disagreement	*un désaccord*
a veto	*un veto*
a shift	*un glissement*
a swing	*un virage*
a turnaround	*un revirement, une volte-face*
a split	*une division*
a speech	*un discours*
an orator ['ɔrətə]	*un orateur*
an asset	*un atout*
charisma [kæ'rizmə]	*le charisme*
a dogma	*un dogme*
a duty	*un devoir*
a task	*une tâche*
an agenda [ə'dʒendə]	*un ordre du jour, un programme*

a campaign [kæm'pein]	*une campagne*
a tactic	*une tactique*
a catchword	*un mo d'ordre*
a survey ['sə:vei]	*une étude*
a poll [pəul]	*un sondage, un scrutin*
an election	*une élection*
a subscription	*une souscription*
a candidate	*un candidat*
a seat	*un siège*
a constituency (GB)	*une circonscription électorale*
a constituent	*un électeur, un administré*
a slogan	*un slogan*
a poster	*une affiche*
a billboard	*un panneau d'affichage*
a programme	*un programme*
a polling station	*un bureau de vote*
a polling booth	*un isoloir*
a ballot paper	*un bulletin*
a ballot box	*une urne*
political	*politique*
left-wing	*de gauche*
right-wing	*de droite*
idealistic [ai,diə'listik]	*idéaliste*
utopian [ju:'təupiən]	*utopique*
nationalist	*nationaliste*
republican	*républicain*
democratic	*démocratique*
constitutional	*constitutionnel*
liberal	*libéral*
radical	*radical, extrémiste*
leftist	*gauchiste*
anarchic [æ'na:kik]	*anarchiste, anarchique*
absolute	*absolu*
dictatorial	*dictatorial*
arbitrary	*arbitraire*
moderate	*modéré*
loyal ['lɔiəl]	*loyal*
opposed (to)	*opposé, hostile (à)*
popular	*populaire*
unpopular	*impopulaire*
reliable, trustworthy	*digne de confiance*
dedicated	*dévoué*
corrupt [kə'rʌpt]	*corrompu*
tough [tʌf]	*dur*
resolute	*résolu*
charismatic	*charismatique*
creative [kri(:)'eitiv]	*créatif*
imaginative	*imaginatif*

to lead*	*être à la tête de, mener*	to challenge	*défier, mettre au défi*
to found [faund]	*fonder*	to oppose	*s'opposer à*
to set* up	*créer, mettre en place*	to rule out	*écarter*
to support, to back	*soutenir, apporter son soutien*	to smear [smiə]	*éclabousser (scandale)*
to vote for	*voter pour*	to trigger (off)	*déclencher*
to elect [i'lekt]	*élire*	to demonstrate	*manifester*
to appeal (to)	*séduire, plaire*	to campaign	*faire campagne*
to join	*adhérer*	to launch [lɔ:ntʃ]	*lancer*
to endorse	*adhérer à, cautionner*	to run* for	*être candidat à*
to criticize	*critiquer*	to survey	*étudier, faire une étude*
to divide	*diviser*	to rally	*rassembler*
to split	*diviser (en deux camps)*	to soar [sɔ:]	*grimper (ex. sondages)*
to question	*contester*	to sink*	*plonger, sombrer*

Expressions

a political party	*un parti politique*
a party official	*un responsable du parti*
the party executives	*les états-majors*
the rank-and-file	*la base*
a rank-and-file / grassroots militant	*un militant de base*
an election campaign	*une campagne électorale*
to be politically-minded	*s'intéresser à la politique*
political asylum	*l'asile politique*
a political refugee	*un réfugié politique*
a political analyst / expert / commentator	*un politologue*
a policy maker	*un décideur / responsable politique*
opposition parties	*les partis de l'opposition*
the shadow cabinet (GB)	*le cabinet fantôme*
a foreign policy	*une politique étrangère*
a domestic policy	*une politique intérieure*
an economic policy	*une politique économique*
political circles	*les milieux politiques*
the right wing	*l'aile droite*
the left wing	*l'aile gauche*
the Social Democratic Party	*le parti social-démocrate*
the Labour Party (GB)	*le parti travailliste*
the Conservative Party (the Tories) (GB)	*le parti conservateur*
the Liberal Party (the Whigs) (GB)	*le parti libéral*
the Democratic Party (US)	*le parti démocrate*
the Republican Party (US)	*le parti républicain*
freedom of speech	*la liberté de parole*
an opinion poll	*un sondage d'opinion*
to carry out a survey	*faire une étude*
to take to the streets	*descendre dans la rue*
to be critical of	*critiquer, trouver à redire*

to come under fire	*être vivement critiqué*
to come to a deadlock	*aboutir à une impasse*
to come to an agreement	*parvenir à un accord*
to take up the challenge	*relever le défi*
to be power-hungry	*être assoiffé de pouvoir*
to seize power	*s'emparer du pouvoir*
a military coup	*un coup d'État militaire*
to be in power	*être au pouvoir*
to deliver a speech	*faire un discours*
to go to the polls	*aller voter*
general elections	*élections législatives*
local elections	*élections municipales*
to run for president	*être candidat aux élections présidentielles*

Phrases

The public does not approve of the Prime Minister's uncompromising attitude.
Le public n'est pas d'accord avec l'attitude intransigeante du Premier ministre.

Freedom of information is a fundamental aspect of American democracy.
La liberté d'information est un aspect fondamental de la démocratie américaine.

In the States, the presidential term of four years begins on January 20th.
Aux États-Unis, le mandat présidentiel de quatre ans commence le 20 janvier.

The United Kingdom is a parliamentary monarchy.
Le Royaume Uni est une monarchie parlementaire.

In Britain, there has to be a General Election at least every five years.
En Grande Bretagne, il doit y avoir des élections législatives au moins tous les cinq ans.

American voters are vocal about their views on public issues.
Les électeurs américains n'hésitent pas à exprimer leur opinion au sujet des questions publiques.

In the United States, it is possible for a candidate to run for office in a general election without the backing of a political party.
Aux États-Unis, un candidat peut se présenter aux élections sans l'appui d'un parti politique.

An informed electorate is the surest guarantee of the survival of democracy.
Un electorat informé est la garantie la plus sûre de la survie de la démocratie.

The majority is deeply divided over the issue of abortion.
La majorité est fortement divisée sur la question de l'avortement.

Nowadays, most of the speeches and statements of government officials are broadcast by the media.
De nos jours, la plupart des discours et déclarations des responsables du gouvernement sont diffusés par les médias.

Exercices

I. Retrouver l'adjectif :

1. attractive and desirable but impracticable
2. unstable
3. throughout the country
4. based on opinion or impulse, not on reason
5. able to put thoughts and feelings into clear speech
6. unyielding
7. in favour of progress and reform and opposed to privilege
8. showing patriotic feelings
9. very firm
10. true and faithful

II. Retrouver les 10 expressions correctes :

a party service / the general hall / the civil poll / red tax / freedom paper / the right tape / income election / the city wing / an opinion official / a ballot of speech

III. Traduire en anglais :

1. Les membres de la Chambre des Représentants servent des mandats de deux ans.
2. La constitution américaine accorde tous les pouvoirs législatifs au Congrès.
3. Les députés britanniques sont très bruyants quand ils s'opposent à un projet de loi.
4. Les partis politiques sont la base du système politique américain.
5. Les négociations avec les syndicats sont dans l'impasse.
6. Beaucoup d'électeurs critiquent la politique étrangère du gouvernement.
7. Les militants de base sont descendus dans la rue, ce qui a surpris les dirigeants du parti.
8. Le parlement a écarté une augmentation de l'impôt sur le revenu.
9. Il a adhéré au parti travailliste quand il avait 20 ans.
10. Cet homme politique corrompu a été contraint de démissionner.

VIII. THE WORLD

29. Nations and countries
Nations et pays

(the) earth [ə:θ]	*la terre*
a land	*une terre, un pays*
the fatherland	*la (mère) patrie*
a people	*un peuple*
a nation	*une nation*
a state	*un État*
a continent	*un continent*
an isle [ail]	*une île*
an island	*une île, un îlot*
the mainland	*le continent (opposé à une île)*
a country	*un pays*
a capital	*une capitale*
a border, a frontier	*une frontière*
a boundary	*une limite, une frontière*
a district	*un arrondissement, une zone, un quartier*
a county [‘kaunti]	*un comté*
a province	*une province*
a territory	*un territoire*
a colony	*une colonie*
a colonist, a settler	*un colon*
a colonizer	*un colonisateur*
a language, a tongue	*une langue*
a patriot [‘peitriət]	*un patriote*
patriotism	*le patriotisme*
the national anthem [‘ænθəm]	*l'hymne national*
a nationalist	*un nationaliste*
a chauvinist	*un chauvin*
the poles	*les pôles*
the north	*le nord*
the south	*le sud*

the east	*l'est*
the west	*l'ouest*
northern [‘nɔ:ðən]	*septentrional*
southern [‘sʌðən]	*méridional*
eastern	*oriental*
western	*occidental*
urban	*urbain*
major [‘meidʒə]	*majeur*
main	*principal*
minor	*secondaire, mineur*
small	*petit*
tiny [‘taini]	*minuscule*
rural	*rural*
populous	*peuplé*
uninhabited	*inhabité*
territorial	*territorial*
national	*national*
nationalistic	*nationaliste*
patriotic	*patriotique*
chauvinistic	*chauvin*
north (of)	*au nord (de)*
south (of)	*au sud (de)*
east (of)	*à l'est (de)*
west (of)	*à l'ouest (de)*
to lie* [lai]	*se trouver, être*
to be situated	*être situé*
to inhabit	*habiter*
to settle	*coloniser*
to stretch, to spread*	*s'étendre*
to limit	*limiter*
to conquer	*conquérir*
to annex	*annexer*
to link	*relier*

Countries of the world and their peoples

Pays	*Adjectif*	*Nom*
Type 1 : l'adjectif et le nom se terminent en «-an » (pluriel en « –ans » ; exemple : « an Afghan », « the Afghans »). N'oubliez pas que tous les adjectifs et noms de nationalité commencent par une lettre majuscule !		
Afghanistan [æf'gænistæn]	Afghan	an Afghan
Argentina [ˌa:dʒən'ti:nə]	Argentinian	an Argentinian
Bahamas [bə'ha:məs]	Bahamian	a Bahamian
Barbados [ba:'beidəuz]	Barbadian	a Barbadian
Belarus	Belorussian /Byelorussian	a Belorussian /a Byelorussian
Belgium	Belgian	a Belgian
Belize [be'li:z]	Belizian	a Belizian
Bosnia-Herzegovina	Bosnian	a Bosnian
Botswana	Botswanan	a Tswana
Brazil [brə'zil]	Brazilian	a Brazilian
Brunei	Bruneian	a Bruneian
Burundi	Burundian	a Burundian
Cameroon	Cameroonian	a Cameroonian
Canada ['kænədə]	Canadian	a Canadian
Cape Verde Islands	Cape Verdean	a Cape Verdean
Chad	Chadian	a Chadian
Chile ['tʃili]	Chilean	a Chilean
Croatia	Croat / Croatian	a Croat /a Croatian
Djibouti	Djiboutian	a Djiboutian
Dominican Republic	Dominican	a Dominican
Ecuador	Ecuadorean	an Ecuadorean
Egypt ['i:dʒipt]	Egyptian	an Egyptian
El Salvador	Salvadorean	a Salvadorean
Fiji	Fijian	a Fijian
Germany	German	a German
Ghana	Ghanaian	a Ghanaian
Grenada	Grenadian	a Grenadian
Haiti	Haitian	a Haitian
Honduras	Honduran	a Honduran
Hungary ['hʌŋgəri]	Hungarian	a Hungarian
Iran [iə'ra:n]	Iranian	an Iranian
Italy	Italian	an Italian

Jordan	Jordanian	a Jordanian
Laos	Laotian	a Laotian
Madagascar	Malagasay / Madagascan	a Malagasay / a Madagascan
Malawi	Malawian	a Malawian
Maldives	Maldivian	a Maldivian
Mali	Malian	a Malian
Mauritius	Mauritian	a Mauritian
Mexico	Mexican	a Mexican
Monaco	Monegasque / Monacan	a Monegasque / a Monacan
Morocco [mə'rɔkəu]	Moroccan	a Moroccan
Mozambique	Mozambican	a Mozambican
Norway	Norwegian	a Norwegian
Panama	Panamanian	a Panamanian
Papua New Guinea	Guinean / Papua New Guinean	a Guinean / a Papua New Guinean
Paraguay	Paraguayan	a Paraguayan
Peru [pə'ru:]	Peruvian	a Peruvian
Saudi Arabia	Saudi Arabian / Saudi	a Saudi Arabian / a Saudi
Serbia	Serb / Serbian	a Serb / a Serbian
Sierra Leone	Sierra Leonian	a Sierra Leonian
Singapore	Singaporean	a Singaporean
Slovenia	Slovene / Slovenian	a Slovene / a Slovenian
Trinidad and Tobago	Trinidadian	a Trinidadian
Ukraine	Ukrainian	a Ukrainian
Uruguay	Uruguayan	a Uruguayan
Zaire	Zaïrean	a Zaïrean
Zimbabwe	Zimbabwean	a Zimbabwean

En ce qui concerne les pays figurant dans la liste suivante, il suffit d'ajouter la lettre « n » pour obtenir l'adjectif et le nom. Exemple : « Albania+n » Þ « Albanian », « an Albanian » :

Albania, Algeria [æl'dʒiəriə], Andorra, Angola, Armenia, Australia, Austria *(l'Autriche),* Bolivia, Bulgaria, Cambodia, Colombia, Costa Rica, Cuba ['kju:bə], Dominica, Eritrea, Estonia, Ethiopia [,iθi'əupjə], the Gambia, Georgia, Guatemala, Guinea ['gini, India, Indonesia, Jamaica, Kenya ['kenjə], Latvia, Liberia, Lithuania, Macedonia, Malaysia [mə'leiziə], Mauritania, Moldova, Mongolia, Namibia, Nicaragua, Nigeria [nai'dʒiəriə], North Korea, Romania, Rwanda, South Africa, South Korea, Syria, Tanzania, Tunisia [tju(:)'niziə], Uganda, Venezuela, Samoa, Zambia.

Type 2 : l'adjectif et le nom se terminent en « -ese ». Attention : le nom est invariable.		
Burkina	Burkinese	a Burkinese
Burma ['bə:mə]	Burmese	a Burmese
China ['tʃainə]	Chinese	a Chinese
Congo	Congolese	a Congolese
Guyana	Guyanese	a Guyanese
Lebanon	Lebanese	a Lebanese
Malta ['mɔ:ltə]	Maltese	a Maltese
Portugal	Portuguese	a Portuguese
Sudan [su(:)'da:n]	Sudanese	a Sudanese
Surinam [,suəri'næm]	Surinamese	a Surinamer /a Surinamese
Togo	Togolese	a Togolese

En ce qui concerne les pays figurant dans la liste suivante, il suffit d'ajouter la terminaison « -ese » pour obtenir l'adjectif et le nom :

Benin, Bhutan, Gabon, Japan [dʒə'pæn], Nepal [ni'pɔ:l], Senegal, Sudan, Taiwan, Vietnam.

Type 3 : l'adjectif et le nom se terminent en « -i ». Le nom est variable : « an Israeli », « Israelis ».		
Somalia	Somali	a Somali
Swaziland	Swazi	a Swazi
Thailand	Thai	a Thai

En ce qui concerne les pays figurant dans la liste suivante, il suffit d'ajouter la terminaison « -i » pour obtenir l'adjectif et le nom :

Bahrain, Bangladesh, Iraq, Israel, Kuwait, Oman, Pakistan, Qatar, Yemen.

Type 4 : adjectifs en « -ish », noms variables.		
Britain	British	a Briton
Denmark	Danish	a Dane
England	English	an Englishman, an Englishwoman
Finland	Finnish	a Finn
(the Republic of) Ireland	Irish	an Irishman, an Irishwoman
Poland	Polish	a Pole
Scotland	Scottish	a Scot
Spain	Spanish	a Spaniard
Sweden ['swi:dn]	Swedish	a Swede
Turkey ['tə:ki]	Turkish	a Turk

Type 5: cas divers.		
Cyprus ['saiprəs]	Cypriot	a Cypriot
the Czech Republic	Czech	a Czech
France	French	a Frenchman, a Frenchwoman
Greece	Greek	a Greek

Iceland	Icelandic	an Icelander
Kazakhstan	Kazakh	a Kazakh
Luxemb(o)urg		a Luxemb(o)urger
Montenegro	Montenegrin	a Montenegrin
New Zealand		a New Zealander
Niger	Nigerien	a Nigerien
Norway	Norwegian	a Norwegian
the Philippines [ˈfilipi:nz]	Philippine	a Filipino
Slovakia [sləuˈveikĭə]	Slovak	a Slovak
Sri Lanka	Sri Lankan	a Sri Lankan
Switzerland	Swiss	a Swiss
Tajikistan	Tajik / Tadjik	a Tajik / a Tadjik
the Netherlands (Holland)	Dutch	a Dutchman, a Dutchwoman
Turkmenistan	Turkmen / Turkoman	a Turkmen / a Turkoman
Uzbekistan	Uzbek	an Uzbek
Wales	Welsh	a Welshman, a Welshwoman
Yugoslavia [ˈju:gəuˈsla:vjə]	Yugoslav	a Yugoslav

Western Europe — *l'Europe occidentale*
West Europeans — *les Européens de l'Ouest*
Eastern Europe — *l'Europe orientale*
East Europeans — *les Européens de l'Est*
Southern France — *le midi de la France*
Northern Italy — *l'Italie du Nord*
Southern Africa — *le Sud de l'Afrique*
South Africa — *l'Afrique du Sud*
the Northern Hemisphere — *l'hémisphère nord*
the Southern Hemisphere — *l'hémisphère sud*
South America — *l'Amérique du Sud*
North America — *l'Amérique du Nord*
Northern Ireland — *l'Irlande du Nord*
the North Pole — *le Pôle Nord*
the South Pole — *le Pôle Sud*
South East Asia — *l'Asie du Sud-Est*
the Near-East — *le Proche-Orient*
the Middle-East — *le Moyen-Orient*
the Far-East — *l'Extrême-Orient*
the West Indies — *les Antilles*
the northern coast — *le littoral nord*
northern lights — *l'aurore boréale*

Expressions

America from coast to coast — *l'Amérique de l'Atlantique au Pacifique*
a desert island — *une île déserte*
rural districts — *les zones rurales*
urban districts — *les zones urbaines*
a sparsely populated district — *une zone peu peuplée*
a densely populated district — *une zone très peuplée*
a land of opportunity — *une terre où chacun a sa chance*
to go West — *aller vers l'Ouest*
to lie (to the) north of — *être (se trouver) au nord de*
to lie in the north of — *se situer dans le nord de*
territorial claims — *des revendications territoriales*
a bone of contention — *une pomme de discorde*
to be poles apart — *être aux antipodes (l'un de l'autre)*
Mother Earth — *la terre nourricière*
to take French leave — *filer à l'anglaise*

Phrases

Pakistan lies to the north west of India.
Le Pakistan est situé au nord-ouest de l'Inde.

New Delhi, the federal capital, is situated in the north of India.
New Delhi, la capitale fédérale, se trouve au nord de l'Inde.

The first rail link under the English Channel eventually opened in 1994.
La première liaison ferroviaire sous la Manche fut enfin ouverte en 1994.

American pioneers went west to settle new territories.
Les pionniers américains allaient vers l'ouest pour coloniser de nouveaux territoires.

Since the 1900s Hispanics have crossed the US border in increasing numbers.
Depuis les années 1900 un nombre croissant d'hispaniques a franchi la frontière des États Unis.

President Kennedy declared that space was to be America's New Frontier.
C'est le Président Kennedy qui déclara que l'espace devait être une Nouvelle Frontière pour l'Amérique.

Europeans found it hard to choose their capital between Brussels, Luxemburg and Strasburg.
Les Européens eurent du mal à choisir leur capitale entre Bruxelles, Luxembourg et Strasbourg.

Throughout their history Balkan peoples have disagreed on their boundaries.
Tout au long de leur histoire les peuples balkaniques n'ont pu s'entendre au sujet de leurs frontières.

From 1870 the Suez Canal cut the passage to India by half.
À partir de 1870 le canal de Suez réduisit de moitié la durée de la traversée vers l'Inde.

It appeared that neither the British nor the Chinese were ready to compromise over Hong Kong.
Il apparut que ni les Britanniques ni les Chinois n'étaient disposés à un compromis au sujet de Hong Kong.

Exercices

I. Traduire :

1. les Polonais
2. un Marocain
3. les Hollandais
4. deux Espagnols
5. quelques Suisses

II. Name the countries the following landmarks belong to :

1. The Riviera 2. The Hague 3. The Rhine 4. Vienna 5. Warsaw 6. Algiers 7. Beijing 8. The Balearic Islands 9. Oporto 10. Athens 11. The Urals 12. Cairo 13. Antwerp 14. The Azores 15. Dunkirk

III. Reformuler les phrases en utilisant les mots donnés entre parenthèses :

1. The two countries still totally disagree as to the central issue of diplomatic representation. (poles)

2. Israel is unlikely to accept to discuss Syrian demands for land. (claims)
3. Nowadays even sparsely populated Southern Sahara has become a subject of dispute. (bone)
4. Both candidates declared it was essential that the USA should remain a country where everyone had a chance to succeed. (opportunity)
5. Singapore has now such a large population that birth control has become compulsory. (densely)

IV. Compléter les phrases suivantes :

1. The 1898 treaty stipulated that Hong Kong was to be handed over to ... in 1997.
2. The only uninhabited continent, ..., is said to be now threatened by ‘civilization’.
3. Hundreds of thousands of ... are said to have left the region north of Hanoi in the hope of making it to the west.
4. Of all ... cities Cairo is undoubtedly the most severely overpopulated.
5. Unlike their Swedish neighbours, the ... intend to reject the moratorium on whale hunting.

30. Travel
Les voyages

a tourist [‘tuərist]	*un touriste*
a travel agent	*un agent de voyages*
a travel agency [‘eidʒənsi]	*une agence de voyages*
a break	*un court repos*
a trip	*un voyage, une excursion*
a journey [‘dʒə:ni]	*un voyage, un trajet*
a voyage [‘vɔi:dʒ]	*un voyage (par mer)*
a ticket	*un billet*
a ticket barrier	*un portillon*
the fare	*le prix du billet*
a reservation	*une réservation*
luggage [‘lʌgidʒ]	*les bagages*
a piece of luggage	*un bagage*
a suitcase [‘sju:tkeis]	*une valise*
a trunk	*une malle*
hassle	*les tracas*
a delay	*un retard*
a cancellation	*une annulation*
a package holiday [‘pækidʒ]	*un voyage organisé*
a tour operator	*un voyagiste*

a holiday	*des vacances / un jour de congé*
the holidays	*les vacances*
a holiday-maker	*un vacancier*
a destination	*une destination*
a location	*un lieu, une situation*
adventure [əd’ventʃə]	*l’aventure*
an adventurer	*un aventurier*
an explorer	*un explorateur*
a foreigner, an alien [‘fɔrinə] [‘eiljən]	*un étranger*
a border	*une frontière*
customs	*la douane*
a customs officer	*un douanier*
a time chedule [‘ʃedju:l]	*un horaires*
a passport	*un passeport*
a visa	*un visa*
an identity card	*une carte d’identité*
a traveller’s cheque	*un chèque de v*
a foreign currency	*une devise étrangère*
the exchange rate	*le taux de change*
smuggling	*la contrebande*

a place	*un endroit*
a landscape	*un paysage*
the scenery ['si:nəri]	*le paysage*
a sight	*une attraction touristique*
a monument	*un monument*
a museum	*un musée*
a beauty spot	*un site naturel*

Land travel — ***Voyages terrestres***

driving	*faire de la voiture*
riding	*l'équitation*
cycling	*le cyclisme*
walking	*la marche*
hiking ['haikiŋ]	*la randonnée (à pied)*
trekking	*la randonnée (en montagne)*
camping	*le camping*
a tour [tuə]	*une visite, un périple*
a drive	*une promenade en voiture*
a ride	*une ballade à cheval*
an excursion	*une sortie, une excursion*
a resort [ri'zɔ:t]	*un lieu de villégiature*
a spa [spa:]	*une ville thermale*
a beach	*une plage*
a camp site	*un terrain de camping*
a caravan site	*un camping pour caravanes*
a route [ru:t]	*un itinéraire*
a coach trip	*une excursion en car*
a busload	*un car entier*
rail	*le rail*
the railways, the railroad (US)	*les chemins de fer*
a station	*une gare*
the ticket office	*le guichet*
a 1st class carriage	*une voiture de 1re classe*
a single ticket	*un aller simple*
a return ticket	*un aller et retour*
a sleeper	*un wagon-lit*
a ticket collector	*un contrôleur*
a conductor	*un chef de train*
a hotel	*un hôtel*
a motel	*un motel*
a youth hostel	*une auberge de jeunesse*
an inn	*une auberge*
accommodation	*l'hébergement*
a vacancy ['veikənsi]	*une chambre à louer*
the reception desk	*la réception*
a single room	*une chambre à un lit*
a double room	*une chambre à deux lits*
full board	*pension complète*
half board	*demi-pension*
a stay	*un séjour*

Sea travel — ***Voyages maritimes***

sailing	*la navigation (à voile)*
a crossing	*une traversée*
a passage ['pæsidʒ]	*une traversée, un voyage*
a cruise [kru:z]	*une croisière*
a liner	*un paquebot*
an anchor ['æŋkə]	*une ancre*
a berth [bə:θ]	*une couchette*
a passenger	*un passager*
a harbour ['ha:bə]	*un port*
a stopover	*une halte*

Air travel — ***Voyages aériens***

a plane, an airplane (US)	*un avion*
flying	*voyager en avion*
a flight	*un vol*
an airport	*un aéroport*
an air terminal	*une aérogare*
departure [di'pa:tʃə]	*le départ*
arrival [ə'raivəl]	*l'arrivée*
a boarding pass card	*une carte/ d'embarquement*
a gate	*une porte*
take-off	*le décollage*
landing	*l'atterrissage*
a schedule	*un horaire*
an airliner	*un avion de ligne*
a steward ['stju:əd]f	*un steward*
a stewardess	*une hôtesse*
airfares	*les tarifs aériens*
hand luggage	*les bagages à main*
picturesque	*pittoresque*
exotic	*exotique*
posh	*cossu*
far	*loin, lointain*
remote [ri'məut]	*lointain, reculé*
distant	*éloigné*
close [kləus]	*proche*
neighbouring	*avoisinant*
foreign, alien	*étranger*

touristy	*trop fréquenté*
crowded ['kraudid]	*encombré (de monde)*
adventurous	*aventureux*
abroad, overseas	*à l'étranger*
overnight	*de nuit*
overland	*par voie de terre*
via	*via, par*
to (un)pack	*(dé)faire ses valises*
to journey, to travel	*voyager*
to leave*	*partir*
to start (out, off)	*se mettre en route*
to get* on / off	*monter / descendre*
to embark	*embarquer*
to disembark	*débarquer*
to miss	*manquer*
to catch*	*prendre*
to fly*	*voyager en avion*
to sail	*voyager par bateau*
to drive*	*aller en voiture*
to ride*	*aller à cheval (à moto, à bicyclette)*
to hitchhike	*faire de l'auto-stop*
to take*off	*décoller*
to land	*atterrir*
to check in	*enregistrer*
to declare [di'klɛə]	*déclarer*
to proceed	*aller, avancer*
to book	*réserver*
to hire ['haiə], to rent	*louer*
to cancel	*annuler*
to visit	*visiter*
to discover	*découvrir*
to explore	*explorer*
to escape	*s'échapper*
to get* away	*partir, se libérer*
to attract	*attirer*
to cater (for, to)	*pourvoir à, satisfaire*

Expressions

the tourist industry	*l'industrie du tourisme*
the hotel industry	*l'industrie hôtelière*
touristy places	*des endroits (trop) touristiques*
faraway places	*des terres lointaines*
distant shores	*des rivages lointains*
a trip to India	*un voyage en Inde*
a round trip	*un voyage aller et retour*
along the coast	*le long de la côte*
through the jungle	*à travers la jungle*
across the desert	*à travers le désert*
over the sea	*par-delà la mer*
over / across the Atlantic	*outre Atlantique*
a change of scenery	*un dépaysement*
off the beaten track	*hors des sentiers battus*
on horseback / on foot	*à cheval / à pied*
the check-in time	*l'heure d'enregistrement*
the sailing time	*l'heure de départ (bateau)*
to be early / late	*être en avance / en retard*
on my way to Edinburgh	*en route pour Édimbourg*
to be bound for	*être en route pour, en partance pour*
a roadside inn	*une auberge au bord de la route*
a luxury hotel	*un hôtel de luxe*
a Bed and Breakfast	*une chambre d'hôte*
a guest house	*une pension de famille*
No Vacancies	*complet*
to be on holiday	*être en vacances*
to go sightseeing	*faire du tourisme*
to travel abroad	*voyager à l'étranger*
to catch a train	*prendre le train*

to visit places of historical interest	*visiter des lieux historiques*
to get away from it all	*partir en laissant tous ses soucis derrière soi*
to be in need of a break	*avoir besoin de repos*
to stay overnight	*passer la nuit*
to put someone up	*héberger quelqu'un*
to travel light	*voyager avec peu de bagages*
to travel first class	*voyager en première classe*
to travel by train / by plane	*voyager en train / en avion*
he travelled on the 8 o'clock train	*il a pris le train de huit heures*
to travel on the cheap	*voyager en faisant le minimum de dépenses*
to travel on a British passport	*voyager avec un passeport britannique*
to go on a round-the-world cruise	*faire une croisière autour du monde*
to go on a camping holiday	*passer ses vacances en faisant du camping*
to pitch a tent	*monter une tente*
to round Cape Horn	*doubler le Cap Horn*
to sail round the globe	*faire le tour du monde en bateau*
to cross a border	*passer une frontière*
the passport control	*le contrôle des passeports*
to go through the customs	*passer la douane*
«Nothing to declare»	*« Rien à déclarer »*
«Goods to declare»	*« Marchandises à déclarer »*
to cancel a flight	*annuler un vol*
to cater for tourists	*pourvoir aux besoins des touristes*
to cater to tourists' tastes	*satisfaire aux goûts des touristes*

Phrases

He's gone to London on a business trip.
Il est (parti) à Londres en voyage d'affaires.

He's been to London several times lately.
Il est allé à Londres plusieurs fois ces derniers temps.

When will you come over to the continent?
Quand viendras-tu sur le continent ?

Wasn't the journey across India by train too tiring?
Le voyage en train à travers l'Inde n'a-t-il pas été trop fatigant ?

Can you put us up for the night?
Peux-tu nous héberger pour la nuit ?

I like package holidays provided everything is included.
J'aime bien les voyages organisés, à condition que tout soit compris.

No hassle, no extras, that's my idea of a holiday!
Pas de soucis, pas de suppléments, voilà comment je conçois les vacances !

How many pieces of luggage have you got?
Combien de bagages avez-vous ?

What's the bus fare from Rheims to London?
Combien coûte le billet de car entre Reims et Londres ?

If you are to hitchhike you'd better travel light.
Si tu dois faire du stop, tu ferais mieux de ne pas être chargé.

Exercices

I. Compléter les phrases en utilisant les prépositions suivantes : at - by - away - to - from - round - through - on - over - with

1. The Smiths are not here at the moment, they are ... holiday abroad.
2. Did you have a nice trip ... Australia?
3. We shall call ... Canterbury ... our way north.
4. I hate taking so much luggage ... the customs.
5. Magellan first sailed ... the world in 1520.
6. You can cross the USA ... coast ... coast ... bus.
7. You should come ... to England next year and stay a few days ... us.
8. He drove all ... Europe in his old van.
9. You need a few days in the Caribbean sun to get ... from it all.
10. She travelled ... a British passport, but she was of Russian origin.

II. Apparier un élément de la colonne de gauche avec un élément de la colonne de droite pour former des ensembles cohérents :

It was to have been the holiday of a lifetime	last year it was the Seychelles and this year Malaysia.
If you are one for cabarets and nightclubs	please now proceed to gate number 3.
Since you intend to travel in the North of England	the farther you fly the cheaper it is.
The Smiths always choose exotic destinations ;	you should go and visit London by night.
Our holiday in Majorca was a great success,	unfortunately tragedy struck soon after they started.
If you compare transatlantic air fares with European ones, the conclusion is obvious :	no wonder it attracts so many tourists.
This is a nice part of the world :	as the engine broke down just outside Jaipur.
I'm afraid the train from Delhi will be 3 hours late	no-one would have thought then that 3 decades later it would take airliners a few hours to fly from Paris to New York.
Calling all passengers to Bombay, Flight AI 235 :	you should stop at Durham, it is worth a visit.
In the 30s liners crossed the Atlantic in little less than a week ;	we enjoyed every moment of it.

III. Compléter le texte à l'aide de la liste suivante : bound / fares / first-class / liner / return / sailed / tickets / travellers / view / voyage

Legend has it that the adjective "posh" comes from "Port side Out, Starboard Home".

At the time of the British empire, ... to India ... aboard ships ... for Bombay. Those who could afford high ... and who wanted to have a pleasant ... booked a ... cabin on the port side (left hand side) of the ... on their way out of England : thus they had a ... of the coasts of Europe and Africa.

On their ... passage to England, they chose the starboard side for the same reason.

Those POSH ... were the most expensive, hence the association of POSH with luxury.

31. Haves and have-nots
Les nantis et les démunis

the rich, the wealthy	*les riches*
the poor	*les pauvres*
the well-to-do, the well-off	*les gens aisés*
wealth	*la richesse*
affluence	*l'abondance, l'aisance*
riches [‘ritʃiz]	*les richesses*
prosperity	*la prospérité*
an upstart	*un parvenu*
luxury [‘lʌkʃəri]	*le luxe*
a billionaire	*un milliardaire*
the Establishment	*les pouvoirs établis*
the upper classes	*les couches supérieures de la société*
status [‘steitəs]	*le standing*
the lower classes	*les couches inférieures de la société*
the deprived	*les déshérités*
the needy	*les nécessiteux*
the poor	*les pauvres*
the underprivileged	*les défavorisés*
the destitute	*les indigents*
the homeless	*les sans abri*
poverty	*la pauvreté*
hardship, deprivation	*la privation*
destitution	*le dénuement, l'indigence*
wretchedness	*la misère, l'extrême pauvreté*
squalor [‘skwɔlə]	*la misère noire*
the scum [skʌm]	*la racaille*
a plight	*une situation critique, désespérée*
homelessness	*le fait d'être sans toit*
a beggar [‘begə]	*un mendiant*
a shelter	*un abri*
a soup kitchen	*une soupe populaire*
a shanty town	*un bidonville*
a slum [slʌm]	*un taudis*
misfits	*les inadaptés*
an underdog	*un opprimé*
a dropout	*un marginal*
an outcast	*un paria*
a failure [‘feiljə]	*un raté, un échec*
a tramp	*un clochard*
a drug addict	*un drogué*
rejection	*le rejet, l'exclusion*
loneliness	*la solitude*
the Third World	*le tiers monde*
a power	*une puissance*
influence	*l'influence*
pressure [‘preʃə]	*la pression, des pressions*
debt [det]	*la dette*
a gap	*un écart*
plenty	*l'abondance*
scarcity [‘skɛəsiti]	*le manque, la pénurie*
rural exodus	*l'exode rural*
a shortage	*une pénurie*
starvation	*l'inanition, la famine*

famine ['fæmin]	*la famine*
drought [draut]	*la sécheresse*
malnutrition	*la malnutrition*
a commodity	*une denrée*
help, aid	*l'aide*
a charity	*un organisme humanitaire*
emergency relief	*l'aide d'urgence*
natives and immigrants	*autochtones et immigrés*
immigration	*l'immigration*
a quota	*un quota*
a sweatshop	*un atelier clandestin*
exploitation	*l'exploitation*
a ghetto	*un ghetto*
race relations	*les relations raciales*
discrimination	*la discrimination*
segregation	*la ségrégation*
(a) prejudice	*(un) des préjugés*
persecution	*la persécution*
racism	*le racisme*
Blacks	*les Noirs*
Whites	*les Blancs*
a negro ['ni:grəu]	*un noir*
a slave	*un esclave*
slavery	*l'esclavage*
coloured people	*les gens de couleur*
a gipsy	*un gitan*
a Jew [dʒu:]/a Jewess	*un juif/une juive*
a concentration camp	*un camp de concentration*
civil rights	*les droits civiques*
abolition [ə'bɔ:ʃən]	*l'abolition*
equal rights	*l'égalité des droits*
equality	*l'égalité*
inequalities	*les inégalités*
settlers and aborigenes	*colons et indigènes*
the (Red) Indians	*les indiens (peaux rouges)*
a territory	*un territoire*
the Frontier	*la limite des terres colonisées (US)*
the Wild West	*le Far West*
a pioneer [,paiə'niə]	*un pionnier*
a reservation	*une réserve*
a nomad	*un nomade*
a tribe	*une tribu*
the prairie	*la prairie*
a genocide ['dʒenəusaid]	*un génocide*
a mass-killing	*une tuerie*
a slaughter ['slɔ:tə]	*une tuerie, un carnage*
a massacre ['mæsəkə]	*un massacre*
a totalitarian regime	*un régime totalitaire*

an oppressed minority	*une minorité opprimée*
the Red Cross	*la Croix Rouge*
the French Doctors	*les médecins français (MSF, etc.)*
a civilian	*un civil*
an uprising	*un soulèvement*
an opponent	*un opposant*
a dissenter	*un dissident religieux*
an ordeal [ɔ:'di:l]	*une (rude) épreuve*
an exodus ['eksədəs]	*un exode*
an exile ['eksail]	*un exilé*
an expatriate	*un expatrié*
wealthy, affluent	*riche*
well-off, well-to-do	*aisé*
prosperous	*prospère*
extravagant	*dépensier, prodigue*
extravagantly	*avec prodigalité*
contemptuous	*méprisant*
contemptuously	*avec mépris*
migrant ['maigrənt]	*migrant*
native ['neitiv]	*indigène*
illegal(ly)	*illégal(ement)*
downtrodden	*opprimé*
developed	*développé*
industrialized	*industrialisé*
underdeveloped	*sous-développé*
developing	*en voie de développement*
discriminatory	*discriminatoire*
racial ['reiʃəl]	*racial*
racially	*sur le plan racial*
egalitarian	*égalitaire*
prejudiced	*plein de préjugés*
poor(ly)	*pauvre(ment)*
destitute	*démuni de tout*
wretched ['retʃid]	*misérable*
miserable	*malheureux, triste*
precarious [pri'kɛəriəs]	*précaire*
desperate(ly) ['despərit(li)]	*désespéré(ment)*
rejected [ri'dʒektid]	*rejeté*
starving	*mourant de faim*
well-fed	*bien nourri*
ill-fed	*mal nourri*
scanty	*insuffisant*
scarce	*peu abondant*
plentiful	*abondant*
sympathetic(ally)	*bienveillant (avec bienveillance)*
compassionate	*compatissant*
awful(ly)	*affreux, terrible(ment)*
dreadful(ly)	*épouvantable(ment)*
appalling(ly) [ə'pɔ:liŋ(li)]	*effroyable(ment)*

ruthless(ly) [‘ru:θlis(li)]	*impitoyable(ment)*
merciless(ly)	*implacable(ment)*
to own [əun]	*posséder*
to show* off wealth	*étaler ses biens*
to scorn	*mépriser*
to deprive	*priver*
to dispossess [‘dispə’zes]	*déposséder*
to need	*avoir besoin de*
to beg	*mendier*
to reject [‘ri:dʒekt]	*rejeter*
to shelter	*abriter*
to fail	*rater, échouer*
to starve	*mourir de faim*
to intervene [,intə’vi:n]	*intervenir, s’interposer*
to distribute, to deal* out	*distribuer*
to provide, to supply	*fournir*
to relieve	*soulager*
to exploit, to sweat	*exploiter*
to toil	*travailler dur*

to discriminate (against)	*faire de la discrimination (contre)*
to segregate	*pratiquer la ségrégation*
to flee*	*fuir*
to migrate	*se déplacer*
to emigrate	*émigrer*
to persecute	*persécuter*
to revolt	*se révolter*
to oppress	*opprimer*
to torture [‘tɔ:tʃə]	*torturer*
to suppress	*réprimer*
to crush [krʌʃ]	*écraser, réprimer*
to seize [si:z]	*saisir*
to annex [ə’neks]	*annexer*
to conquer	*conquérir*
to exterminate	*exterminer*
to decimate	*décimer*
to outlaw [‘aut-lɔ:]	*mettre hors-la-loi*
to deport [di’pɔ:t]	*déporter*
to displace	*déplacer*

Expressions

the affluent society	*la société d’abondance*
a status symbol	*un signe de réussite sociale*
to grow (get) rich	*s’enrichir*
to make a fortune	*faire fortune*
the standard of living	*le niveau de vie*
to exert pressure on	*exercer des pressions sur*
high-income brackets/groups	*les tranches de revenus élevés*
low-income brackets/groups	*les tranches de revenus bas*
a widening gap between rich and poor	*un écart grandissant entre les riches et les pauvres*
to be in need/want of something	*avoir besoin de quelque chose*
to be in dire straits	*être dans une situation désespérée*
to go busking	*mendier en faisant de la musique*
state allowances	*allocations de l’État*
social benefits	*les prestations sociales*
unemployment benefits	*l’allocation chômage*
to seek shelter	*chercher un abri*
the urban poor	*les pauvres des villes*
to feel rejected	*se sentir rejeté/exclu*
to live on the fringe of society	*vivre en marge de la société*
fringe groups	*les groupes (de) marginaux*
refugee camps	*des camps de réfugiés*
to dispatch emergency relief/aid	*expédier de l’aide d’urgence*
financial aid	*des aides financières*
to starve to death	*mourir de faim*
innocent civilians	*des civils innocents*
the starving Ethiopian populations	*les populations affamées d’Éthiopie*

displaced populations	*des populations déplacées*
to flee (from) oppression	*fuir l'oppression*
sweated workers	*des travailleurs exploités*
slave wages	*un salaire de misère*
migrant workers	*des travailleurs migrants*
an illegal immigrant	*un immigré clandestin*
an immigration quota	*un quota d'immigration*
an anti-immigrant feeling	*un sentiment anti-immigrés*
to be deported back home	*être déporté dans son pays d'origine*
to feel discriminated against	*se sentir l'objet de discrimination*
to be racially prejudiced	*avoir des préjugés raciaux*
an Indian reservation	*une réserve d'Indiens*
political exile	*l'exil politique*
political asylum	*l'asile politique*
to be under foreign rule	*être sous l'autorité/ la domination étrangère*
to be under someone's thumb	*être sous la coupe de quelqu'un*
to suppress a revolt/an uprising	*réprimer une révolte/un soulèvement*
to deprive someone of his liberty	*priver quelqu'un de sa liberté*

Phrases

Beggars can't be choosers.
Qui quémande ne peut choisir.

The rich get richer and the poor get poorer.
Les riches s'enrichissent et les pauvres s'apauvrissent.

Our affluent society often proves merciless to misfits.
Notre société d'abondance se révèle souvent impitoyable pour les marginaux.

White settlers decimated native tribes to annex their land.
Les colons blancs décimèrent les tribus indigènes afin d'annexer leurs territoires.

American blacks think they have not yet achieved economic equality.
Les Noirs américains estiment qu'ils ne sont pas encore parvenus à l'égalité sur le plan économique.

Stopping the rural exodus has now become a priority.
Arrêter l'exode rural est désormais une priorité.

Soup kitchens open each winter to feed the urban poor.
Des soupes populaires ouvrent chaque hiver pour nourrir les pauvres des villes.

The existence of ghettos casts a shadow on the American ideal of the Melting Pot.
L'existence de ghettos bat en brèche l'idéal américain du Creuset des Peuples.

Religious dissenters were either ruthlessly persecuted or forced to emigrate.
Les dissidents religieux étaient soit impitoyablement persécutés soit forcés d'émigrer.

The uprising was crushed by the army and ended in mass slaughter.
Le soulèvement fut réprimé par l'armée et se termina en carnage.

Exercices

I. Compléter les phrases suivantes :

Before being granted political (1)... he will have to prove that he was persecuted in his native country.

As a prominent member of the (2)... he naturally was a strong advocate of order based on hierarchy.

Unfortunately it seems that the gap between developed and underdeveloped countries has recently (3)... again.

In the 1920s farmers from Oklahoma (4)... the Dust Bowl for California.

The falling of prices of such (5)... as cocoa or coffee aggravated the debt of (6)... - ... countries.

The (7)... rights movement succeeded in making the middle classes aware of racial (8)... .

The United Nations decided that it had a right to (9)... pressure on tyrants in order to protect (10)... minorities.

II. Remettre les mots dans l'ordre correct :

1. seek / homeless / tube / destitute / the / winter / shelter / in / in / and / stations
2. American / parked / last / 20th / at / were / reservations / Indians / the / the / the / on / beginning / century / of
3. workshops / he / sweating / in / fortune / his / made / clandestine / textile / a / immigrants
4. wealth / do / if / off / show / what / people / their / not / would / they / could / affluent / ?
5. lavishly / guests / point / she / always / made / her / a / entertaining / of
6. fringe / live / addicts / feel / often / and / rejected / drug / the / of / on / society
7. shanty / big / displaced / gather / towns / cities / in / outside / populations / and
8. quotas / USA / were / 1923 / in / in / first / immigration / implemented / the
9. abolished / places / was / 60s / officially / public / segregation / the / in / in
10. themselves / commodity / pay / developing / unable / when / fell / debt / countries / their / found / to / prices

III. Reformuler les phrases en utilisant les mots entre parenthèses à la forme donnée :

1. American blacks still complain of being the victims of discrimination. (discriminated)
2. In order to survive he played music and begged in the streets of New York. (busking)
3. Those who could not reach the refugee camps just died of starvation. (death)
4. Even though he was no supporter of apartheid, there is no denying that he had a racial bias. (prejudiced)
5. The peasants who were hit by poverty moved to the overcrowded cities. (stricken)
6. He became rich selling sun lamps in Northern England. (fortune)

7. The Red Cross was called on to send aid as quickly as possible to relieve the displaced populations. (emergency)
8. Many intellectuals lost their freedom for expressing political opinions hostile to the military regime. (deprived)
9. Many lives will be lost if we cannot bring villagers the food and medicine they need. (supply)
10. The brutal massacre of young protesters by the military marked the beginning of the revolution. (slaughtering)

32. Meteorology and space
La météorologie et l'espace

Weather	***Le temps***
a forecast	*une prévision*
the weatherman	*M. Météo*
a thermometer	*un thermomètre*
a barometer	*un baromètre*
the sky	*le ciel*
a cloud	*un nuage*
the sun	*le soleil*
sunrise	*le lever du soleil*
the dew [dju:]	*la rosée*
sunset	*le coucher du soleil*
sunshine	*l'ensoleillement*
a sunbeam	*un rayon de soleil*
the dogdays	*la canicule*
a heatwave	*une vague de chaleur*
a drought [draut]	*une sécheresse*
a climate [‘klaimit]	*un climat*
a depression	*une dépression*
rain	*la pluie*
the rainy season	*la saison des pluies*
a raindrop	*une goutte de pluie*
rainfall	*les précipitations*
a rainbow	*un arc-en-ciel*
a shower [‘ʃau-ə]	*une averse*
a downpour [‘daunpɔ:]	*une forte averse*
a puddle	*une flaque d'eau*
the monsoon [mɔn'su:n]	*la mousson*
a storm	*une tempête*
a thunderstorm	*un orage*
lightning	*les éclairs, la foudre*
a flash	*un éclair*
a flood [flʌd]	*une inondation*
snow [snəu]	*la neige*
a snowfall	*une chute de neige*
a snowflake	*un flocon de neige*
a snowball	*une boule de neige*
a snowman	*un bonhomme de neige*
a snowstorm	*une tempête de neige*
a snowdrift	*une congère*
an avalanche [‘ævəla:nʃ]	*une avalanche*
sleet	*grésil, neige fondue*
the thaw [θɔ:]	*le dégel*
hail	*la grêle*
a hailstone	*un grêlon*
frost	*le gel*
hoarfrost	*le givre*
an icicle	*un petit glaçon, une chandelle de glace*
a haze	*une brume légère*
mist	*la brume*
fog	*le brouillard*
a draught [dra:ft]	*un courant d'air*
wind	*le vent*
a breeze	*une brise*
a gale [geil]	*un coup de vent, un grand vent*
a blizzard	*un blizzard*
a hurricane [‘hʌrikən]	*un ouragan*
a tornado	*une tornade*
a typhoon [tai'fu:n]	*un typhon*
a landslide	*un glissement de terrain*
an earthquake	*un tremblement de terre*
a volcano	*un volcan*
an eruption	*une éruption*
lava [‘la:və]	*la lave*
ashes	*des cendres*

a tide	*une marée*	rainy, wet	*pluvieux*
a tidal wave	*un raz-de-marée*	foul [faul], dreadful	*affreux*
sunny	*ensoleillé*	soaked	*trempé*
fine, fair	*beau*	thunderstruck	*foudroyé*
glorious	*magnifique*	to warn	*prévenir*
unsettled	*variable*	to forecast*	*prévoir*
bright	*clair, radieux*	to rain	*pleuvoir*
dry	*sec*	to drizzle	*bruiner*
cloudy	*nuageux*	to pour [pɔ:] down	*tomber à verse*
overcast	*couvert*	to hail [heil]	*grêler*
dull [dʌl]	*gris, triste*	to break* out	*éclater*
rainy	*pluvieux*	to rumble	*gronder*
windy ['windi]	*venteux*	to blow*	*souffler*
(it's) windy	*il fait du vent*	to snow	*neiger*
foggy	*brumeux*	to shine*	*briller*
(it's) foggy	*il y a du brouillard*	to dazzle	*éblouir*
snowy	*neigeux, enneigé*	to rise*	*se lever*
stormy, thundery	*orageux*	to set*	*se coucher*
close [kləus]	*lourd*	to thaw, to melt	*fondre*
stifling ['staifliŋ]	*étouffant*	to freeze*	*geler*
icy ['aisi]	*couvert de glace, glacial*	to whirl [wə:l]	*tourbillonner*
		to clear up	*s'éclaircir*
frosty	*gelé, glacial*	to clear away	*se dégager*
chilly	*frisquet*	to lift	*se lever (brouillard)*
cold	*froid*	to ease off	*s'atténuer (vent)*
wintry	*hivernal*	to pick up	*se renforcer (vent)*
cool	*frais*	to die down	*tomber (vent)*
warm	*chaud (agréable)*	to swell*	*grossir (rivière)*
mild [maild]	*doux*	to overflow	*déborder*
temperate	*tempéré*	to flood	*inonder*
hot	*chaud (forte chaleur)*	to carry along	*emporter*
sweltering	*accablant*	to quake [kweik]	*trembler*
scorching	*torride*	to shake*	*secouer*
humid, damp	*humide*	to erupt [i'rʌpt]	*entrer en éruption*

The universe — *L'univers*

(the) Earth	*la Terre*	a collision	*une collision*
the globe	*le globe*	an impact	*un impact*
a light-year	*une année lumière*	a cataclysm	*un cataclysme*
an earthling	*un terrien*	the atmosphere ['ætməsfiə]	*l'atmosphère*
an astronomer	*un astronome*		
a planet	*une planète*	the stratosphere	*la stratosphère*
a satellite ['sætəlait]	*un satellite*	outer space	*l'espace interstellaire*
a galaxy	*une galaxie*	the cosmos	*le cosmos*
a revolution	*une révolution*	radiation [ˌreidi'eiʃən]	*la radiation*
an orbit	*une orbite*		
a cycle	*un cycle*	an observatory	*un observatoire*
the moon	*la lune*	a telescope	*un télescope*
moonlight	*le clair de lune*	an eclipse	*une éclipse*
a star	*une étoile*	a ring	*un anneau*
a constellation	*une constellation*	Mercury	*Mercure*
a meteor ['mi:tjə]	*un météore*	Venus ['vi:nəs]	*Vénus*
a meteorite ['mi:tjərait]	*un météorite*	Pluto ['plu:təu]	*Pluton*
		Saturn ['sætən]	*Saturne*
a comet	*une comète*	Jupiter	*Jupiter*
an asteroid	*un astéroïde*	Mars [ma:z]	*Mars*
a fireball	*une boule de feu*	a Martian	*un Martien*

Uranus ['juərənəs]	*Uranus*	cosmic	*cosmique*
Neptune	*Neptune*	solar	*solaire*
gravity	*la pesanteur*	boundless	*sans limites*
gravitation	*la gravitation*	infinite ['infinit]	*infini*
weightlessness	*l'apesanteur*	earthbound	*en direction de la terre*
a cosmonaut	*un cosmonaute*		
an astronaut	*un astronaute*	extra-terrestrial	*extraterrestre*
a spaceship	*un vaisseau spatial*	electromagnetic	*électromagnétique*
a rocket	*une fusée*	to spin*	*tourner*
a shuttle	*une navette*	to revolve [ri'vɔlv]	*graviter*
a heat shield	*un bouclier thermique*	to attract	*attirer*
a space flight	*un vol spatial*	to twinkle	*scintiller*
a lunar module	*un module lunaire*	to collide [kə'laid]	*entrer en collision*
a moon walk	*une marche sur la lune*	to burn*	*se consumer*
		to break* up	*se fragmenter*
global	*mondial, planétaire*	to expand [iks'pænd]	*se développer, grandir*
universal	*universel*	to launch [lɔːntʃ]	*lancer*
gravitational	*gravitationnel*		

Expressions

an observation satellite	*un satellite d'observation*
the mean temperature	*la température moyenne*
high pressure	*haute pression*
low pressure	*basse pression*
a weather report	*un bulletin météorologique*
weather conditions	*les conditions météorologiques*
a harsh climate	*un climat rude*
a sunny spell	*une période ensoleillée*
a bright / sunny interval	*une éclaircie*
black ice	*le verglas*
below freezing point	*en dessous de zéro*
a flash of lightning	*un éclair*
a peal / clap of thunder	*un coup de tonnerre*
struck by lightning	*foudroyé*
a lightning conductor	*un paratonnerre*
to rain heavily	*pleuvoir fortement*
a heavy shower	*une forte averse*
to be pouring with rain	*pleuvoir à verse*
to get wet	*se faire mouiller*
to get soaked	*se faire tremper*
soaked to the skin	*trempé jusqu'aux os*
a heatwave	*une vague de chaleur*
sunny periods	*des périodes ensoleillées*
bright intervals	*de belles éclaircies*
a snow report	*un avis d'enneigement*
hard packed snow	*de la neige tassée*
high / low temperatures	*des hautes / basses températures*
sub-zero temperatures	*des températures au-dessous de zéro*
a gust of wind	*un coup de vent, une bourrasque*
an easterly / westerly wind	*un vent d'est / d'ouest*
a gale warning	*un avis de tempête*
a force 8 gale	*un vent de force 8*

the big bang	*le big-bang*
a black hole	*un trou noir*
the solar system	*le système solaire*
a solar eclipse	*une éclipse solaire*
a lunar eclipse	*une éclipse de lune*
a celestial body	*un astre*
the Milky Way	*la Voie Lactée*
the Great Bear, the Plough	*la Grande Ourse*
the Lesser Bear	*la Petite Ourse*
a shooting star	*une étoile filante*
the space age	*l'ère spatiale*
a space program	*un programme spatial*
a launch pad	*une aire de lancement*
a space laboratory, a skylab	*un laboratoire spatial*
to reach for the stars	*partir à la conquête de l'espace*
interstellar space	*l'espace intersidéral*
to go into orbit	*se mettre en orbite*
a heat shield	*un bouclier thermique*
a splash down	*un amerrissage*
a flying saucer	*une soucoupe volante*
little green men	*des petits hommes verts*
a U.F.O. (Unidentified Flying Object)	*un OVNI*

Phrases

It is raining cats and dogs.
Il tombe des cordes.

It never rains but it pours.
Un malheur ne vient jamais seul.

Every cloud has a silver lining.
Toute chose a son bon côté.

March winds and April showers bring forth May flowers.
Après la pluie le beau temps.

To be as right as rain.
Se porter comme un charme.

Let's hope the fog will lift soon.
Espérons que le brouillard va bientôt se lever.

Dark clouds are looming on the horizon.
De sombres nuages se profilent à l'horizon.

Space is filled with objects that threaten the Earth.
L'espace est plein d'objets qui menacent la planète Terre.

Some day, an asteroid or a comet will be on a collision course with the Earth.
Un jour, un astéroïde ou une comète sera sur une trajectoire de collision avec la terre.

Thousands of meteorites as big as a lump of coal fall every year, usually harmlessly.
Des milliers de météorites gros comme un morceau de charbon tombent chaque année, habituellement sans causer de dégâts.

Exercices

I. Compléter les phrases suivantes :

1. As the roof badly could barely withstand the rain, there was a ... of water in the middle of the floor.
2. Outlook : a few showers with ... intervals.
3. The ... temperature in Alaska is incredibly low.
4. He had left his umbrella at home and he got ... to the skin.
5. Please drive carefully : there will be some ... ice on the roads early in the morning.
6. It got so dark at midday that everyone thought of a ... eclipse.
7. Have you heard the weather ... : it's going to rain all day again!
8. He claims he saw a flying ... land in his field last night.
9. The ... wave flooded all coastal cities.
10. Looking through his ..., he was able to see some distant planets.

II. Retrouver l'adjectif :

1. drenched
2. not wet
3. changeable
4. uncomfortably warm
5. very cloudy
6. giving the feeling that breathing is difficult
7. marked by strong wind, heavy rain or snow or hail
8. without limits
9. of the sun
10. originating or existing outside the earth

III. Retrouver la préposition ou la postposition :

1. The weather cleared ... in the afternoon.
2. It poured ... rain all day.
3. He was struck ... lightning as he was working in his field.
4. Most meteorites break ... before they reach the atmosphere.
5. The high winds eased ... after a few hours.
6. The climate is very harsh in that country and the temperature is usually ... freezing point.
7. It rained heavily and he got soaked ... the skin.
8. The whole village was swept ... a landslide.
9. The rocket will go ... orbit as soon as it leaves the atmosphere.
10. It kept pouring ... and we had to cancel the barbecue party.

IX. TRADE

33• Economic issues
Les questions économiques

the economy	*l'économie*
economics	*la science économique*
trade	*le commerce, les échanges*
barter	*le troc*
bargaining	*le marchandage*
goods, wares	*des marchandises, des produits*
a product	*un produit*
a commodity	*une denrée, une marchandise*
business ['biznis]	*les affaires*
a businessman	*un homme d'affaires*
a business	*un commerce, une affaire*
marketing	*la mercatique*
management	*l'organisation, la gestion*
the management	*la direction, les administrateurs*
a boss	*un patron*
a manager	*un directeur*
an entrepreneur	*un chef d'entreprise*
an industrialist	*un industriel*
a magnate, a tycoon ['mægneit], [tai'ku:n]	*un magnat*
imports	*les importations*
exports	*les exportations*
protectionism	*le protectionnisme*
customs tariffs	*les tarifs douaniers*
tariff barriers/walls ['bæriəz]	*les barrières tarifaires*
a quota	*un contingent*
a ban (on), an embargo	*un embargo*
a blockade	*un blocus*
a freeze	*un gel*
a field, a domain	*un domaine*
a sector	*un secteur*
a market	*un marché*
an outlet	*un débouché*
a niche [ni:ʃ]	*un créneau*
a prospect, an outlook	*une perspective*
a tendency, a trend	*une tendance*

a forecast, an estimate	*une prévision*
a survey	*une étude*
a goal, a target	*un objectif*
a scheme, a project [ski:m]	*un projet, un plan d'action*
a policy	*une politique*
a meeting	*une réunion*
the agenda [ə'dʒendə]	*l'ordre du jour*
a package ['pækidʒ]	*un train de mesures*
talks	*des négociations*
a representative	*un représentant*
a deal	*un accord, une transaction*
an agreement	*un accord*
a contract	*un contrat*
a treaty	*un traité*
a deadline	*une date limite*
deregulation	*la déréglementation*
a criterion (criteria) [krai'tiəriən]	*un critère*
a standard	*une norme*
statistics	*les statistiques*
an index	*un indice*
figures ['figə]	*les chiffres*
a chart [tʃa:t]	*un tableau*
a graph [gra:f]	*une courbe*
a diagram	*un organigramme*
growth	*la croissance*
a pace	*un rythme, une cadence*
a budget	*un budget*
a currency ['kʌrənsi]	*une devise*
speculation	*la spéculation*
a speculator	*un spéculateur*
inflation	*l'inflation*
a revaluation	*une réévaluation*
a deficit	*un déficit*
a creditor	*un créancier*
an imbalance	*un déséquilibre*
accountancy	*la comptabilité*
an accountant	*un comptable*
the cost	*le coût*
expenditures [iks'penditʃəz]	*les dépenses*

overheads	*les frais généraux*
taxes	*les impôts, les taxes*
a loss	*une perte*
a bankruptcy ['bæŋkrəptsi]	*une faillite*
gains, profits	*les gains, les bénéfices*
profitability	*la rentabilité*
a margin ['ma:dʒin]	*une marge*
a turnover	*un chiffre d'affaires*
benefits	*les avantages*
cash	*les liquidités*
stock	*le stock*
assets ['æsets]	*l'actif*
toxic assets	*des actifs toxiques*
liabilities [,laiə'bilitiz]	*le passif*
an investment	*un investissement*
an investor	*un investisseur*
an outlay	*une mise de fonds*
sponsoring, sponsorship	*le parrainage*
a stake	*une participation, une mise*
a tender, a bid	*un appel d'offre, une soumission*
a merger ['mə:dʒə]	*une fusion*
a takeover	*un rachat, une absorption*
a partner	*un associé*
partnership	*le partenariat*
an incentive	*une stimulation*
a subsidy	*une subvention*
competition	*la concurrence*
competitiveness	*la compétitivité*
self-sufficiency	*l'autosuffisance*
a decrease	*une diminution*
a fall	*une chute*
an increase	*une augmentation*
a rise	*une hausse*
stagnation	*la stagnation*
a slack, a slowdown	*un ralentissement*
a downturn, a downswing	*une baisse d'activité*
a recession	*une récession*
a crisis ['kraisis] (crises) [kraisi:z]	*une crise*
a depression	*une dépression*
a slump	*un marasme*
a bust	*un effondrement*
a crash	*un krach*
a squeeze	*des mesures d'austérité, un resserrement*
a remedy ['remidi]	*une solution*
a recovery,	*une reprise,*
an upturn, a takeoff	*un redémarrage*
a boom [bu:m]	*un boom, un essor*

a monopoly	*un monopole*
a multinational	*une multinationale*
a company, a corporation	*une compagnie*
a firm, a concern	*une firme, une entreprise*
an undertaking, an enterprise	*une entreprise, une affaire*
a trust	*un cartel*
capital, funds	*les capitaux, les fonds*
finance [fai'næns]	*les finances*
a bank	*une banque*
a loan [ləun]	*un prêt*
a rate	*un taux*
a borrower	*un emprunteur*
interest	*l'intérêt, les intérêts*
a debt [det]	*une dette*
a savings bank	*une caisse d'épargne*
a deposit account	*un compte de dépôt*
a current account	*un compte courant*
a cheque, a check (US)	*un chèque*
a cheque book	*un carnet de chèques*
a cashier [kə'ʃiə], a teller	*un caissier*
a withdrawal	*un retrait*
a statement	*un relevé de compte*
an overdraft	*un découvert*
a credit card	*une carte de crédit*
the Stock Exchange	*la Bourse*
the quotation	*la cote*
a bond	*une obligation*
a security	*un titre, une valeur*
a share	*une action*
a shareholder	*un actionnaire*
a dividend	*un dividende*
a broker	*un courtier*
a stockbroker	*un agent de change*
financial	*financier*
commercial	*commercial*
economic	*économique*
economical, cost-saving	*économique (qui permet d'économiser)*
state-owned	*nationalisé*
subsidized	*subventionné*
private	*privé*
franchised	*franchisé*
self-employed	*à son compte*
greedy	*cupide*
costly	*coûteux*
managerial	*directorial*
competitive	*compétitif*
fierce/cut-throat/unfair	*féroce / acharnée / (concurrence) déloyale*
profit-making, profitable	*rentable, lucratif*

tax-free	*non imposé*
duty-free	*détaxé*
index-linked	*indexé*
due [dju:]	*exigible*
overdue	*échu, arriéré*
(in)solvent	*(in)solvable*
bankrupt	*en faillite*
debt-ridden	*criblé de dettes*
low, weak	*faible*
sluggish, slack	*stagnant, peu actif*
faltering	*défaillant*
ailing ['eiliŋ]	*en difficulté*
stable	*stable*
steady ['stedi]	*régulier, stable*
sound [saund]	*sain*
safe	*sûr*
risky	*hasardeux*
brisk	*actif*
keen	*vif*
buoyant [bɔiənt]	*animé, très actif*
fast-growing	*en pleine expansion*
flourishing, ['flɔriʃiŋ] thriving	*florissant, prospère*
average ['ævəridʒ]	*moyen*
plummeting ['plʌmitiŋ]	*en chute libre*
zooming, rocketing	*qui grimpe en flèche*
gloomy	*sombre, morose*
dramatic [drə'mætik]	*considérable*
sweeping	*énorme*
bearish ['bɛəriʃ]	*orienté à la baisse (marché)*
bullish	*orienté à la hausse*
to trade (in)	*faire le commerce (de)*
to import	*importer*
to export	*exporter*
to supply	*fournir*
to meet*	*satisfaire, honorer*
to bargain	*négocier, marchander*
to barter ['ba:tə]	*troquer*
to compete (with)	*être en concurrence (avec)*
to undertake*	*entreprendre*
to found	*fonder*
to manage, to run*	*diriger, gérer*
to plan	*planifier*
to settle	*régler*
to iron out [aiən]	*aplanir*
to streamline, to slim down	*dégraisser*
to free	*libérer*
to freeze*	*geler*
to handle	*traiter, manipuler*
to implement	*mettre en œuvre*
to expand [iks'pænd]	*être en expansion*
to boom	*être en plein essor*
to thrive, to flourish ['flʌriʃ]	*prospérer*
to diversify [dai'və:sifai]	*(se) diversifier*
to update	*moderniser*
to upgrade	*améliorer*
to sponsor	*patronner*
to grant	*accorder*
to subsidize	*subventionner*
to fund	*financer*
to loan	*prêter*
to borrow	*emprunter*
to invest	*investir*
to boost [bu:st]	*stimuler, relancer*
to denationalize	*dénationaliser*
to take* over	*racheter, reprendre*
to merge [mə:dʒ]	*fusionner*
to benefit (from)	*bénéficier (de)*
to earn [ə:n]	*gagner*
to break* even	*rentrer dans ses frais*
to cash	*encaisser*
to tax	*imposer*
to levy	*prélever, percevoir*
to jeopardize	*mettre en danger*
to harm	*nuire*
to decline	*être en déclin*
to slump	*s'effondrer*
to plummet	*dégringoler*
to pick up	*redémarrer*
to take* off	*décoller*
to skyrocket, to soar [sɔ:]	*grimper en flèche*
to narrow	*(se) réduire*
to widen	*(s')élargir*
to cut* (down), to curtail [kə:'teil]	*diminuer, réduire*
to speculate	*spéculer*
to devalue	*dévaluer*
to revalue	*réévaluer*

Expressions

a (free) market economy	*une économie de type libéral*
a (centrally) planned economy	*une économie de type planifié*
a mixed economy	*une économie de type mixte*
a free-trade area	*une zone de libre-échange*

the black market	*le marché noir*
foreign trade	*le commerce extérieur*
a trade agreement	*un accord commercial*
the trade gap	*le déficit commercial*
the balance of trade, the trade balance	*la balance commerciale*
the trade surplus	*l'excédent commercial*
domestic trade	*le commerce intérieur*
the Gross National Product (GNP)	*le Produit National Brut (PNB)*
the Gross Domestic Product (GDP)	*le Produit Intérieur Brut (PIB)*
the per capita income	*le revenu par habitant*
supply and demand	*l'offre et la demande*
market research	*l'étude de marché*
to penetrate a market	*conquérir un marché*
to phase out of the market	*retirer progressivement du marché*
a bear market	*un marché orienté à la baisse*
a bull market	*un marché orienté à la hausse*
to allow goods in	*laisser entrer des marchandises*
to do business with	*entretenir des relations commerciales avec*
unfair trade practices	*des pratiques commerciales déloyales*
rules and regulations	*la réglementation*
the growth index	*l'indice de croissance*
the ups and downs	*les hauts et les bas*
austere times	*une période d'austérité*
the oil shock	*le choc pétrolier*
the Stock Exchange crash	*le krach boursier*
to be at a standstill	*être au point mort*
to be in the red	*être en déficit*
the exchange rate	*le taux de change*
a hard currency	*une devise forte*
a soft currency	*une devise faible*
the primary/secondary/tertiary sector	*le secteur primaire/secondaire/tertiaire*
to set up/to start a business	*créer une société*
to raise capital	*trouver des fonds*
cost savings	*la réduction des coûts*
gross profit	*la marge brute*
overhead costs	*les frais généraux*
tax evasion	*la fraude fiscale*
profit-sharing	*la participation aux bénéfices*
to share in the profits	*participer aux bénéfices*
to suffer a loss	*subir des pertes*
to foot the bill	*régler la note*
a chartered accountant	*un expert-comptable*
to wind up a business	*liquider une affaire*
to go out of business	*fermer, cesser ses activités*
decision making	*la prise de décision*
a decision-maker	*un décideur*
a round-table discussion	*une table ronde*
to make/strike a deal	*conclure un marché*
the Board of Directors	*le conseil d'administration*
the Chairman of the Board	*le président du conseil d'administration*
the C.E.O. (Chief Executive Officer) (US), the managing director (GB)	*le P.D.G.*
the chief of staff, the head of personnel	*le chef du personnel*
a company car	*une voiture de société*

a business trip — *un voyage d'affaires*
a state-owned company — *une société d'état*
a small or medium-sized company — *une P.M.E.*
a family firm — *une entreprise familiale*
a takeover bid — *une O.P.A.*
a lame duck — *un canard boiteux*

Phrases

In China, commercial interests go hand in hand with diplomatic concerns.
En Chine, les intérêts commerciaux vont de pair avec les préoccupations diplomatiques.

Business is very slack as the market is at its weakest.
Comme le marché est à son niveau le plus faible, les affaires ne marchent pas.

Switching from a planned economy over to free enterprise is a difficult process.
Le passage du dirigisme économique à la libre entreprise est un processus difficile.

Lewis overspent and, as a result, found that his account was in the red.
Lewis a trop dépensé et, en conséquence, il s'est aperçu que son compte était à découvert.

The world is undergoing the most severe economic hardships since World War II.
Le monde connaît les difficultés économiques les plus sévères depuis la Seconde Guerre mondiale.

They failed to meet the targets set by the International Monetary Fund.
Ils n'ont pas réussi à atteindre les objectifs fixés par le Fonds Monétaire International.

Soaring prices and a worthless currency have reduced their standard of living to a bare minimum.
La flambée des prix et une devise sans valeur ont réduit leur niveau de vie à un strict minimum.

They have spent their life savings on having a house built in the country.
Ils ont dépensé les économies de toute une vie pour se faire construire une maison à la campagne.

US companies accuse state-owned firms of receiving multi-billion-dollar subsidies.
Les compagnies américaines accusent les sociétés étatisées de recevoir des milliards de dollars de subventions.

During the boom years, Japan's domestic market, rather than exports, drove the economy.
Pendant les années de prospérité, c'est le marché intérieur japonais, plutôt que les exportations, qui ont fait marcher l'économie.

Exercices

I. Retrouver les mots répondant aux définitions suivantes :

1. the exchange of goods for other goods
2. a situation in which you are forced to sell your property to pay your creditors
3. a sum of money that is lent
4. money granted by the government to an industry that needs help

5. periodical payment to shareholders
6. the possession of the sole right to supply
7. unlawful buying and selling of goods
8. fixed limit of time
9. amount spent
10. quantity of goods allowed to enter a country

II. Retrouver la postposition ou la préposition :

1. The UN imposed a ban ... arms imports.
2. That firm was taken ... by an American company.
3. They are expecting sales to take ... during the Christmas period.
4. Business is very low, but experts forecast that it will pick ... in the spring.
5. The negotiations with the management are ... a standstill.
6. They have benefited ... the new economic policy.
7. The boss has decided that expenditures are to be cut ... .
8. My account is always ... the red at the end of the month.
9. He set ... his firm when he was twenty.
10. The workers told the management they wanted a share ... the profits.

III. Traduire en anglais :

1. Pour trouver des fonds, le conseil d'administration a été contraint de vendre une partie du stock.
2. Les actionnaires ont bénéficié du redémarrage économique.
3. Suite à une mauvaise gestion, cette compagnie a fait faillite.
4. Le P.D.G. est parti en voyage d'affaires aux États-Unis.
5. Ils ont entrepris de trouver de nouveaux débouchés.
6. Leur nouvelle politique vise à stimuler le marché extérieur.
7. Le produit intérieur brut est en déclin depuis plusieurs mois.
8. Leurs bénéfices ont dégringolé après le choc pétrolier.
9. L'état accorde de moins en moins de subventions.
10. La vente de marchandises détaxées représente la moitié de leur chiffre d'affaires.

34. Shopping
Les achats

a shop	*un magasin*	a delivery	*une livraison*
a sale	*une vente*	a market	*un marché*
a purchase ['pə:tʃəs]	*un achat*	a stall [stɔ:l]	*un étal*
a (department) store	*un grand magasin*	a supermarket	*un supermarché*
		a hypermarket	*un hypermarché*
a chain store	*une chaîne*	a trolley ['trɔ:li]	*un chariot*
a branch [bra:ntʃ]	*une succursale*		

a shop window	*une vitrine, une devanture*
a sign [sain]	*une enseigne*
an escalator	*un escalier mécanique*
a lift	*un ascenseur*
an item ['aitəm], an article	*un article*
a range, a line	*une gamme*
packaging	*le conditionnement*
a paper bag	*un sac en papier*
a fashion	*une mode*
a craze, a fad	*une vogue*
a price	*un prix*
a make	*une marque (produits manufacturés)*
a brand	*une marque (nourriture, pr. chimiques)*
sales	*les soldes*
a crowd [kraud]	*une foule*
a rush	*une ruée*
a discount	*une ristourne*
a bargain	*une affaire, une offre exceptionnelle*
a special offer	*une offre spéciale*
a display	*un étalage, une exposition*
a shelf (shelves)	*une étagère*
a counter	*un comptoir*
a department	*un rayon*
a showroom	*une salle d'exposition*
a basement ['beismənt]	*un sous-sol*
the cash desk, the checkout (supermarket)	*la caisse*
a cashier [kæ'ʃiə]	*un caissier, une caissière*
a queue [kju:]	*une queue*
a shop assistant	*un vendeur*
a shopkeeper	*un commerçant*
a retailer	*un détaillant*
a dealer	*un concessionnaire*
a wholesaler	*un grossiste*
a middleman	*un intermédiaire*
a rep(resentative)	*un représentant*
teleshopping	*la télévente*
a customer, a client, a patron ['peitrən]	*un client*
a shopper, a buyer, a purchaser	*un acheteur*
a consumer	*un consommateur*
a shoplifter	*un voleur à l'étalage*
Shops	*Les magasins*
a baker	*un boulanger*
a baker's shop	*une boulangerie*
a cake shop	*une pâtisserie*
a butcher ['butʃə]	*un boucher*
a butcher's shop	*une boucherie*

a grocer ['grəusə]	*un épicier*
a grocer's shop	*une épicerie*
a greengrocer	*un marchand de légumes*
a delicatessen	*une épicerie fine*
the milkman	*le laitier*
a cheese shop	*une fromagerie*
a cheesemonger	*un marchand de fromages*
a fishmonger	*un poissonnier*
a fishmonger's shop	*une poissonnerie*
a confectioner	*un confiseur*
a confectioner's shop, a sweet shop	*une confiserie*
a tobacconist	*un marchand de tabac*
a tobacconist's shop	*un bureau de tabac*
a bookseller	*un libraire*
a bookshop	*une librairie*
a stationer ['steiʃənə]	*un papetier*
a stationer's shop	*une papeterie*
a newsagent	*un marchand de journaux*
a chemist ['kemist]	*un pharmacien*
a chemist's shop, a pharmacy	*une pharmacie*
a clothes shop	*un magasin de vêtements*
a fashion boutique	*une boutique de mode*
a dummy ['dʌmi]	*un mannequin*
a dry cleaner's	*une teinturerie*
a laundry ['lɔ:ndri]	*une blanchisserie*
a launderette	*une laverie automatique*
a hairdresser, a barber (US)	*un coiffeur*
a hairdressing salon ['sælɔ̃:ŋ]	*un salon de coiffure*
a beauty salon	*un salon de beauté*
a shoe-repair shop	*une cordonnerie*
a hardware shop	*une quincaillerie*
a flower shop, a florist's shop	*un fleuriste*
a computer shop	*un magasin d'informatique*
a record shop ['rekɔ:d]	*un magasin de disques*
an antique(s) shop	*un antiquaire*
an antique dealer	*un marchand d'antiquités*
a junk shop	*une brocante*
a furniture shop	*un magasin de mobilier*
an off-licence, a wine shop, a liquor store (US) ['likə]	*un magasin de vins et alcools*
the undertaker's	*l'entreprise de pompes funèbres*

Note : Les constructions génitives deviennent généralement des cas possessifs incomplets ("You go to the baker's to buy a loaf of bread", "She met her friend at the butcher's"). Dans les autres cas, le mot "shop" ne peut être omis ("I bought a lovely bottle of claret at the wine shop").

cheap, inexpensive	*bon marché*
low [ləu]	*bas*
dirt cheap	*à très bas prix, donné*
shoddy	*de mauvaise qualité*
defective, faulty	*défectueux*
worthless	*sans valeur*
old-fashioned	*démodé*
genuine ['dʒenjuin]	*authentique*
new	*neuf*
second hand	*d'occasion*
soiled	*sali*
discounted, reduced	*à prix réduit*
moderate ['mɔdəreit]	*modéré*
economical [,i:kə'nɔmikəl]	*économique, économe*
high	*élevé*
expensive, dear	*cher*
costly, pricey	*coûteux*
overpriced	*dont le prix est excessif*
fair	*raisonnable*
extravagant [iks'trævigənt]	*dépensier, gaspilleur*
free, costless	*gratuit*
returnable, refunded	*consigné, remboursé*
self-service	*libre service*
well stocked	*bien achalandé*
convenient [kən'vi:njənt]	*pratique*
attractive	*attirant, séduisant*
tempting	*tentant*
custom-made, customized ['kʌstəmaizd]	*sur mesure*
flourishing, prosperous	*florissant, prospère*
crowded	*plein de monde*
noisy	*bruyant*
bankrupt	*en faillite*

to buy*, to purchase ['pə:tʃəs]	*acheter*
to choose*	*choisir*
to consume	*consommer*
to bargain	*marchander*
to shop	*faire ses courses, des achats*
to patronize	*accorder sa clientèle à*
to order	*commander*
to pay*	*payer*
to cost*	*coûter*
to spend*	*dépenser*
to open	*ouvrir*
to close	*fermer*
to sell*	*vendre*
to reduce	*réduire*
to complain	*se plaindre*
to return, to take* back	*rapporter*
to refund ['ri'fʌnd]	*rembourser*
to check	*vérifier*
to mend	*réparer*
to cash	*encaisser*
to supply	*fournir, approvisionner*
to charge (for)	*faire payer*
to label ['leibl]	*étiqueter*
to wrap [ræp]	*envelopper*
to pack	*emballer*
to weigh [wei]	*peser*
to deliver	*livrer*
to send*	*envoyer*
to receive	*recevoir*
to trade in, to deal* in	*faire le commerce de*
to manage, to run*	*diriger, gérer*
to stock, to store	*stocker*
to display	*exposer*

Expressions

to go shopping	*faire les commissions*
to go window-shopping	*faire du lèche-vitrines*
to shop around	*chercher des bonnes occasions*
to go on a shopping spree	*faire des achats extravagants*
home-shopping	*les achats à domicile*
a mail-order company	*une maison de vente par correspondance*

a price tag	*une étiquette portant le prix*
a bar code	*un code barres*
a shopping centre, a shopping mall	*un centre commercial*
a shopping arcade	*une galerie marchande*
a sports shop	*un magasin d'articles de sport*
a camera store	*un magasin d'appareils photo*
a D.I.Y. store	*un magasin de bricolage*
a flea market	*un marché aux puces*
a junk shop	*une brocante*
the purchasing/spending power	*le pouvoir d'achat*
the Consumer Price Index (C.P.I.)	*l'indice des prix à la consommation*
consumer habits	*les habitudes de consommation*
consumer protection	*la protection des consommateurs*
consumer trends	*les tendances de consommation*
a consumer group	*une association de consommateurs*
price regulation	*la réglementation des prix*
to pay cash	*payer comptant*
to pay on delivery	*payer à la livraison*
free of charge	*sans frais*
Value-Added Tax (V.A.T.)	*la T.V.A.*
to buy on credit	*acheter à crédit*
hire purchase	*l'achat à crédit*
a down payment	*un premier versement*
a credit card	*une carte de crédit*
to pay with plastic money	*payer avec une carte de crédit*
a credit freeze	*un gel du crédit*
terms of payment	*des conditions de paiement*
a quality standard	*une norme de qualité*
the quality/price ratio, the value for money	*le rapport qualité/prix*
a range of goods	*une ligne de produits*
a free sample	*un échantillon gratuit*
a clearance sale	*des soldes, une liquidation*
out of stock	*en rupture de stock*
to slash/to undercut prices	*sacrifier les prix*
a (good) bargain	*une bonne affaire*
a self-service store	*un magasin libre-service*
the fish counter	*la poissonnerie (supermarché)*
the shoe department	*le rayon des chaussures*
to meet customers' needs	*satisfaire les besoins des clients*
a cut in prices	*une réduction des prix*

Phrases

The customer is always right.
Le client a toujours raison.

John went to the hairdresser's yesterday to have his hair cut.
John est allé chez le coiffeur hier pour se faire couper les cheveux.

The January sales always attract huge crowds of shoppers.
Les soldes de janvier attirent toujours des foules énormes d'acheteurs.

These cheap TV sets are selling like hot cakes.
Ces postes de télévision bon marché se vendent comme des petits pains.

This fabric is sold by the metre. *Ce tissu se vend au mètre.*

She no longer uses her credit card as she tends to spend more than she can afford.
Comme elle a tendance à dépenser plus qu'elle ne peut se le permettre, elle n'utilise plus sa carte de crédit.

He goes round all the stores hunting for a bargain.
Il fait tous les grands magasins en quête de la bonne affaire.

Most of the items on display were going for a song. and people were snatching them up.
La plupart des articles exposés coûtaient un bouchée de pain et les gens se les arrachaient.

If you are sold a faulty article, don't hesitate to take it back and complain to the store manager.
Si l'on vous vend un article défectueux, n'hésitez pas à le rapporter et à vous plaindre au directeur du magasin.

He had put in an order with a mail-order company, but the goods were not delivered in due time.
Il avait fait une commande auprès d'une société de vente par correspondance, mais les marchandises ne furent pas livrées en temps voulu.

Exercices

I. Compléter les phrases suivantes :

1. The store detective caught a ... red-handed as the latter was trying to steal a pair of gloves.
2. She went on a shopping ... and came back loaded with parcels.
3. If you find our price ... than any competitor's, we'll lower it!
4. Nowadays, most customers tend to shop for goods that are good ... for money.
5. As the guarantee had run out, they ... her £20 for the repair.
6. They often give you free ... as you go into the supermarket.
7. He went to the ... store to buy a repair kit.
8. He wanted to buy some salmon, but he couldn't find the fish ... .
9. She bought an antique lamp at the ... market.
10. As he could not afford a new one, he bought his fridge ... .

II. Quels sont les adjectifs correspondant aux définitions suivantes ?

1. having no value
2. wasting money
3. made according to your requirements
4. not wasteful
5. dirty
6. full of people
7. out of date

8. true
9. suitable, handy
10. of poor quality

III. Retrouver la préposition ou la postposition :

1. He bought his car ... credit.
2. What do you trade ...?
3. Customers are expecting a cut ... prices.
4. That percolator was very good value ... money.
5. It is always worth shopping ... : you find bargains!
6. He said he would pay ... delivery.
7. They sent him the parcel free ... charge.
8. Since you don't like it, why don't you take it ... to the shop?
9. Tomatoes are sold ... the pound.
10. I think he deals ... used cars.

35• Advertising
La publicité

advertising, publicity	*la publicité*
an advertiser, an adman	*un publicitaire*
a publicist	*un agent de publicité*
an advertisement, an advert, an ad	*une publicité*
a commercial, a spot ad	*un spot publicitaire*
a commercial break	*une page de publicité*
a flash	*un flash*
a (video) clip	*un clip*
a jingle	*un couplet publicitaire*
hype [haip]	*le battage publicitaire*
teasing	*l'aguichage*
a campaign	*une campagne*
promotion	*la promotion*
a strategy	*une stratégie*
a target	*une cible*
design [di'zain]	*la conception*
a concept	*un concept*
a designer	*un stylicien, un concepteur*
a graphic designer	*un graphiste*
a sitter, a model	*un modèle*
a close-up	*un gros plan*
punch	*le dynamisme*
a challenge	*un défi*
a logo	*un logo*
a motto, a slogan	*un slogan*
a follow-up	*une relance*
a survey ['sə:vei]	*une étude*
a poll [pəul]	*un sondage*
an interviewer	*un enquêteur*
a questionnaire	*un questionnaire*
a reply coupon	*un coupon-réponse*
a user ['ju:zə]	*un utilisateur*
a leaflet, a flyer	*un prospectus*
a sticker	*un autocollant*
a folder	*un dépliant*
a booklet, a brochure ['brəuʃjuə]	*une brochure*
a poster, a bill	*une affiche*
a billboard, a hoarding	*un panneau publicitaire*
the cityscape	*le paysage urbain*
a drawing	*un dessin*
a caption	*une légende*
a pun	*un jeu de mots*
a trick	*une astuce*
a box	*un encadré*

a coupon, a voucher	*un bon de réduction*
a discount	*un rabais*
a rebate	*une ristourne*
a prize	*un prix, un lot*
a special offer	*une promotion*
a label [‘leibl]	*une étiquette (descriptive)*
a (price) tag	*une étiquette (prix)*
packaging	*l'emballage, le conditionnement*
a trial [‘traiəl]	*un essai*
manipulating	*manipulateur*
deceptive, [di’septiv]	
misleading	*mensonger*
deceitful [di’si:tful]	*trompeur*
shocking	*choquant*
clumsy	*maladroit*
far-fetched	*exagéré*
flashy	*tape-à-l'œil*
gaudy [‘gɔ:di]	*criard*
incredible	*incroyable*
formal	*guindé*
odd	*bizarre*
realistic	*réaliste*
lifesize	*en taille réelle*
truthful	*véridique*
appealing	*attirant*
eye-catching, catchy	*accrocheur*
entertaining	*divertissant*
funny	*amusant*
comical	*comique*
efficient	*efficace*
effective	*qui à de l'effet*
relevant [‘relivənt]	*pertinent*
convincing	*convaincant, persuasif*
clever	*astucieux, ingénieux*
cunning [‘kʌniŋ]	*habile, rusé*
outstanding	*remarquable*
creative	*créatif*
imaginative	*imaginatif*
ubiquitous [ju(:)’bikwitəs]	*omniprésent*

to advertise	*faire la publicité pour*
to promote,to publicize	*promouvoir*
to launch [lɔ:ntʃ]	*lancer*
to sponsor	*commanditer*
to market	*commercialiser*
to position	*positionner*
to design	*concevoir*
to target [‘ta:git]	*cibler*
to focus (on)	*se concentrer (sur)*
to broadcast*	*diffuser*
to communicate	*communiquer*
to saturate	*saturer*
to suggest	*suggérer*
to underline, to emphasize	*souligner*
to enhance	*mettre en valeur*
to reinforce	*renforcer*
to influence	*influencer*
to convince	*convaincre*
to compel	*forcer*
to achieve [ə’tʃi:v]	*réussir*
to manipulate	*manipuler*
to condition, to brainwash	*conditionner*
to call on	*faire appel à*
to stir, to rouse [rauz]	*éveiller, faire naître*
to appeal to	*attirer*
to embody	*incarner*
to exhibit	*exposer, montrer*
to entertain	*divertir*
to distort	*déformer*
to deceive	*tromper*
to bother [‘bɔðə]	*déranger*
to assume [ə’sju:m]	*supposer*
to energize	*dynamiser*
to boost [bu:st]	*donner un coup de fouet*
to test	*essayer*
to select	*choisir*
to compete with	*concurrencer*

Expressions

a bus shelter	*un abribus*
urban furniture	*le mobilier urbain*
an advertising agency	*une agence publicitaire*
an advertising campaign	*une campagne publicitaire*
an advertising blitz	*un matraquage publicitaire*
a brand image	*une image de marque*
a quality standard	*une norme de qualité*
an advertising medium	*un support publicitaire*

a market survey	*une étude des supports publicitaires*
to air a commercial	*diffuser un message publicitaire*
a commercial break	*une page publicitaire*
peak viewing time, prime time	*les heures de grande audience*
audience rating	*l'indice d'écoute*
sandwich board advertising	*de la publicité par homme sandwich*
advertising space	*l'espace publicitaire*
comparative advertising	*la publicité comparative*
deceptive advertising	*la publicité mensongère*
adverse publicity	*de la contre-publicité*
a give-away paper	*un journal gratuit*
direct mail advertising	*la publicité par correspondance*
a reply card	*une carte-réponse*
a mailing list	*un fichier d'adresses*
a market survey	*une étude de marché*
a brand manager	*un chef de produit*
a field survey	*une étude sur le terrain*
the customer profile	*le profil de la clientèle*
a prospective customer	*un client potentiel*
an age group	*une tranche d'âge*
a cross section	*un échantillon représentatif*
an introductory offer	*une offre de lancement*
a special offer	*une offre spéciale, une promotion*
a free offer	*une offre gratuite*
a sampling demonstration	*une dégustation*
a stamp card	*une carte de fidélité*
a savings voucher	*un bon de réduction*
a sales promotion	*une campagne de vente*
to entice someone into buying	*pousser quelqu'un à acheter*
a buying incentive	*une incitation à l'achat*

Phrases

Advertising can brainwash some consumers into buying useless gadgets.
La publicité peut, par lavage de cerveau, pousser certains consommateurs à acheter des gadgets inutiles.

The more catchy the slogan, the more efficient an advert will be.
Plus le slogan est accrocheur, plus une publicité sera efficace.

I've seen this new brand advertised on television.
J'ai vu de la publicité pour cette nouvelle marque à la télévision.

Some commercials are so cleverly designed that they are quite entertaining.
Certains spots publicitaires sont si habilement conçus qu'ils sont tout-à-fait divertissants.

I hate seeing the walls of our cities plastered with gaudy posters.
Je déteste voir les murs de nos villes tapissés d'affiches criardes.

I don't see why films should be interrupted by commercial breaks.
Je ne vois pas pourquoi les films devraient être interrompus par des pauses publicitaires.

They regularly offer free samples to develop customer loyalty.
Ils offrent régulièrement des échantillons gratuits pour fidéliser la clientèle.

There are two kinds of French ads: one where a woman has her clothes off, the other where she takes them off.
Il y a deux sortes de publicités en France : l'une où une femme n'a pas de vêtements, l'autre où elle les enlève.

The launching of an advertising campaign requires skill and competence.
Le lancement d'une campagne publicitaire demande des capacités et de la compétence.

Owing to increasing advertising rates, more and more companies resort to sport sponsorship.
À cause de l'augmentation des tarifs publicitaires, de plus en plus de compagnies ont recours au parrainage sportif.

Exercices

I. Retrouver les dix expressions correctes :

1. urban time 2. a video furniture 3. a free list 4. a brand offer 5. prime survey 6. a buying clip 7. a cross card 8. a stamp incentive 9. a mailing image 10. a field section

II. Quels sont les adjectifs correspondant aux définitions suivantes :

1. intentionally misleading
2. too bright and showy
3. present everywhere
4. exaggerated
5. true to life
6. strange, peculiar
7. persuasive
8. particularly amusing
9. clever at deceiving
10. to the point

III. Remettre les éléments de la colonne de droite dans le bon ordre et traduire les phrases obtenues :

An efficient poster always	search for a key to Europe's single market.
I wonder how my address	ends December 24th.
Many sportsmen are now	required.
Offer	has a catchy slogan.
Advertisers	ended up on their mailing list.
This is the third time this evening	send it in to the following address.

I do not wish to receive	a top priority for a media executive.
Complete the coupon, tear it off and	they have broadcast this commercial.
No stamps	used as advertising media.
Buying the best advertising space is	promotional material from other companies.

36. Popular phrases and sayings
Expressions populaires et dictons

Animal metaphors — ***Métaphores animales***

a red herring	*une manœuvre de diversion*
a white elephant	*une usine à gaz*
a black sheep	*une brebis galeuse*
a dark horse	*un concurrent inattendu*
a loan shark	*un usurier*
a bone of contention	*une pomme de discorde*
free as a bird	*libre comme l'air*
(as) pissed as a newt	*beurré comme un petit Lu*
as mad as a March hare	*fou à lier*
like a bull in a china shop	*comme un éléphant dans un magasin de porcelaine*
to have a bee in one's bonnet	*être obsédé par une idée*
to have bats in the belfry	*avoir une araignée au plafond*
to make a bee line for something	*aller droit vers quelque chose*
to have a frog in one's throat	*avoir un chat dans la gorge*
to shed crocodile tears	*verser des larmes de crocodile*
to be long in the tooth	*avoir l'expérience de l'âge*
to pigeon-hole people	*mettre les gens dans des cases*
to have a bone to pick with someone	*avoir envie d'en découdre avec quelqu'un*
to be as dead as a dodo	*être mort et enterré*
to open a can of worms	*tomber sur un sac de nœuds*
to kill the goose that lays the golden eggs	*tuer la poule aux œufs d'or*
to kill two birds with one stone	*faire d'une pierre deux coups*
to have gooseflesh	*avoir la chair de poule*
to go to bed with the lamb and rise with the lark	*se coucher avec le soleil et se lever aux aurores*
to keep the wolf from the door	*(se) mettre à l'abri du besoin*
I had it straight from the horse's mouth.	*Ce sont des informations de première main.*
I am at the end of my tether.	*Je suis à bout de patience.*
There's a fly in the ointment.	*Il y a un os.*
I smell a rat.	*Je flaire quelque chose de suspect.*
You could have knocked me down with a feather!	*Là tu m'en as bouché un coin !*

It's raining cats and dogs.	*Il pleut comme vache qui pisse.*
You're barking up the wrong tree!	*Tu te trompes d'adversaire !*
We were as snug as a bug in a rug.	*On était bien aises.*
I've known her for donkey's years.	*Je la connais depuis une éternité.*
If pigs could fly...	*Quand les poules auront des dents...*
It's like water off a duck's back.	*Ça ne (lui) fait ni chaud ni froid.*
Birds of a feather flock together.	*Qui se ressemble s'assemble.*
A bird in the hand is worth two in the bush.	*Un tiens vaut mieux que deux tu l'auras.*
The early bird catches the worm.	*L'avenir appartient à ceux qui se lèvent tôt.*
One swallow doesn't make a summer.	*Une hirondelle ne fait pas le printemps.*
If you run after two hares, you will catch neither.	*Il ne sert à rien de courir deux lièvres à la fois.*
Don't look a gift horse in the mouth.	*À cheval donné, on ne regarde pas les dents.*
Barking dogs seldom bite.	*Chien qui aboie rarement mord.*
Her bark is worse than her bite.	*Elle parle fort mais elle n'est pas méchante.*
He that would hang his dog gives out first that he is mad.	*Qui veut pendre son chien prétend qu'il a la rage.*
There's more than one way to skin a cat.	*Il y a plusieurs manières de s'y prendre.*
It's the last straw that breaks the (laden) camel's back.	*C'est la goutte d'eau qui fait déborder le vase.*
A fox is not taken twice in the same snare.	*On ne m'y (l'y) reprendra pas.*
Who keeps company with the wolves will learn to howl.	*À fréquenter les bandits, on le devient soi-même.*
The law catches flies but lets hornets go free.	*La justice prend le menu fretin mais laisse échapper les gros poissons.*
When the cat's away the mice will play.	*Quand le chat n'est pas là les souris dansent.*

Bodily metaphors ***Métaphores corporelles***

a private eye	*un détective privé*
a peeping Tom	*un petit curieux (un voyeur)*
a leap in the dark	*un saut dans l'inconnu*
a tongue-in-cheek remark	*une remarque ironique (au deuxième degré)*
an Achilles' heel	*un point faible (talon d'Achille)*
a stumbling block	*une pierre d'achoppement*
a blackleg	*un jaune (non gréviste)*
without batting an eyelid	*sans sourciller (imperturbablement)*
off the cuff	*sans notes, ex abrupto*
by rule of thumb	*de manière empirique*
to be under someone's thumb	*être sous la coupe de quelqu'un*
to be born with a silver spoon in one's mouth	*naître dans la soie*
to toe the line	*obtempérer, se mettre au pas*
to have cold feet	*avoir la trouille*
to put one's foot in it	*faire une gaffe*
to sleep tight	*dormir à poings fermés*
to set off on the wrong foot	*prendre un mauvais départ*

to be alive and kicking	*être (encore) bien vivant*
to jump on the bandwagon	*suivre le mouvement*
to pay on the nail	*payer rubis sur l'ongle*
to pay through the nose	*payer les yeux de la tête*
to keep a stiff upper lip	*rester flegmatique*
to be caught red-handed	*être pris la main dans le sac*
to be dressed up to the nines	*être sur son trente-et-un*
to give someone a good dressing-down	*remonter les bretelles à quelqu'un*
to put one's money where one's mouth is	*agir conformément à ses paroles*
to have a chip on one's shoulder	*en vouloir au monde entier / chercher querelle à tout le monde*
to let one's hair down	*se détendre*
to pull someone's leg	*se payer la tête de quelqu'un*
Pull the other one!	*À d'autres ! (Tu te payes ma tête !)*
Keep your shirt on!	*On se calme !*
It's no skin off my nose!	*C'est pas mon problème !*
My heart skipped a beat.	*J'ai eu un coup au cœur.*
Here's mud in your eye!	*À la tienne, Étienne !*
She is the spitting image of her mother.	*C'est sa mère tout craché.*
She is the apple of his eye.	*Elle est la prunelle de ses yeux.*
She looks as if butter would not melt in her mouth.	*Elle a des airs de sainte-nitouche.*
She is dressed to kill.	*Habillée comme ça, elle va faire des ravages.*
She can twist him around her little finger.	*Elle fait de lui ce qu'elle veut.*
He has feet of clay.	*C'est un colosse aux pieds d'argile.*
Beauty is only skin deep.	*La beauté n'est pas tout.*
The way to a man's heart is through his stomach.	*C'est par les petits plats qu'on retient un mari.*
Desperate diseases must have desperate cures.	*À maux extrêmes, remèdes extrêmes.*
Hungry bellies have no ears.	*Ventre affamé n'a pas d'oreilles.*
In the country of the blind the one-eyed man is king.	*Au royaume des aveugles, les borgnes sont rois.*
Once bitten, twice shy.	*Chat échaudé craint l'eau froide.*

Culinary metaphors	***Métaphores culinaires***
a pot boiler	*une œuvre alimentaire*
a flash in the pan	*un feu de paille*
pie in the sky	*des châteaux en Espagne*
the upper crust	*les gens de la haute*
the icing on the cake	*la cerise sur le gâteau*
to eat humble pie	*faire amende honorable*
to bite off more than one can chew	*avoir les yeux plus grands que le ventre*
to have one's cake and eat it too	*avoir le beurre et l'argent du beurre*
to take a remark with a pinch of salt	*ne pas prendre une remarque pour argent comptant*
to be awarded the wooden spoon	*gagner la cuiller de bois (arriver bon dernier)*

to bring home the bacon	*faire bouillir la marmite*
to have a finger in every pie	*être mêlé à toutes les affaires*
Not a sausage!	*Pas un radis !*
I haven't got a bean!	*J'ai pas un radis !*
Never a square meal...	*Jamais un repas digne de ce nom...*
Let's take pot luck!	*À la fortune du pot !*
That's a fine kettle of fish!	*Nous voilà dans de beaux draps !*
I've got other fish to fry.	*J'ai d'autres chats à fouetter.*
He chickened out of it.	*Il s'est dégonflé.*
She doesn't mince her words.	*Elle ne mâche pas ses mots.*
She knows on which side her bread is buttered.	*Elle sait où est son intérêt.*
He is on the gravy train.	*Il a trouvé le filon.*
There's no such a thing as a free lunch.	*Tout se paie.*
It's the pot calling the kettle black.	*C'est l'hôpital qui se moque de la charité.*
The proof of the pudding is in the eating.	*La qualité se révèle à l'usage.*
Too many cooks spoil the broth.	*On n'arrive à rien quand tout le monde s'en mêle.*

Domestic metaphors ***Métaphores domestiques***

cold comfort	*une maigre consolation*
a basket case	*une personne émotionnellement instable*
by hook or by crook	*coûte que coûte*
to carry the can	*porter le chapeau*
to sit on the fence	*rester neutre, ne pas se prononcer*
to have a skeleton in the cupboard	*avoir des secrets (de famille) à cacher*
to wash one's dirty linen in public	*laver son linge sale en public*
to get out of bed on the wrong side	*se lever du mauvais pied*
to jump out of the frying pan into the fire	*tomber de Charybde en Scylla*
to kick the bucket	*casser sa pipe*
Walls have ears.	*Les murs ont des oreilles.*
A watched pot never boils.	*Pour celui qui est impatient, chaque seconde est une éternité.*
A woman's work is never done.	*Une femme a toujours à faire dans sa maison.*
The pitcher goes so often to the well that it is broken at last.	*Tant va la cruche à l'eau qu'à la fin elle se casse.*
There's many a slip twixt cup and lip.	*Il y a loin de la coupe aux lèvres.*

Military metaphors ***Métaphores militaires***

a pitched battle	*une bataille rangée / une bagarre générale*
a blonde bombshell	*une blonde canon*
a battle axe	*une mégère*
the rank-and-file	*le gros de la troupe, les sans grade*
a last-ditch attempt	*une tentative désespérée*
the parting shot	*la flèche du Parthe*
point blank	*à bout portant*
lock, stock and barrel	*dans son intégralité*

to hold the fort	*résister / tenir la boutique*
to bury the hatchet	*enterrer la hache de guerre*
to pass muster	*être acceptable*
to pass with flying colours	*passer (un examen) avec les honneurs*
to be on the warpath	*être sur le sentier de la guerre*
to beat a hasty retreat	*battre en retraite (précipitamment)*
to throw down the gauntlet	*lancer un défi*
to take up the gauntlet	*relever le défi*
to be hoist with one's own petard	*être pris à son propre piège*
Forewarned is forearmed.	*Un homme averti en vaut deux.*
All is fair in love and war.	*À la guerre comme en amour, tout est permis.*
Money is the sinews of war.	*L'argent, c'est le nerf de la guerre*

Musical metaphors ***Métaphores musicales***

to be as fit as a fiddle	*se porter comme un charme*
to play second fiddle	*jouer les seconds couteaux*
to put the damper on	*mettre une sourdine*
to face the music	*affronter l'adversité*
to play by ear	*jouer d'oreille, s'adapter aux circonstances*
to blow one's own trumpet	*vanter ses propres mérites*
It rings true / It has the ring of truth.	*Cela sonne vrai.*
It's going for a song.	*Ça part pour une bouchée de pain.*
He that sings on Friday will weep on Sunday.	*Tel qui rit vendredi, dimanche pleurera.*
He who pays the piper calls the tune.	*L'argent, c'est le pouvoir.*

Nautical metaphors ***Métaphores nautiques***

spick and span	*nickel, impeccable*
shipshape (and Bristol fashion)	*en ordre impeccable*
in the offing	*imminent / en perspective*
to be under the weather	*ne pas être dans son assiette*
to be left high and dry	*être laissé en rade*
to be in the doldrums	*être en plein marasme*
to know the ropes	*connaître (toutes) les ficelles*
Down the hatch!	*Cul sec !*
Everything is above board.	*Il n'y a rien à cacher. / C'est au-dessus de tout soupcon.*
We are all in the same boat.	*On est tous dans le même bateau.*
The rats are deserting the sinking ship.	*Les rats abandonnent le navire.*
A great ship asks deep waters.	*Un grand bateau demande des eaux profondes.*
The worse the passage, the more welcome the port.	*Plus dure est la traversée, plus désirable est le port.*

Rural metaphors ***Métaphores de la vie rurale***

an old chestnut	*un marronnier (une histoire rebattue)*
to spill the beans	*vendre la mèche / vider son sac*
to beat around the bush	*tourner autour du pot*
to nip in the bud	*tuer dans l'œuf*

to grasp the nettle	*prendre le taureau par les cornes*
to call a spade a spade	*appeler un chat un chat*
to separate the wheat from the chaff	*séparer le bon grain de l'ivraie*
to get hold of the wrong end of the stick	*comprendre de travers*
to put the cart before the horse	*mettre la charrue avant les bœufs*
to hear something on the grapevine	*apprendre quelque chose par la rumeur publique*
to make hay while the sun shines	*saisir l'occasion au vol*
to count one's chickens before they are hatched	*vendre la peau de l'ours avant de l'avoir tué*
It's going haywire.	*Ça part en quenouille.*
Never put all your eggs in the same basket.	*Ne jamais mettre tous ses œufs dans le même panier.*
There's no use crying over spilt milk.	*Ce qui est fait est fait. (inutile de le regretter)*
Fling dirt enough and some will stick.	*Médisez, il en restera toujours quelque chose.*
Old muck-hills will bloom.	*Les plus belles fleurs poussent sur le fumier.*

Social metaphors ***Métaphores de la vie sociale***

the lord of the manor	*le maître des lieux*
a spin doctor	*un consultant en communication*
an iron hand in a velvet glove	*une main de fer dans un gant de velours*
to be as drunk as a Lord	*être saoul comme une bourrique*
to live in an ivory tower	*se retirer dans sa tour d'ivoire*
to keep up with the Joneses	*ne pas être en reste avec les voisins*
to be at someone's beck and call	*être au service de quelqu'un*
to be in someone's black books	*être en disgrâce*
to put in one's two-penny's worth	*rajouter son grain de sel*
to be in the limelight	*être sous les feux de la rampe*
They are as thick as thieves.	*Ils s'entendent comme larrons en foire. (Ils sont très complices.)*
Blood is thicker than water.	*La voix du sang est la plus forte.*
Beggars cannot be choosers.	*Faute de grive on mange du merle.*
Better the devil you know than the devil you don't.	*Mieux vaut un démon connu qu'un démon inconnu.*
A king without learning is but a crowned ass.	*Un roi ignorant n'est qu'un âne couronné.*
The cowl does not make the monk.	*L'habit ne fait pas le moine.*
Charity begins at home	*Charité bien ordonnée commence par soi-même.*
Familiarity breeds contempt.	*Nul n'est prophète en son pays.*
He who laughs last laughs longest.	*Rira bien qui rira le dernier.*
You can't teach your grandmother to suck eggs.	*On n'apprend pas aux vieux singes à faire la grimace.*
It's too late to spare when the bottom is bare.	*Il est trop tard pour épargner quand on a perdu sa chemise.*
Out of sight, out of mind.	*Loin des yeux, loin du cœur.*
The more, the merrier.	*Plus on est de fous plus on rit.*

Crafts and trades ***Les métiers***

a knock-on effect	*un effet domino*

at full blast	*à plein tube / à fond la caisse*
(as) mad as a hatter	*fou à lier*
a baker's dozen	*treize à la douzaine*
to be given the sack / to get the axe	*se faire virer*
to run out of steam	*s'épuiser / être en baisse de régime*
to have too many irons in the fire	*vouloir trop en faire*
to go against the grain	*contrarier la nature*
to give someone short shrift	*négliger quelqu'un / traiter quelqu'un par dessus la jambe*
He is a chip off the old block.	*C'est bien le fils de son père.*
Back to the drawing-board!	*Il va falloir revoir la copie !*
Mind your own business!	*Occupe-toi de tes affaires (oignons) !*
A stitch in time saves nine.	*Un point à temps en vaut cent.*
A bad workman always blames his tools.	*Un mauvais ouvrier accuse ses outils.*
An old poacher makes the best keeper.	*Un ancien braconnier fait un bon garde-chasse.*

Nature ***La nature***

a storm in a teacup	*une tempête dans un verre d'eau*
the tip of the iceberg	*la partie emergée de l'iceberg*
to break the ice	*briser la glace*
to be over the moon	*être enchanté*
to be on cloud nine	*être aux nues*
to leave no stone unturned	*remuer ciel et terre*
to go west	*passer l'arme à gauche / se perdre*
to be sold down the river	*se faire rouler dans la farine*
to have the choice between a rock and a hard place	*devoir choisir entre la peste et le choléra*
to make a mountain out of a molehill	*(se) faire une montagne de rien*
He can't see the wood for the trees.	*C'est l'arbre qui lui cache la forêt.*
A rolling stone gathers no moss.	*Pierre qui roule n'amasse pas mousse.*
Every cloud has a silver lining.	*À quelque chose malheur est bon.*
It never rains but it pours.	*Un malheur n'arrive jamais seul.*
There's no rose without a thorn.	*Il n'y a pas de rose sans épine.*
Great oaks from little acorns grow.	*Les petits ruisseaux font les grandes rivières.*
Still waters run deep.	*Il faut se méfier de l'eau qui dort.*

Sports and games ***Les sports et les jeux***

a hat trick	*le coup du chapeau (réussir à trois reprises)*
the Mexican wave	*la ola*
to start from scratch	*partir de rien*
to have the upper hand	*avoir le dessus*
to win hands down	*gagner sans coup férir (les doigts dans le nez)*
to throw in the towel	*jeter l'éponge*
to be saved by the bell	*être sauvé par le gong*
to lose one's marbles	*perdre la boule*
She's still got all her marbles.	*Elle a encore toute sa tête.*

It is too dicey.	*C'est trop risqué.*
The die is cast. / The dice are cast.	*Les dés sont jetés.*
The game is up.	*L'affaire est éventée.*
Back to square one.	*Retour à la case départ.*
Give us a break, will you!	*Lâche-nous un peu, s'il te plaît !*
Put your skates on!	*Grouille-toi !*
Pull your socks up!	*Remue-toi !*
It had been on the cards for a long time!	*C'était joué d'avance !*

The passing of time ***Le passage du temps***

at the eleventh hour	*au dernier moment / in extremis*
to strike while the iron is hot	*battre le fer tant qu'il est chaud*
to have one foot in the grave	*avoir un pied dans la tombe*
Once in a blue moon.	*Tous les 36 du mois.*
Better late than never.	*Mieux vaut tard que jamais.*
Dead men tell no tales.	*Les morts ne parlent pas.*
Rome was not built in a day.	*Paris ne s'est pas construit en un jour.*
Youth will have its swing.	*Il faut que jeunesse se passe.*
Time and tide wait for no man.	*On ne peut pas arrêter le temps.*

Sundry ***Divers***

the full Monty	*la totale / le grand jeu*
beyond the pale	*hors-limites*
castles in the air	*des châteaux en Espagne*
as ugly as sin	*laid comme un pou*
to burn one's bridges	*brûler ses vaisseaux*
to leave someone in the lurch	*laisser quelqu'un dans une situation difficile*
to be in a shambles	*être en pleine pagaille*
to be all at sixes and sevens	*ne pas savoir où donner de la tête*
to put someone in the picture	*mettre quelqu'un au parfum*
to speak double Dutch	*parler le zoulou / un langage incompréhensible*
to pass the buck	*se débarrasser de la patate chaude*
to get off scot free	*s'en tirer à bon compte*
to be penny wise, pound foolish	*faire des économies de bouts de chandelle*
And to add insult to injury...	*Et pour comble d'insulte...*
Mum's the word.	*Motus et bouche cousue.*
Mind your Ps and Qs!	*Surveille ton langage !*
He's gone round the bend.	*Il débloque.*
She's a carbon copy of her mother.	*C'est la copie conforme de sa mère.*
It hangs by a thread.	*Ça ne tient qu'à un fil.*
All roads lead to Rome.	*Tous les chemins mènent à Rome.*
All that glitters is not gold.	*Tout ce qui brille n'est pas or.*
There is no accounting for taste.	*Les goûts et les couleurs ne se discutent pas.*
God helps them that help themselves.	*Aide-toi, le ciel t'aidera.*
Nothing ventured, nothing gained.	*Qui ne tente rien n'a rien.*
The road to hell is paved with good intentions.	*L'enfer est pavé de bonnes intentions*

Verbes irréguliers figurant dans les listes

to abide	abode (ou reg.)	abode (ou reg.)
to arise	arose	arisen
to babysit	babysat	babysat
to be	was	been
to bear	bore	borne (to be born : naissance)
to beat	beat	beaten
to become	became	become
to beget	begot	begotten
to begin	began	begun
to bend	bent	bent
to bet	bet	bet
to bind	bound	bound
to bite	bit	bitten
to blow	blew	blown
to break	broke	broken
to breed	bred	bred
to bring	brought	brought
to broadcast	broadcast	broadcast
to build	built	built
to burn	burnt (ou reg.)	burnt (ou reg.)
to burst	burst	burst
to buy	bought	bought
can	could	
to cast	cast	cast
to catch	caught	caught
to choose	chose	chosen
to cling	clung	clung
to come	came	come
to cost	cost	cost
to creep	crept	crept
to cut	cut	cut
to deal	dealt	dealt
to dig	dug	dug
to do	did	done
to draw	drew	drawn
to dream	dreamt (ou reg.)	dreamt (ou reg.)
to drink	drank	drunk
to drive	drove	driven
to dwell	dwelt (ou reg.)	dwelt (ou reg.)
to eat	ate	eaten
to fall	fell	fallen
to feed	fed	fed
to feel	felt	felt
to fight	fought	fought
to find	found	found
to flee	fled	fled
to fly	flew	flown
to forbid	forbade	forbidden
to forecast	forecast	forecast
to foresee	foresaw	foreseen
to foretell	foretold	foretold
to forget	forgot	forgotten

to forgive	forgave	forgiven
to freeze	froze	frozen
to get	got	got
to give	gave	given
to go	went	gone
to grind	ground	ground
to grow	grew	grown
to hang	hung	hung (reg. en cas de pendaison)
to have	had	had
to hear	heard	heard
to hew	hewed	hewn
to hide	hid	hidden
to hit	hit	hit
to hold	held	held
to hurt	hurt	hurt
to keep	kept	kept
to kneel	knelt	knelt
to know	knew	known
to lay	laid	laid
to lead	led	led
to leap	leapt (ou reg.)	leapt (ou reg.)
to learn	learnt	learnt
to leave	left	left
to lend	lent	lent
to let	let	let
to lie	lay	lain
to light	lit (ou reg.)	lit (ou reg.)
to lose	lost	lost
to make	made	made
may	might	
to mean	meant	meant
to meet	met	met
to mislead	misled	misled
to mistake	mistook	mistaken
to mow	mowed	mown (ou reg.)
to overcome	overcame	overcome
to overdo	overdid	overdone
to overtake	overtook	overtaken
to overthrow	overthrew	overthrown
to pay	paid	paid
to put	put	put
to quit	quit	quit
to read	read	read
to rebuild	rebuilt	rebuilt
to ride	rode	ridden
to ring	rang	rung
to rise	rose	risen
to run	ran	run
to rewrite	rewrote	rewritten
to saw	sawed	sawn (ou reg.)
to say	said	said
to see	saw	seen
to seek	sought	sought
to sell	sold	sold
to send	sent	sent
to set	set	set

to shake	shook	shaken
to shear	sheared	shorn (ou reg.)
to shed	shed	shed
to shine	shone	shone
to shoot	shot	shot
to show	showed	shown
to shrink	shrank	shrunk
to shut	shut	shut
to sing	sang	sung
to sink	sank	sunk
to sit	sat	sat
to slay	slew	slain
to sleep	slept	slept
to slide	slid	slid
to smell	smelt	smelt
to sow	sowed	sown (ou reg.)
to speak	spoke	spoken
to spell	spelt	spelt
to spend	spent	spent
to spill	spilt	spilt
to spin	spun	spun
to split	split	split
to spoil	spoilt (ou reg.)	spoilt (ou reg.)
to spread	spread	spread
to spring	sprang	sprung
to stand	stood	stood
to steal	stole	stolen
to stick	stuck	stuck
to sting	stung	stung
to stink	stank	stunk
to strike	struck	struck
to swear	swore	sworn
to sweep	swept	swept
to swell	swelled	swollen (ou reg.)
to swim	swam	swum
to take	took	taken
to teach	taught	taught
to tear	tore	torn
to tell	told	told
to think	thought	thought
to throw	threw	thrown
to tread	trod	trodden
to undergo	underwent	undergone
to understand	understood	understood
to undertake	undertook	undertaken
to unwind	unwound	unwound
to upset	upset	upset
to wake	woke	woken
to wear	wore	worn
to weave	wove	woven
to weep	wept	wept
to win	won	won
to wind	wound	wound
to withdraw	withdrew	withdrawn
to write	wrote	written

Aubin
IMPRIMEUR

Achevé d'imprimer en septembre 2018
N° d'impression 1809.0112
Dépôt légal, septembre 2018
Imprimé en France